Siegel's

CORPORATIONS AND OTHER BUSINESS ENTITIES

Essay and Multiple-Choice Questions and Answers

Fifth Edition

BRIAN N. SIEGEL
J.D., Columbia Law School

LAZAR EMANUEL
J.D., Harvard Law School

Revised by

Theresa A. Gabaldon
Lyle T. Alverson Professor of Law
The George Washington University Law School

Published by Wolters Kluwer Law & Business in New York.

Wolters Kluwer Law & Business serves customers worldwide with CCH, Aspen Publishers, and Kluwer Law International products. (www.wolterskluwerlb.com)

To contact Customer Service, e-mail customer.service@wolterskluwer.com, call 1-800-234-1660, fax 1-800-901-9075, or mail correspondence to:

> Wolters Kluwer Law & Business
> Attn: Order Department
> PO Box 990
> Frederick, MD 21705

The authors gratefully acknowledge the assistance of the California Committee of Bar Examiners, which provided access to questions on which some of the essay questions in this book are based.

Printed in the United States of America.

1 2 3 4 5 6 7 8 9 0

ISBN 978-1-4548-0927-2

This book is intended as a general review of a legal subject. It is not intended as a source of advice for the solution of legal matters or problems. For advice on legal matters, the reader should consult an attorney.

About Wolters Kluwer Law & Business

Wolters Kluwer Law & Business is a leading global provider of intelligent information and digital solutions for legal and business professionals in key specialty areas, and respected educational resources for professors and law students. Wolters Kluwer Law & Business connects legal and business professionals as well as those in the education market with timely, specialized, authoritative content and information-enabled solutions to support success through productivity, accuracy, and mobility.

Serving customers worldwide, Wolters Kluwer Law & Business products include those under the Aspen Publishers, CCH, Kluwer Law International, Loislaw, Best Case, ftwilliam.com, and MediRegs family of products.

CCH products have been a trusted resource since 1913 and are highly regarded resources for legal, securities, antitrust and trade regulation, government contracting, banking, pension, payroll, employment and labor, and healthcare reimbursement and compliance professionals.

Aspen Publishers products provide essential information to attorneys, business professionals, and law students. Written by preeminent authorities, the product line offers analytical and practical information in a range of specialty practice areas from securities law and intellectual property to mergers and acquisitions and pension/benefits. Aspen's trusted legal education resources provide professors and students with high-quality, up-to-date and effective resources for successful instruction and study in all areas of the law.

Kluwer Law International products provide the global business community with reliable international legal information in English. Legal practitioners, corporate counsel ,and business executives around the world rely on Kluwer Law journals, looseleafs, books, and electronic products for comprehensive information in many areas of international legal practice.

Loislaw is a comprehensive online legal research product providing legal content to law firm practitioners of various specializations. Loislaw provides attorneys with the ability to quickly and efficiently find the necessary legal information they need, when and where they need it, by facilitating access to primary law as well as state-specific law, records, forms and treatises.

Best Case Solutions is the leading bankruptcy software product to the bankruptcy industry. It provides software and workflow tools to flawlessly streamline petition preparation and the electronic filing process, while timely incorporating ever-changing court requirements.

ftwilliam.com offers employee benefits professionals the highest quality plan documents (retirement, welfare, and non-qualified) and government forms (5500/PBGC, 1099, and IRS) software at highly competitive prices.

MediRegs products provide integrated health care compliance content and software solutions for professionals in healthcare, higher education and life sciences, including professionals in accounting, law and consulting.

Wolters Kluwer Law & Business, a division of Wolters Kluwer, is headquartered in New York. Wolters Kluwer is a market-leading global information services company focused on professionals.

Introduction

Although law school grades are a significant factor in obtaining a summer internship or entry position at a law firm, no formalized preparation for finals is offered at most law schools. For the most part, students are expected to fend for themselves in learning how to take a law school exam. Ironically, law school exams may bear little correspondence to the teaching methods used by professors during the school year. At least in the first year, professors require you to spend most of your time briefing cases. This is probably not great preparation for issue-spotting on exams. In briefing cases, you are made to focus on one or two principles of law at a time; thus, you don't get practice in relating one issue to another or in developing a picture of an entire problem or the entire course. When exams finally come, you're forced to make an abrupt 180-degree turn. Suddenly, you are asked to recognize, define, and discuss a variety of issues buried within a single multi-issue fact pattern. Alternatively, you may be asked to select among a number of possible answers, all of which look inviting but only one of which is right.

The comprehensive course outline you've created so diligently, and with such pain, means little if you're unable to apply its contents on your final exams. There is a vast difference between reading opinions in which the legal principles are clearly stated and applying those same principles to hypothetical essay exams and multiple-choice questions.

The purpose of this book is to help you bridge the gap between memorizing a rule of law and ***understanding how to use it*** in an exam. After an initial overview describing the exam-writing process, you see a large number of hypotheticals that test your ability to write analytical essays and to pick the right answers to multiple-choice questions. ***Read them—all of them!*** Then review the suggested answers that follow. You'll find that the key to superior grades lies in applying your knowledge through questions and answers, not through rote memory.

GOOD LUCK!

Table of Contents

Preparing Effectively for Essay Examinations

The "ERC" Process 1

Issue-Spotting...3

How to Discuss an Issue 4

Structuring Your Answer 8

Discuss All Possible Issues 10

Delineate the Transition from One Issue to the Next 11

Understanding the "Call" of a Question 11

The Importance of Analyzing the Question Carefully Before Writing 12

When to Make an Assumption...13

Case Names 14

How to Handle Time Pressures 14

Formatting Your Answer...15

The Importance of Reviewing Prior Exams 15

As Always, a Caveat 16

Essay Questions

Question 1 (Fiduciary Duties and Liabilities of Directors and Officers) 21

Question 2 (Choice of Business Entity) 22

Question 3 (Derivative Action, Fiduciary Duties and Liabilities of
Directors and Officers, Fiduciary Duties of Shareholders, Removal,
Voting, Dividends, Inspection of Books and Records).........................23

Question 4 (Powers of the Board of Directors, Fiduciary Duties
and Action) 25

Question 5 (Fiduciary Duties of Shareholders, Preemptive Rights, Merger,
Fiduciary Duties and Liabilities of Directors and Officers, Ultra Vires
Doctrine) 26

Question 6 ('34 Act Registration, Sarbanes-Oxley Requirements,
Dodd-Frank Requirements, Voting, Proxy, Fiduciary Duties and
Liabilities of Directors and Officers, Powers of Officers)...................27

Question 7 (Fiduciary Duties and Liabilities of Directors and Officers,
Powers of Officers, Agency, Insider Trading).....................................28

Question 8 (Derivative Action, Fiduciary Duties and Liabilities of
   Directors and Officers, Powers of Board of Directors) 29

Question 9 (Derivative Action, Fiduciary Duties and Liabilities of
   Directors and Officers, Preemptive Rights, Insider Trading).............................30

Question 10 (Piercing the Corporate Veil, Defective Incorporation,
   Watered Stock, Fiduciary Duties and Liabilities of Directors
   and Officers)..31

Question 11 (General Partnerships, Limited Liability Partnerships,
   Choice of Business Entity)..32

Question 12 (Fiduciary Duties and Liabilities of Directors and Officers,
   Preemptive Rights, Insider Trading) 34

Question 13 (Derivative Action, Fiduciary Duties and Liabilities of
   Directors and Officers, Compensation of Directors and Officers,
   Indemnification of Directors and Officers, Transfer of Stock)..........................35

Question 14 (Derivative Action, Dividends, Fiduciary Duties and
   Liabilities of Directors and Officers)..36

Question 15 (Sale of Stock, Watered Stock, Dividends, Preemptive
   Rights, Proxy) 37

Question 16 (Preincorporation Contract, Partnership, De Jure
   Corporation, Defective Incorporation, Piercing the Corporate
   Veil, Watered Stock) 38

Question 17 (Derivative Action, Fiduciary Duties and Liabilities of
   Directors and Officers, Agency, Powers of Officers, Preincorporation
   Contract) 39

Question 18 (Proxy, Removal, Ultra Vires Doctrine, *Pari Delicto*
   Doctrine) 40

Question 19 (Removal, Insider Trading)..41

Question 20 (Transfer of Stock, Dividends, Voting, Dissolution
   of Corporation)...42

Question 21 (Purpose, Deadlock, Dissolution, Limited Liability
   Companies, Limited Liability Partnerships, Choice of Business).....................43

Question 22 (Dividends, Powers of Board of Directors, Sale of Stock,
   Compensation of Directors and Officers) 44

Question 23 (Insider Trading)...45

Question 24 (Limited Liability Companies, Authority of Members,
   Piercing the Veil of the Limited Liability Company, Misrepresentation of
   Authority)...46

Question 25 (Dividends, Fiduciary Duties and Liabilities of Directors and Officers, Duties of Directors to Multiple Classes, Amendment of Articles, Unanimous Written Consent)..48

Question 26 (Treatment of Limited Liability Company as Corporation for Purposes of Statute, Authority of Members, Ultra Vires and the Limited Liability Company, Fiduciary Duties and Liabilities of Members) 50

Question 27 (Charitable Contributions, Ultra Vires Doctrine, Meetings of Directors, Notice, Quorum and Voting Requirements, Derivative Action, Fiduciary Duties and Liabilities of Directors and Officers)..................52

Essay Answers

Answer to Question 1 55
Answer to Question 2 59
Answer to Question 3 63
Answer to Question 4 66
Answer to Question 5 69
Answer to Question 6 72
Answer to Question 7 77
Answer to Question 8 80
Answer to Question 9 83
Answer to Question 10 86
Answer to Question 11 91
Answer to Question 12 95
Answer to Question 13 99
Answer to Question 14 102
Answer to Question 15 106
Answer to Question 16 109
Answer to Question 17 113
Answer to Question 18 116
Answer to Question 19 120
Answer to Question 20 123
Answer to Question 21 126
Answer to Question 22 130
Answer to Question 23 133
Answer to Question 24 136

Answer to Question 25 139

Answer to Question 26 143

Answer to Question 27 146

Multiple-Choice Questions

Questions 1 through 105 (Corporations)...153

Questions 106 through 120 (Unincorporated Entities and Choice of Business).......207

Multiple-Choice Answers

Answers to Questions 1 through 105 (Corporations) 217

Answers to Questions 106 through 120 (Unincorporated Entities
    and Choice of Business)..262

Index

Alphabetical index, listing issues and cases by the number of the
    question raising the issue or citing the case.......................................271

Preparing Effectively for Essay Examinations

To achieve superior scores on essay exams, a law student must (1) learn and understand "blackletter" principles and rules of law for each subject; (2) analyze how those principles of law arise within a test fact pattern; and (3) clearly and succinctly discuss each principle and how it relates to the facts. One of the most common misconceptions about law school is that you must memorize each word on every page of your casebooks or outlines to do well on exams. The reality is that you can commit an entire casebook to memory and still do poorly on an exam. Our review of hundreds of student answers has shown us that most students can recite the rules. The students who do **best** on exams are able to analyze how the rules they have memorized relate to the facts in the questions, and they are able to communicate their analysis to the grader. The following pages cover what you need to know to achieve superior scores on your law school essay exams.

The "ERC" Process

To study effectively for law school exams you must be able to "ERC" (*E*lementize, *R*ecognize, and *C*onceptualize) each legal principle covered in your casebooks and course outlines. *Elementizing* means reducing each legal theory and rule you learn to a concise, straightforward statement of its essential elements. Without knowledge of these elements, it's difficult to see all the issues as they arise.

For example, if you are asked, "What is a corporation *de facto*?" it is **not** enough to say, "A corporation *de facto* is one that is implied in fact even though it doesn't really exist." This might (or might not) impress a grader with your facility in an ancient language, but it would also leave him or her wondering if you had attended class. An accurate description of the corporation *de facto* concept would go something like this: "As a matter of common law, a corporation that has failed to satisfy statutory formation requirements nonetheless will be recognized if there was a good faith attempt to comply with applicable statutory requirements and actual use of the corporate structure." This formulation correctly shows several things. First (and very importantly), corporation *de facto* is a common law doctrine which may be overcome by statute. In addition, there are distinct elements that must be satisfied before the doctrine can be successfully invoked. They can be compressed into two elements or split out into three. The two-element version goes like this: (1) There was a ***good faith attempt to comply***

1

with applicable statutory requirements and (2) *actual use of the corpo-rate structure.* There is a three-element version as well: (1) There was a *good faith attempt to comply* with (2) *applicable statutory requirements* and (3) *actual use of the corporate structure.* It should be obvious that graders are unlikely to care which version you adopt. The three-element version simply gives you more analytic prompts than the other version. *Recognizing* means perceiving or anticipating which words or ideas within a legal principle are likely to be the source of issues and how those issues are likely to arise within a given hypothetical fact pattern. With respect to the corporation *de facto* concept, there are three *potential* issues as to whether such a corporation would be recognized as a matter of common law, *as well as* the very important question of whether the common law has been preempted by statute. The three issues may be stated as questions in which-ever order makes sense. Thus: Was there a statute under which a corpora-tion could be formed? (Note that the answer to this question will usually be "yes.") Was the person seeking protection under the doctrine attempting in good faith to comply with the statute? Did the person seeking protection thereafter act as if a corporation existed? *Conceptualizing* means imagin-ing situations in which each of the elements of a rule of law can give rise to factual issues. *Unless you can imagine or construct an application of each element of a rule, you don't truly understand the legal principles behind the rule!* In our opinion, the inability to conjure up hypothetical fact pat-terns or stories involving particular rules of law foretells a likelihood that you will miss issues involving those rules on an exam. It's *crucial* (1) to *recognize* that issues result from the interaction of facts with the words defining a rule of law and (2) to develop the ability to *conceptualize* or *imagine* fact patterns using the words or concepts within the rule.

For example, a set of facts illustrating the "good faith attempt to comply" element of the corporation *de facto* concept might be the following:

> A wishes to form a corporation for the purpose of protecting herself against individual liability. She purchases a book that explains how the process works. It includes a form to be filled out and the information that the form can be filed by mail. A quit reading the book at that point. If she continued, she would have found out that, in her jurisdiction, corporations do not come into existence until the Secretary of State issues a certificate of incorporation. A decides to call the new corporation "A Corp.," and fills out the form accordingly. She then places it in the mail. The same day, believing that she has successfully formed A Corp, she enters into a con-tract with B, signing it as "A, President of A Corp." When B subsequently tries to sue A, A will argue that she had the subjective, honest belief that she formed A Corp., and that should be all that is required. B will argue

that, notwithstanding A's honesty, reading only part of the book, and thus failing to wait until receiving the certificate of incorporation before acting in the corporate name, is not a good faith attempt at compliance.

An illustration of how the "actual use of the corporate structure" requirement might generate an issue is the following:

> X and Y have been partners in a general partnership for years. They become aware that incorporation would give them the benefit of limited liability for at least some business obligations. They obtain a form for articles of incorporation and fill in the blanks. X delivers the articles personally to the Secretary of State's office, where he is told that the articles are fine and there is nothing else he has to do. Unfortunately, the person who talked to him was not the person in charge of checking the articles for compliance with statutory requirements. When the articles are checked two days later by the appropriate person, a mistake is discovered and the articles are rejected. Notice is sent to X but is lost in the mail. X and Y thereafter continue to conduct their business much as they did before. They do not elect a board of directors or issue stock, but they do establish a corporate bank account. They also enter all contracts in the corporate name. One of these contracts is with Z. When Z sues X personally, Z will argue that there was inadequate use of the corporate structure. X will respond that having a corporate bank account and entering contracts in the corporate name should be adequate; the requirement is "actual use," not "perfect use." Z could counter that opening bank accounts and signing contracts are not matters of "structure."

"Mental games" such as these must be played with every element of every rule you learn.

Issue-Spotting

One of the keys to doing well on an essay examination is issue-spotting. In fact, issue-spotting is *the* most important skill you will learn in law school. If you recognize a legal issue, you can find the applicable rule of law (if there is one) by researching the issue. But if you fail to see the issues, you won't learn the steps that lead to success or failure on exams or, for that matter, in the practice of law. It is important to remember that (1) an issue is a question to be decided by the judge or jury and (2) a question is "in issue" when it can be disputed or argued about at trial. The bottom line is that *if you don't spot an issue, you can't raise it or discuss it.*

The key to issue-spotting is to learn to approach a problem in the same way an attorney does. Let's assume you've been admitted to practice and a client enters your office with a legal problem involving a dispute. He will recite his facts to you and give you any documents that may be pertinent. He will then want to know if he can sue (or be sued, if your client seeks to avoid liability). To answer your client's questions intelligently, you will have to decide the following: (1) what principles or rules can possibly be asserted by your client; (2) what defense or defenses can possibly be raised to these principles; (3) what issues may arise if these defenses are asserted; (4) what arguments each side can make to persuade the fact finder to resolve the issue in his favor; and (5) finally, what the *likely* outcome of each issue will be. *All the issues that can possibly arise at trial will be relevant to your answers.*

How to Discuss an Issue

Keep in mind that *rules of law are the guides to issues* (i.e., an issue arises where there is a question whether the facts do, or do not, satisfy an element of a rule); a rule of law *cannot dispose of an issue* unless the rule can reasonably be *applied to the facts.*

A good way to learn how to discuss an issue is to study the following mini-hypothetical and the two student responses that follow it.

Mini-Hypothetical

A decides to form a corporation to protect herself from liability for the obligations of the new wedding consultant business that she plans to start. She feels the matter is somewhat pressing because she already has entered into a contract leasing office space from B. The lease is to commence on the first day of the following month. A signed the contract as "A, agent for A Perfect Wedding, a corporation to be formed, which will be the obligor." She did ask B if that form of signature was all right. B responded "That's fine, I understand." Before the first day of the following month, A obtains a form for articles of incorporation and fills it out for A Perfect Wedding, Inc. Believing in good faith that she has done everything required to form a corporation, A immediately enters into a contract with C pursuant to which C will print a large quantity of A Perfect Wedding letterhead. This contract is signed by A as "A, President of A Perfect Wedding." A's business plan fizzles out before the end of the month and she decides not to make any payments under either contract.

Discuss the rights of B and C against A.

Pertinent Principles of Law:

1. In the event a promoter acts on behalf of a corporation not yet formed, under circumstances making it clear that the other party knows the

corporation does not yet exist, the promoter is bound unless there is an agreement to the contrary.

2. The common law doctrine of corporation *de facto* provides that even though not all statutory formation requirements have been satisfied, a separate corporate entity will be recognized if there was a good faith attempt to comply with applicable statutory requirements and actual use of the corporate structure.

3. The doctrine of corporation by estoppel will, as justice requires, sometimes prevent one who has held him- or herself out as willing to rely only on corporate credit from attempting to bind an individual.

4. In most jurisdictions, statutes provide that anyone purporting to act on behalf of a corporation that has not satisfied statutory requirements will be personally bound. In many jurisdictions, there is a qualification referring to anyone purporting to act on behalf of a corporation *knowing* it has not satisfied statutory requirements.

First Student Answer

Is A personally liable to B?

This question raises issues of promoter's liability and corporation *de facto*. A promoter is liable for debts entered into in the corporate name before the corporation is formed. Thus, A may be liable to both B and C. There is an exception, though, for contracts that are entered into on behalf of a corporation *de facto*. This would probably be good against C, but not against B. The contract with B was entered before A even tried to form a corporation. The doctrine requires that there be a good faith attempt to comply with applicable statutory requirements and actual use of the corporate structure. On the other hand, A might argue that B knew the corporation wasn't formed and orally agreed not to hold A liable. B would disagree.

Is A personally liable to C?

As stated above, the doctrine of corporation *de facto* might help A in a suit by C. A acted in good faith, believing that she had formed a corporation. The second element, actual use of corporate structure, could be a problem. The question does not indicate that she made any use of the corporate structure at all, other than signing in the corporation's name. C would argue that's not sufficient. It's important to note, though, that not every jurisdiction still recognizes *de facto* corporations. In many places there are statutes saying that if you act on behalf of a corporation before it is formed you will be liable. This would answer the question for both B and C. Another possibility is corporation by estoppel.

Second Student Answer

Liability to B

In the event a promoter acts on behalf of a corporation not yet formed, under circumstances making it clear that the other party knows the corporation does not yet exist, the promoter is bound unless there is an agreement to the contrary. Based on the facts given, both the discussion and form of signature gave B clear notice that no corporation had yet been formed. B will argue this means that A is bound. A will argue, however, that B's comment, "That's fine, I understand," constitutes an agreement not to hold A personally liable. B would respond that his response was too ambiguous to be regarded as anything more than an acknowledgement that he understood the corporation was not yet formed, which would simply trigger the general rule. This argument might very well prevail.

B might try to strengthen B's position by invoking the statute that exists in most states providing that someone purporting to act on behalf of a corporation not yet formed is personally liable. A will respond that "purporting to act" fairly is understood as "leading the other party to believe the corporation exists." A will further argue that everyone is supposed to know that you can't bind a corporation before it exists, so saying they are acting for a corporation that clearly does not exist does not suggest you are acting on its behalf. Although a sensible argument, this will do nothing to help A out with respect to the general rule on promoter's liability.

Liability to C

The common law doctrine of corporation *de facto* provides that even though not all statutory formation requirements have been satisfied, a separate corporate entity will be recognized if (1) there was a good faith attempt to comply with applicable statutory requirements and (2) actual use of the corporate structure. With respect to the first element, A might argue that she acted in good faith in filling out the articles; she simply didn't know about the requirement that they be filed. She might also point out that whether they were or weren't filed really doesn't make any difference to B. B will argue that if you don't even investigate the statutory requirements, you cannot claim that you acted in good faith. With respect to the second element, A will claim that she entered the contract in the corporation's name and that is the only thing that should matter to B. B will respond that A didn't even use a corporate designation like "Inc. or Corp." B might also make a policy argument to the effect that the corporation *de facto* doctrine should only be applied to help those who are really trying to do things right, but simply encountered some sort of technical difficulty. B's arguments are probably the stronger.

A might also try to assert the doctrine of corporation by estoppel. This occasionally has been used, as justice requires, to prevent someone who has held himself out as willing to rely only on corporate credit from attempting to bind an individual. B will argue that because of the lack of clarity with respect to what kind of entity A Perfect Wedding was this doctrine should not apply. A will respond that most people would assume that if someone is a "President," a corporation is involved. Once again, B probably has the stronger argument.

In any event, in most jurisdictions, statutes intended to clarify the common law provide that anyone purporting to act on behalf of a corporation that has not satisfied statutory requirements will be personally bound. In many jurisdictions, there is a qualification referring to anyone purporting to act on behalf of a corporation *knowing* it has not satisfied statutory requirements. The version adopted by the relevant state could be critical. If there is no knowledge requirement, it certainly seems that A purported to act on behalf of a non-existent corporation. If there is a knowledge requirement, the facts lead us to believe that knowledge did not exist; A acted innocently. Thus, by negative implication, it would seem that the statute is telling us A should not be liable. B would argue that the statute means A is not liable by reason of the statute; the common law requirements of corporation *de facto* should then be invoked to resolve the matter. Once again, B's argument seems stronger.

Critique

Let's start by examining the First Student Answer. Although its labeling separates "B" issues and "C" issues, the discussion wanders a bit between the two. In addition, a failure to think very long about the question seems to have led the author into discussing the doctrine of corporation *de facto* with respect to B, even though it is not relevant. As First Student eventually recognizes, there has to be an attempt to incorporate before the doctrine is triggered. There was no such attempt before the contract with B was entered, so raising it here gets no points.

The First Student Answer also wanders back and forth between its invocation of the general rule on promoter's liability and the corporation *de facto* doctrine. As a result, it fails to directly connect the general rule on promoter's liability and its own stated exception (agreement to the contrary). Moreover, failing to engage directly with B's own words means that the back and forth about "A will argue" and "B will disagree" is not very meaningful. In general, saying that one party will disagree with the other is not going to get points – you have to describe the basis for the disagreement.

The First Student Answer really should have set out the elements of corporation *de facto* in its discussion of liability to C. The discussion of the doctrine itself is not bad, although it does fail to recognize that A never did use a corporate designation in signing the contract. First Student manifests awareness of the statutes that arguably preempt the common law doctrine, but does not make any serious attempt to apply the statutes to the facts. Saying that the statutes "answer[s] the question" is not going to get many points without explaining why.

Finally, sticking a line about corporation by estoppel on at the end is not very effective. It does not really show that First Student understands the doctrine and makes no attempt to apply it to the facts. In addition, it gives First Student no opportunity to show how the statutes affect the doctrine. On the other hand, if you notice an issue or remember a rule of law only as your time is running out, it is better to write it down than to leave it out entirely.

The Second Student Answer is much better. Keeping the discussions of B and C truly separate worked well, since they did in fact present different issues. Second Student also made it clear how exceptions and general rules related to each other and did a good job of working facts into the analysis. There is a fine line to be observed between repeating the facts and actually integrating them into the legal analysis, and Second Student succeeded. (Incidentally, in addition to being a better exam writer, it does seem that Second Student knew more than First Student about statutory variations and had a clearer understanding of what the statutes actually mean).

Structuring Your Answer

Graders will give high marks to a clearly written, well-structured answer. Each issue you discuss should follow a specific and consistent structure that a grader can easily follow.

The Second Student Answer basically utilizes the *I-R-A-A-O format* with respect to each issue. In this format, the *I* stands for *Issue*; the *R* for *Rule of law*; the first *A* for *one side's Argument*; the second *A* for *the other party's rebuttal Argument*; and the *O* for your *Opinion as to how the issue would be resolved*. The *I-R-A-A-O* format emphasizes the importance of (1) discussing *both* sides of an issue and (2) communicating to the grader that, where an issue arises, an attorney can only advise his or her client as to the *probable* decision on that issue.

A somewhat different format for analyzing each issue is the *I-R-A-C format*. Here, the *I* stands for *Issue*; the *R* for *Rule of law*; the *A* for *Application of the facts to the rule of law*, and the *C* for *Conclusion. I-R-A-C* is a legitimate approach to the discussion of a particular issue, within the time constraints imposed by the question. The *I-R-A-C format* must be applied to each issue in the question; it is not the solution to the entire answer. If there are six issues in a question, for example, you should offer six separate, independent *I-R-A-C* analyses.

We believe that the *I-R-A-C* approach is preferable to the *I-R-A-A-O* formula. However, either can be used to analyze and organize essay exam answers. Whatever format you choose, however, you should be consistent throughout the exam and remember the following rules:

First, *analyze all of the relevant facts*. Facts have significance in a particular case *only as they come under the applicable rules of law*. The facts presented must be analyzed and examined to see if they do or do not satisfy one element or another of the applicable rules, and the essential facts and rules must be stated and argued in your analysis.

Second, you must communicate to the grader the *precise rule of law* controlling the facts. In their eagerness to commence their arguments, students sometimes fail to state the applicable rule of law first. Remember, the *R* in either format stands for *Rule of law*. Defining the rule of law *before* an analysis of the facts is essential in order to allow the grader to follow your reasoning.

Third, it is important to treat *each side of an issue with equal detail*. If a hypothetical describes how an elderly woman was forced to eat cat food because the directors of a corporation in which she had invested did not declare dividends, your sympathies might understandably fall on the side of the old woman. The grader will nevertheless expect you to see and make every possible argument for the other side. Don't permit your personal viewpoint to affect your answer! A good lawyer never does! When discussing an issue, always state the arguments for each side.

Finally, don't forget to *state your opinion or conclusion* on each issue. Keep in mind, however, that your opinion or conclusion is probably the *least* important part of an exam answer. Why? Because your professor knows that no attorney can tell his or her client exactly how a judge or jury will decide a particular issue. By definition, an issue is a legal dispute that can go either way. An attorney, therefore, can offer the client only his or her best opinion about the likelihood of victory or defeat on an issue. Because the decision on any issue lies with the judge or jury, no attorney can ever be absolutely certain of the resolution.

Discuss All Possible Issues

As we've noted, a student should draw *some* type of conclusion or opinion for each issue raised. Whatever your conclusion on a particular issue, it is essential to anticipate and discuss *all of the issues* that would arise if the question were actually tried in court.

Let's assume that a hypothetical about the duty of care involves issues pertaining to what the duty requires, what constitutes breach, proximate causation, and statutory or other limitations on damages. If the defendant prevails on any one of these issues, he or she may avoid liability. Nevertheless, even if you feel strongly that the duty would have required no different action on the part of the defendant, you *must* go on to discuss all of the other potential issues as well (breach, proximate causation, and limitations on damages). If you were to terminate your answer after a discussion of duty alone, you'd receive an inferior grade. Why should you have to discuss every possible issue if you are relatively certain that the outcome of a particular issue would be dispositive of the entire case? Because at the commencement of litigation, neither party can be *absolutely positive* about which issues he or she will prevail upon at trial. We can state with confidence that every attorney with some degree of experience has won issues he or she thought he or she would lose, and has lost issues on which victory seemed assured. Because one can never be absolutely certain how a factual issue will be resolved by the fact finder, a good attorney (and exam writer) will consider *all* possible issues.

To understand the importance of discussing all of the potential issues, you should reflect on what you will do in the actual practice of law. If you represent the defendant, for example, it is your job to raise every possible defense. If there are five potential defenses, and your pleadings rely on only three of them (because you're sure you will win on all three), and the plaintiff is somehow successful on all three issues, your client may well sue you for malpractice. Your client's contention would be that you should be liable because if you had only raised the two additional issues, you might have prevailed on at least one of them, and therefore liability would have been avoided. It is an attorney's duty to raise *all* legitimate issues. A similar philosophy should be followed when taking essay exams.

What exactly do you say when you've resolved the initial issue in favor of the defendant, and discussion of any additional issues would seem to be moot? The answer is simple. You begin the discussion of the next issue with something like, "Assuming, however, the plaintiff prevailed on the foregoing issue, the next issue would be . . . ." The grader will understand and appreciate what you have done.

The corollary to the importance of raising all potential issues is that you should avoid discussion of obvious nonissues. Raising nonissues is detrimental in three ways: First, you waste a lot of precious time; second, you usually receive absolutely no points for discussing an issue that the grader deems extraneous; and third, it suggests to the grader that you lack the ability to distinguish the significant from the irrelevant. The best guideline for avoiding the discussion of a nonissue is to ask yourself, "Would I, as an attorney, feel comfortable about raising that particular issue or objection in front of a judge?"

Delineate the Transition from One Issue to the Next

It's a good idea to make it easy for the grader to see the issues you've found. One way to accomplish this is to cover no more than one issue per paragraph. Another way is to underline each issue statement. Provided that time permits, we recommend that you use both techniques. The essay answers in this book contain numerous illustrations of these suggestions.

One frequent student error is to write two separate paragraphs in which all of the arguments for one side are made in the initial paragraph, and all of the rebuttal arguments by the other side are made in the next paragraph. This organization is *a bad idea*. It obliges the grader to reconstruct the exam answer in his or her mind several times to determine whether all possible issues have been discussed by both sides. It will also cause you to state the same rule of law more than once. A better-organized answer presents a given argument by one side and follows that immediately in the same paragraph with the other side's rebuttal to that argument.

Understanding the "Call" of a Question

The statement *at the end* of an essay question or of the fact pattern in a multiple-choice question is sometimes referred to as the "call" of the question. It usually asks you to do something specific such as "discuss," "discuss the rights of the parties," "list X's rights," "advise X," "give the best grounds on which to find the shareholder's agreement unenforceable," "state what D can be held liable for," "discuss whether dividends can be compelled," and so forth. The call of the question should be read carefully because it tells you exactly what you're expected to do. If a question asks, "what are X's rights against Y?" or "what is X liable to Y for?" you don't have to spend a lot of time on Y's rights against Z. You will usually receive absolutely no credit for discussing issues or facts that are not required by the call. On the other hand, if the call of an essay question is simply "discuss" or "discuss the rights of the parties," then **all** foreseeable issues must be covered by your answer.

Students are often led astray by an essay question's call. For example, if you are asked for "X's rights against Y" or to "advise X," you may think you may limit yourself to X's viewpoint with respect to the issues. This is **not correct**! You cannot resolve one party's rights against another party without considering the issues that would arise (and the arguments the other side would assert) if litigation occurred. In short, although the call of the question may appear to focus on the rights of one of the parties to the litigation, a superior answer will cover all the issues and arguments that person might **encounter** (not just the arguments he or she would **make**) in attempting to pursue his or her rights against the other side.

The Importance of Analyzing the Question Carefully Before Writing

The overriding **time pressure** of an essay exam is probably a major reason why many students fail to analyze a question carefully before writing. Five minutes into the allocated time for a particular question, you may notice that the person next to you is writing furiously. This thought then flashes through your mind: "Oh my goodness, he's putting down more words on the paper than I am, and therefore he's bound to get a better grade." It can be stated **unequivocally** that there is no necessary correlation between the number of words on your exam paper and the grade you'll receive. Students who begin their answer after only five minutes of analysis have probably seen only the most obvious issues and missed many, if not most, of the subtle ones. They are also likely to be less well organized.

Opinions differ as to how much time you should spend analyzing and outlining a question before you actually write the answer. We believe that you should spend at least 12 to 18 minutes analyzing, organizing, and outlining a one-hour question before writing your answer. This will usually provide sufficient time to analyze and organize the question thoroughly **and** enough time to write a relatively complete answer. Remember that each word of the question must be scrutinized to determine if it (1) suggests an issue under the operative rules of law or (2) can be used in making an argument for the resolution of an issue. Because you can't receive points for an issue you don't spot, it is usually wise to read a question **twice** before starting your outline.

When to Make an Assumption

The instructions for a question may tell you to *assume* facts that are necessary to the answer. Even when these instructions are *not* given, you may be obliged to make certain assumptions about missing facts in order to write a thorough answer. Assumptions should be made only when you are told or when you, as the attorney for one of the parties described in the question, would be obliged to solicit additional information from your client. On the other hand, assumptions should *never be used to change or alter the question.* Don't ever write something like "if the facts in the question were . . . , instead of . . . , then . . . would result." If you do this, you are wasting time on facts that are extraneous to the problem before you. Professors want you to deal with *their* fact patterns, not your own.

Students sometimes try to "write around" information they think is missing. They assume that their professor has failed to include every piece of data necessary for a thorough answer. This is generally *wrong.* The professor may have omitted some facts deliberately to see if the student *can figure out what to do* under the circumstances. However, in some instances, the professor may have omitted them inadvertently (even law professors are sometimes human).

The way to deal with the omission of essential information is to describe (1) what fact (or facts) appears to be missing and (2) why that information is important. Take the following hypothetical as an example: X, an elderly widow, is reduced to eating cat food because the directors of Y Corp., in which she has invested her life's savings, have not declared dividends for some time. When X contacts Y Corp., she is told that the directors "have decided declaration of dividends is not appropriate at this time." X separately finds out that the directors all are also employees of Y Corp., making salaries that are not unreasonable. Note that although this basically comes across as a question about the directors' ability to withhold dividends, you have not been told whether Y Corp. has enough earnings to satisfy statutory requirements. That is, perhaps the directors could not declare dividends even if they wanted to. You would need to build some assumption about this into your answer (i.e., Assuming that statutory requirements for the declaration of dividends are satisfied, ...). You would not, however, want to go into detail talking about what those requirements are. Assumptions should be made in a manner that keeps the other issues open (i.e., they lead to a discussion of all other possible issues). Don't assume facts that would virtually dispose of the entire hypothetical in a few sentences. Suppose that in the mini-hypothetical analyzed earlier in this chapter, you had not been told anything about any discussion that A and B might have had about the way that A was signing their contract. Saying "Assuming that A and B had a separate conversation in which B said he would not hold A personally liable," would not be appropriate. So facile an approach would rarely be appreciated by the grader. The proper way to handle this situation would be to state, "Assuming that A and B had no discussion about the method of signature, ..." You've communicated to the grader that you recognize the need to assume an essential fact and that you've assumed it in a way that enables you to proceed to discuss all other issues.

Case Names

A law student is ordinarily *not* expected to recall case names on an exam. The professor knows that you have read several hundred cases for each course and that you would have to be a memory expert to have all of the names at your fingertips. If you confront a fact pattern that seems similar to a case you have reviewed (but you cannot recall its name), just write something like, "One case we've read held that . . . " or "It has been held that . . . ." In this manner, you have informed the grader that you are relying on a case that contained a fact pattern similar to the question at issue.

The only exception to this rule is in the case of a landmark decision (e.g., *Marbury v. Madison*). Landmark opinions are usually those that change or alter established law. These cases are usually easy to identify, because you will probably have spent an entire class period discussing each of them. *Palsgraf v. Long Island Rail Road* is a prime example of a landmark case in Torts; in Corporations, *Meinhard v. Salmon* and *Dodge v. Ford Motor Company* are worth remembering. In these special cases, you may be expected to recall the case by name, as well as the proposition of law it stands for. However, this represents a very limited exception to the general rule that counsels against wasting precious time trying to memorize and reproduce case names.

How to Handle Time Pressures

What do you do when there are five minutes left in the exam and you have only written down two-thirds of your answer? One thing *not* to do is write something like, "No time left!" or "Not enough time!" This gets you nothing but the satisfaction of knowing you have communicated your personal frustrations to the grader. Another thing *not* to do is insert in the exam booklet the outline you may have made on a piece of scrap paper. Professors will rarely look at these.

First of all, it is not necessarily a bad thing to be pressed for time. The person who finishes five minutes early has very possibly missed some important issues. The more proficient you become in knowing what is expected of you on an exam, the greater the difficulty you may experience in staying within the time limits. Second, remember that (at least to some extent) you're graded against your classmates' answers and they're under exactly the same time pressure as you. In short, don't panic if you can't write the "perfect" answer in the allotted time. Nobody does!

The best hedge against misuse of time is to *review as many old exams as possible.* These exercises will give you a familiarity with the process of organizing and writing an exam answer, which, in turn, should result in an enhanced ability to stay within the time boundaries. If you nevertheless find that you have about 15 minutes of writing to do and 5 minutes to do it in, write a paragraph that summarizes the remaining issues or arguments you would discuss if time permitted. As long as you've indicated that you're aware of the remaining legal issues, you'll probably receive some credit for them. Your analytical and argumentative skills will already be apparent to the grader by virtue of the issues that you have previously discussed.

Formatting Your Answer

Make sure that the way you write or type your answer presents your analysis in the best possible light. In other words, if you write, do so legibly. If you type, remember to use many paragraphs instead of just creating a document in which all of your ideas are merged into a single lengthy block of print. Remember, your professor may have a hundred or more exams to grade. If your answer is difficult to read, you will rarely be given the benefit of the doubt. On the other hand, a paper that is easy to read creates a very positive mental impact upon the professor.

The Importance of Reviewing Prior Exams

As we've mentioned, it is *extremely important to review old exams.* The transition from blackletter law to essay exam can be a difficult experience if the process has not been practiced. Although this book provides a large number of essay and multiple-choice questions, ***don't stop here***! Most law schools have recent tests online or on file in the library, by course. If they are available only in the library, we strongly suggest that you make a copy of every old exam you can obtain (especially those given by your professors) at the beginning of each semester. The demand for these documents usually increases dramatically as "finals time" draws closer.

The exams for each course should be scrutinized ***throughout the semester***. They should be reviewed as you complete each chapter in your casebook. Sometimes the order of exam questions follows the sequence of the materials in your casebook. Thus, the first question on a law school test may involve the initial three chapters of the casebook; the second question may pertain to the fourth and fifth chapters; and so forth. In any event, ***don't wait*** until the semester is nearly over to begin reviewing old exams.

Keep in mind that no one is born with the ability to analyze questions and write superior answers to law school exams. Like any other skill, it is developed and perfected only through application. If you don't take the time to analyze numerous examinations from prior years, this evolutionary process just won't occur. Don't just ***think about*** the answers to past exam questions; take the time to ***write the answers down***. It's also wise to look back at an answer a day or two after you've written it. You will invariably see (1) ways to improve your organizational skills and (2) arguments you missed.

As you practice spotting issues on past exams, you will see how rules of law become the sources of issues on finals. As we've already noted, if you don't ***understand*** how rules of law translate into issues, you won't be able to achieve superior grades on your exams. Reviewing exams from prior years should also reveal that certain issues tend to be lumped together in the same question. For instance, where a fact pattern involves non-declaration of dividends, you probably need to consider both whether the directors are withholding distributions in bad faith and whether the corporation has the statutory ability to make distributions to shareholders. Similarly, questions involving a president taking an act on behalf of a corporation typically will raise issues of both actual and apparent authority. Finally, one of the best means of evaluating if you understand a subject (or a particular area within a subject) is to attempt to create a hypothetical exam for that subject. Your exam should contain as many issues as possible. If you can write an issue-packed exam, you probably know that subject well. If you can't, then you probably haven't yet acquired an adequate understanding of how the principles of law in that subject can spawn issues.

As Always, a Caveat

The suggestions and advice offered in this book represent the product of many years of experience in the field of legal education. We are confident that the techniques and concepts described in these pages will help you prepare for, and succeed at, your exams. Nevertheless, particular professors sometimes have a preference for exam-writing techniques that are not stressed in this book. Some instructors expect at least a nominal reference to the *prima facie* elements of all pertinent legal theories (even though one or more of those principles are *not* placed into issue). Other professors want their students to emphasize public policy considerations in the arguments they make on a particular issue. This book does not stress these individualized preferences. The best way to find out whether your professor has a penchant for a particular writing approach is to ask him or her to provide you with a model answer to a previous exam. If a model answer is not available, speak to second- or third-year students who received a superior grade in that professor's class.

One final point. Although the rules of law stated in the answers to the questions in this book have been drawn from commonly used sources (casebooks, hornbooks, etc.), it is still conceivable that they may be slightly at odds with those taught by your professor. In the area of corporations law, there are differences from jurisdiction to jurisdiction, and your professor will probably advise you to follow the Model Business Corporations Act, Delaware law, or the laws of the state in which you are located. In instances in which a conflict exists between our formulation of a legal principle and the one taught by your professor, *follow the latter*! Because your grades are determined by your professors, their views should always supersede the views contained in this book.

Essay Questions

Question 1

Towncorp is a corporation that is not required to report under the Securities Exchange Act of 1934. During the early to mid-2000s, its directors, including Deanna, authorized the officers to engage in what were known as "hedging" transactions, intended to protect Towncorp against losses in its financial portfolio. The officers thereupon engaged in a series of transactions in various newly designed financial instruments marketed as hedges. They regularly reported to the board on the company's financial condition, giving assurances that Towncorp's portfolio was steadily increasing in value. Deanna, an outside director selected primarily because she was once a prominent government official and now is on the board of a lot of other companies, is not at all financially sophisticated. She reads the materials she is provided and attends all board meetings but does not understand how the hedging transactions really work. She never really makes the slightest attempt to find out, choosing to rely on the expertise of the officers when matters relating to the company's financial condition are discussed. She knows that several of the other companies on the boards of which she sits have engaged in much the same type of hedging transactions. As a matter of fact, a couple of those companies have acted as counter-parties in some of Towncorp's hedges. As it ultimately turns out, the hedging transactions entered by Towncorp have a disastrous impact on the company's portfolio and overall financial condition. When this is revealed, it also is learned that certain officers had assisted another entity with illegal money laundering. This will result in significant sanctions against Towncorp. Inquiry by the board into certain large and dubiously named accounts on the financial statements (i.e., "Miscellaneous Income," and "Other Expenses") might have led to discovery of the illegal activity at a much earlier date. The directors, including Deanna, are told by Towncorp's general counsel that they most certainly can expect to be sued by the shareholders for breaching their fiduciary duties to Towncorp.

Deanna is very concerned about her reputation, as well as the possibility of monetary liability, and has retained you as her own counsel to discuss what her exposure may be. She does not want a discussion relating to the requirements for bringing or maintaining a derivative lawsuit. Neither does she want to hear, at this time, about the possibility of indemnification for any liability or costs she may incur as the result of the prospective litigation.

Question 2

Antonio, Bottom, and Claudius want to form a business entity to commence the business of producing Shakespearean plays and have agreed upon certain goals. These include (in descending order of importance) avoiding individual liability for the obligations of the business, qualifying for pass-through (sometimes known as "conduit") taxation, entitlement to a precisely equal voice in management, and assurance of employment at a guaranteed salary of $75,000 per year. Arguably complicating the picture is the fact that although all will work, Antonio and Bottom also can each invest $500,000. Claudius can contribute only his eye for talent, which is so highly valued by Antonio and Bottom that they are willing to agree to equal profit shares.

Antonio, Bottom, and Claudius have heard about a dizzying assortment of business entities and would like your advice about how each of those entities would lend themselves to achieving their stated goals. They are particularly interested in your explanation of the various merits and demerits of limited partnerships, limited liability partnerships, limited liability limited partnerships, limited liability companies, and corporations, again emphasizing that your advice will be most meaningful in the context of the goals they have described. If there is something else you think they should know, however, please tell them. For instance, if you believe definitions of terms such as "limited liability" or "pass-through taxation" might be useful to a non-lawyer Shakespearean enthusiast, please provide those definitions.

For purposes of preparing this answer, you may assume that the bar authorities in your state take the position that advising multiple parties in the context of business formation does not constitute a sanctionable conflict of interest.

Question 3

Paul owns 250 of the 1,000 issued and authorized shares of Durco, a State X close corporation. The Durco directors are Al, who owns 650 shares of Durco stock, and Baker and Carr, each of whom owns 50 shares. Al offered to buy Paul's Durco shares at a price substantially less than Paul had paid to acquire the stock. Paul refused Al's offer, claiming the offered price was "unfair."

Paul has brought an action in State X court against Durco and its three directors. His complaint alleges the following:

1. The directors acted unreasonably in failing to have Durco distribute as cash dividends approximately $5 million of accumulated earnings.

2. The distribution is being arbitrarily withheld for the benefit of Al.

3. There is an "invalid" agreement among the individual defendants as Durco shareholders, the purpose of which is to maintain Al in office as "managing director" to "supervise and direct the operations and management" of all of Durco's business.

4. Paul has been consistently denied the right to inspect Durco's corporate records during regular working hours or at any other time.

By way of relief, the complaint asks that (1) Al be removed as a director for misconduct, (2) the shareholders' agreement be found invalid, (3) the directors declare and pay a substantial cash dividend, and (4) Paul be permitted to inspect Durco's records during normal business hours.

In their answer, the defendants allege that Paul's action should be considered a derivative action and admit (1) the existence and terms of the shareholders' agreement, (2) withholding of accumulated earnings of approximately $5 million, and (3) denial of access by Paul to Durco's records. They allege by way of affirmative defense that (1) the discretion of the directors to declare dividends has been properly exercised (the business judgment rule); (2) the shareholders' agreement is valid, and, therefore, Al cannot be removed as director, even for cause; and (3) the requested inspection should be denied because Paul wants to inspect the corporate records only for the "improper purpose" of bringing a "strike suit."

The defendants have moved for an order requiring Paul to post security for costs in the pending action.

State X law grants an unqualified right to shareholders of State X corporations to inspect corporate books and records and requires plaintiffs in shareholder derivative actions to provide security for costs.

1. Discuss how the court should rule on the defendants' motion for security for costs.
2. Discuss how the court should rule on each of Paul's requests for relief.

Question 4

The bylaws of Dixie, a publicly held corporation, provide that "the number of directors of the corporation is to be five." Insofar as pertinent, Dixie's articles of incorporation state that the initial board shall consist of the following five named individuals. The articles go on to provide for annual election of directors.

Since its incorporation five years ago, Dixie has been very profitable. Anticipating a hostile takeover attempt, the board voted to increase its size to nine and to stagger the terms of directors so that only three would stand for election each year.

Stan, owner of 29 percent of Dixie's voting stock, demanded that the board call a special meeting of shareholders to disapprove the board's action and to remove the president from office. The board refused to call a meeting for those purposes. It filled the newly created board positions with persons who were experienced in business and were close friends of the original board members. The new board entered into transactions that resulted in financial loss to Dixie, but that made the corporation a less attractive target for takeover.

When Stan filed a derivative suit against Dixie and the directors challenging the board's conduct, the board appointed the new members as a "special litigation committee." Thereafter, the board moved to dismiss the suit because, "based on the recommendation of the special litigation committee, the board has concluded the suit is not in the best interests of Dixie."

1. Discuss whether the board acted lawfully in:
   a. Increasing its size to nine members without a shareholder vote.
   b. Staggering the terms of board members without a shareholder vote.
   c. Refusing to call a special meeting of shareholders.
   d. Filling the newly created board positions without a shareholder vote.
2. Discuss whether the court should grant the board's motion to dismiss.

Do **not** discuss any federal securities law issues.

Question 5

Corp, Inc. (Corp), has 200,000 authorized and outstanding shares of $1 par value stock. Andy, Barb, Carla, and Dave each purchased at par, and each continues to hold, 50,000 shares of Corp. Corp's articles of incorporation prohibit incurring any single debt in excess of $75,000 and require a vote representing 80 percent of outstanding shares to amend the articles. The articles also provide for preemptive rights, cumulative voting, and a board of four directors. Each of the four shareholders has elected him- or herself director at annual shareholders' meetings during each year of Corp's existence.

Corp's board unanimously decided to borrow $100,000 from Lender. Lender took Corp's ten-year note, bearing interest at 20 percent per annum, payable in monthly interest installments. Corp has the option to pay off the note at any time, without penalty. Later, Lender needed funds and approached Andy, Corp's treasurer. Lender offered to sell the note for $90,000. Andy, without consulting Barb, Carla, or Dave, purchased the note for his own account.

The week following Andy's purchase of the note, Rich asked to subscribe to 100,000 shares of Corp stock at $1 per share. Barb, Carla, and Dave approved of Rich's proposal. But, at the annual shareholders' meeting, Andy voted against, and thus defeated, a proposed amendment of the articles of incorporation that would have authorized additional shares free from preemptive rights. Because of the note's high interest, Andy did not want it paid off. The other directors, now aware that Andy had acquired the note, and hoping to use Rich's investment to pay the note, were angered and caused Corp to cease paying the monthly interest installments on the note.

Rich then caused the incorporation of Endrun, Inc. (Endrun), and subscribed to 100,000 of its shares for $100,000. Rich proposes that Corp be merged into Endrun, that each Corp share be converted into an Endrun share, and that Endrun pay the Lender note now held by Andy. Corp's board has approved the merger, 3 to 1, with Andy dissenting.

Assume that the interest rate on the note is **not** usurious. Assume also that there is some reason Corp cannot borrow in order to pay off the note.

1. Discuss whether Andy breached any duty to Corp or his fellow shareholders in voting against the proposal to issue 100,000 shares to Rich.

2. Discuss whether Andy can obtain an injunction to prevent the Corp-Endrun merger.

3. Discuss whether Andy can collect interest payments on Corp's note.

Question 6

Examco, Inc. is a company engaged in the rapidly growing business of exam preparation software. The initial capital of $100,000 with which it started has ballooned to $100,000,000 worth of assets in just a few years. It has a board of directors composed of Pablo (Examco's president), Choi (its chief financial officer), and eleven outsiders (that is, people who are not otherwise employed by Examco).

The board has no committees. All matters coming before it are considered at meetings at which every member seems to feel compelled to express him or herself. They are all getting tired of this and ask Pablo to propose something new. In short order he announces (to the board as well as Examco's workforce) a policy he calls "We can handle this at staff level." For instance, when he decides that executive recruitment and retention is problematic, he creates a new employee benefit of subsidized loans to be extended to all new employees moving to the area. As part of one of the many reports he submits to the board, he does include a line about the new benefit, but no one ever asks about it. After no more than a few months of the new policy, meetings are much shorter, although written reports are much longer.

Suellen, an Examco shareholder, becomes concerned about the overall level of the company's executive compensation. She would like to have the shareholders vote to cut back on benefits programs. Suellen owns a substantial percentage of Examco's stock but not enough for her to control a shareholder vote. She knows that she will have to get a number of the company's 499 other holders of common stock to vote with her and would prefer to piggyback her proposal on management's annual proxy solicitation materials if she can do so.

Suellen seeks your advice about all matters reasonably raised. You should not address procedural enforcement mechanisms (i.e., whether to bring either derivative or individual litigation).

Question 7

Art has been president of Exco, a publicly held corporation with net assets of approximately $50 million, for the past six years. Exco manufactures computers. Two years ago, Art negotiated an agreement for the purchase by Exco of all of the outstanding shares of Yang, Inc. (Yang), a privately held maker of computer components, for $5 million cash. The purchase was completed about 18 months ago. At the time, members of Art's immediate family held Yang's outstanding shares. This information was **not** known except to Art, Yang's management, and Bobbie, an Exco director.

Art negotiated Exco's purchase of Yang stock and executed the purchase agreement on behalf of Exco, relying on his authority as its president. Before the purchase documents were signed, Art discussed the proposed acquisition individually with Bobbie, Curt, and Donna. Curt and Donna are Exco directors who, with Art and Bobbie, comprise a majority of Exco's seven-person board of directors. Bobbie, Curt, and Donna each told Art that he or she approved of the transaction.

After Exco purchased the Yang stock, at the next regular meeting of the Exco board one month later, Art informed all of the directors of the acquisition. While some questions were asked, there was no vote taken on the acquisition at the meeting. Not counting Bobbie, no Exco director was informed of the ownership of Yang stock by Art's family members. Because Bobbie believed the acquisition was beneficial to Exco, she never mentioned her knowledge of the prior ownership of Yang stock by members of Art's family to any of the other Exco directors. The existence of the prior ownership could, however, have been discovered by a review of Yang's corporate records.

Since the stock purchase by Exco, Yang has been consistently and increasingly unprofitable. At the annual Exco shareholders' meeting two months ago, Art, Bobbie, Curt, and Donna were **not** reelected as directors. Last month, Exco's new board replaced Art as president.

1. Discuss whether Exco can rescind the purchase of Yang stock.
2. Discuss whether Exco can recover damages for Yang's unprofitability from any or all of the following:
   a. Art
   b. Bobbie
   c. Curt and Donna

Question 8

Al, Bob, Carla, and Dan own 20 percent each of the outstanding shares of the common stock of Etco, a profitable corporate retailer, and they are the corporation's four directors. Al and Bob are Etco's officers. The remaining 20 percent of the outstanding shares are divided among ten individuals, including Freda, who is a 5 percent shareholder. Etco has only one class of stock.

At a board meeting six months ago, Al announced that he had negotiated a contract to have all of Etco's stores cleaned nightly by XYZ, a partnership jointly owned by Al and Bob. Al disclosed XYZ's ownership at this Etco board meeting, but neither he nor Bob disclosed that the price for cleaning services to be charged Etco by XYZ under the contract was double the market rate. The board approved the contract with XYZ by unanimous vote of all four directors. XYZ immediately began its cleaning services and has been receiving payments under the contract with Etco.

At the same meeting, the Etco board unanimously voted in favor of Carla's proposal to have Etco redeem most of her shares at $25 per share, to provide funds to Carla for a sudden family emergency. At the time, Etco did not have retained earnings equal to the cost of redeeming Carla's stock, but Etco's earnings in the preceding fiscal year, which erased a prior earnings deficit, did exceed the cost of redeeming Carla's stock. Etco's articles of incorporation have no provisions regarding redemption of its stock.

1. Having recently found out about the XYZ contract, Freda has brought a shareholder derivative action against all four directors seeking a judgment rescinding the XYZ contract and for damages to Etco arising from the approval of the contract by the directors. Discuss what the result should be.

2. On her own behalf, Freda has sued Etco and its four directors for a judgment rescinding the redemption of Carla's stock or, in the alternative, requiring redemption by Etco of Freda's stock at $25 per share or for involuntary dissolution of Etco. Discuss what relief, if any, Freda is entitled to in the suit.

Question 9

Four years ago, Paula bought 10,000 shares of the common stock of Deco Corporation (Deco). Two years ago, Deco purchased four retail stores from Savco for $4 million, which was a fair price. Tom, president and a director of Deco, was also a director of Savco. He was absent from the meeting of the Deco board of directors at which the agreement for purchase of the Savco stores was considered. In Tom's absence, the proposed purchase was unanimously approved by the remaining four Deco directors, who constituted a quorum of the board.

About 20 months ago, the Deco directors resolved to issue 25,000 shares of authorized, but unissued, Deco common stock to Smith, in exchange for Greenacre, a store site owned by Smith. The directors did not offer any of the 25,000 shares for acquisition by Deco shareholders before consummating the deal with Smith.

At a special meeting of the Deco board three months ago, Tom advised the board that an audit had established that Deco had incurred a $25 million loss during the preceding fiscal year and that the loss would be publicly announced at the annual Deco shareholders' meeting in two weeks. Tom then tendered his resignation both as president and as a director of Deco, effective immediately, which the board accepted.

Within the two-week period before the stockholders' meeting, Tom sold his 20,000 shares of Deco common stock for $25 per share. After the annual shareholders' meeting, Deco common stock dropped to $10 per share.

Paula died three weeks after the shareholders' meeting. Her daughter, Emma, inherited all of Paula's shares of Deco stock. Emma made three demands on the Deco board of directors, stating that, if each of the demands was not met, she, as a shareholder, would bring appropriate legal action. The demands were as follows:

1. The purchase of the four stores from Savco should be set aside.
2. Emma should be permitted to purchase a number of Deco shares in the same proportion as Paula's 10,000 shares bore to all Deco shares issued and outstanding at the time the shares were transferred to Smith.
3. Deco should bring suit against Tom to recover $300,000, based on the sale of his Deco stock in the two weeks before the annual shareholders' meeting.

Discuss how the Deco directors should respond to each of the demands by Emma.

Question 10

Three years ago, A and B decided to establish Z Corp to manufacture and sell electronic devices. They signed articles of incorporation and established themselves as a two-person board of directors. Each paid $10,000 in cash for 100 shares of the $100 par value common stock of the corporation. However, A and B inadvertently failed to file the articles.

Two and a half years ago, A and B met C, a business consultant whom they hired to advise them on Z Corp's business matters. One month after meeting A and B, C filed Z Corp's articles of incorporation with the secretary of state. Immediately thereafter, C was issued 100 shares of Z Corp common stock: 10 shares in return for services rendered, 40 shares in return for services to be rendered in the future, and 50 shares in return for his personal note to Z Corp for $5,000. C became the third member of the board of directors and was elected treasurer.

One month after filing the articles, C discharged his $5,000 note obligation by transferring office equipment to Z Corp appraised at $6,500 by an independent appraiser. C had purchased this equipment at an auction three months earlier for $1,000.

Two years ago, Z Corp received $10,000 in cash from each of two investors, D, a local banker, and E. Each investor was issued 100 shares of common stock.

About six months ago, it became obvious that Z Corp was experiencing financial difficulty. C heard of a developmental opportunity in a field directly related to Z Corp's operations, but he did *not* advise the other directors because Z Corp lacked sufficient assets to exploit the opportunity. Instead, C, D, and several friends formed a partnership that invested in, and made considerable profit on, the new business opportunity.

Recently, Z Corp's assets became insufficient to discharge its liabilities. Its creditors, many with claims dating back to three years ago, commenced an action against Z Corp and all five shareholders. E has cross-complained against the other four shareholders.

1. Discuss the liabilities, if any, of A, B, C, D, and E to Z Corp's creditors.
2. Discuss the liabilities, if any, of A, B, C, and D to E.

Question 11

Asiago and Brie are partners in a general partnership formed for the purpose of running a cheese shop that imports and sells quality cheese. It carries on business under the name "Asiago, Brie & More." The written partnership agreement specifies that Asiago will contribute $300,000. Brie will provide all necessary labor. Other terms include the following: (1) The partnership will exist for a term of two years, whereupon the partners will determine whether they wish to continue the business. (2) Profits will be split equally.

Almost immediately, Asiago decides that Asiago, Brie & More needs more capital. He therefore invites Edam to contribute $300,000 for a one-third interest in the partnership. Brie objects. Asiago sighs and suggests that the $300,000 be characterized as a loan. Edam said that was fine with him, just so long as he could receive interest in the form of a one-third profit share during the term of the loan (which they agreed would be for the life of the partnership) and be entitled to veto certain uses of his capital. The trio goes forward on that basis. Although Edam never really does any work or makes any decisions, he is fond of hanging around the cheese shop. His name and face are well known to everyone who enters the store, including Colby, the proprietor of CheezRUs (which is Asiago, Brie & More's biggest supplier).

Toward the end of the first year of the partnership's term, Edam and Brie overhear a phone call made by Asiago. Asiago hates the boursin (a type of cheese known for its distinctive odor) that Brie is fond of ordering from CheezRUs and lets her know it. The phone call is to make sure that CheezRUs knows it as well. Asiago tells Colby that he is to deliver no more boursin to Asiago, Brie & More. Before Asiago hangs up, Edam grins and very loudly says, "You've got my vote!" The next day, Brie nonetheless places an order with CheezRUs for $30,000 of boursin. Colby fills the order.

A few days later, Brie takes stock of her situation. She hates Asiago. She also realizes that although she has been working very hard, there are not going to be any profits to share. In fact, the $600,000 from Asiago and Edam has been entirely exhausted and the partnership has no other funds. She believes that, at the least, she should be entitled to a reasonable salary for what she has done.

1. Brie consults you, asking four questions. First, can she get out of the partnership? Second, can she get a salary? Third, who is liable to CheezRUs? Fourth, assuming that Brie would only get out of the partnership if

she is legally entitled to do so, what are her rights and obligations with respect to Asiago and Edam if she does so? If there are any logically prior questions, you should be careful to address them as well.

2. What difference would it have made to your analysis if, instead of carrying on business as a general partnership, Asiago and Brie initially had formed a limited liability partnership?

Question 12

Ajax Mfg. Corp. issued 250,000 shares of $50 par value common stock. Ten thousand of the shares were reacquired and are currently held as treasury stock. After a board meeting at which a number of specific possible Ajax plant expansion sites were discussed, Babb, one of Ajax's nine directors, paid $3,000 to obtain an option to purchase Blackacre, one of those sites, at a purchase price of $120,000. Ajax had allocated $250,000 for site acquisition. When the other directors learned that Babb had acquired the option for Blackacre, they demanded that she assign it to the corporation for the option price of $3,000.

At a subsequent board meeting, the directors voted to purchase Whiteacre for $50,000 from Carl, a director, who had acquired it for $10,000 before becoming a director.

The board also voted to sell the 10,000 treasury shares for $71 per share to Dale, who had been offered employment by Ajax as vice president of finance. Dale had insisted on becoming a shareholder as a condition to accepting the offered employment and agreed to the price of the stock. Earl, an Ajax shareholder, seeks to enjoin this sale, claiming that it violates his preemptive rights.

At the same meeting, the board approved the sale of Greenacre for $50,000. It had been purchased by Ajax five years ago for $70,000.

Fox, vice president of operations for Ajax, heard that Gert, an Ajax shareholder, was annoyed with management and was offering to sell her shares for $65 per share. The latest financial report for Ajax, distributed to all shareholders, indicated that Ajax stock had a book value of $70.50. Fox purchased Gert's shares at her price.

Discuss the following:

1. The demand that Babb assign her option to purchase Blackacre to Ajax.

2. The propriety of Ajax's purchase of Whiteacre from Carl for $50,000.

3. Earl's right to enjoin the sale of 10,000 shares of treasury stock to Dale.

4. The propriety of the sale of Greenacre for $50,000.

5. Fox's liability, if any, by reason of his purchase of Gert's shares.

Question 13

The following actions were taken pursuant to unanimous vote of the directors of Ajax, a corporation:

1. To prevent a minority shareholder from acquiring control, Ajax purchased shares from three shareholders at their asking price of $80 per share. At the time, Ajax's shares had a book value of $92 and a market value of $75 per share.

2. After it was announced that Bob, the longtime treasurer for Ajax, was retiring, Ajax agreed to pay Bob $5,000 annually during his lifetime.

3. Ajax agreed to pay the legal fees and costs of Curt, a vice president, who was being sued in a shareholders' derivative action for making political contributions from corporate funds to candidates designated by other corporations with whom Ajax did business.

4. Ajax adopted a stock option plan for all officers and directors and issued the first set of options.

Pat owns 100 Ajax shares that she acquired before the above events took place. She subsequently purchased 50 additional shares, but has been unable to have the shares transferred to her name because, according to the corporate secretary, the shares are subject to a restrictive shareholders' agreement preventing the transfer. No such restriction appears on the Ajax certificates, including those in Pat's name representing her earlier shareholdings.

Pat feels that all the above-described actions by Ajax and its directors have violated her rights as a shareholder and damaged her. She also wants to know if she is entitled to have the additional 50 shares of Ajax stock registered in her name.

1. Discuss whether Pat has any claim for relief with respect to each of the above-described actions taken by Ajax.

2. Discuss whether Pat has a right to have the 50 shares of Ajax stock registered in her name.

Question 14

Freightco is a State X corporation conducting a trucking business. On June 30 of last year, its board of directors voted to declare a cash dividend of $500,000 from earned surplus and to borrow $1 million to finance an advertising campaign by issuing debentures to be purchased at face value by Landco, a State X corporation conducting a real estate business. Freightco owns 80 percent of the outstanding stock of Landco. Freightco's directors are also the directors of Landco.

An hour after the Freightco board meeting, the Landco board of directors met and voted not to declare any dividend, despite a staff recommendation that a dividend of $1 million be declared. Landco had a sufficient surplus from which such a dividend could be paid. At the same time, the Landco board voted to purchase the Freightco debentures at face value, even though previously issued Freightco debentures with the same terms were selling on the open market at 84 percent of face value. Both the articles and the bylaws of Landco expressly provide that the votes of "interested" directors may count toward a quorum and that "interested" directors may vote on contracts.

Six months after its dividend distribution, Freightco was adjudicated bankrupt. An investigation of Freightco's business affairs disclosed that (1) a report by a specially hired management consulting firm, presented to each director of Freightco before the June 30 board meeting, predicted bankruptcy unless all available capital was allocated to the purchase of new trucks, and (2) only 5 of the 15 Freightco directors actually read the report.

Agee owns 5 percent of the outstanding shares of Landco and also owns Freightco shares. Discuss each claim that Agee may assert either on his own behalf or on behalf of Freightco and Landco and discuss the capacity in which he should assert each claim.

Question 15

Dynamics, Inc., was incorporated two years ago, with an initial authorized capitalization of 10,000 shares of $100 par value common stock. Ames subscribed to 100 shares prior to incorporation; later, but still before Dynamics was incorporated, Ames threatened to withdraw her stock subscription unless she was issued an additional 20 shares at $50 a share. Because Ames's subscription was needed for initial operating capital, the promoters for Dynamics agreed to issue the additional shares to her, and following incorporation, Ames paid $11,000 to Dynamics for which 120 shares marked "fully paid" were issued.

Soon after Dynamics was incorporated, Bates was issued 1,000 shares of stock for transferring to Dynamics his title to Blackacre, which Bates had purchased a year earlier for $55,000.

After issuing a total of 7,500 shares, including the 1,120 shares issued to Ames and Bates, Dynamics could find no other purchasers for its stock.

Last year, its first fiscal year of operations, Dynamics had a net operating loss of $50,000. However, at the end of the year, the board of directors determined that Blackacre was worth $160,000 and, by resolution, directed that its book value be increased to that amount. The board then declared a $2 cash dividend on the 7,500 shares then outstanding.

Last month, without first offering the stock to any other shareholder, Dynamics issued 500 shares of stock to Carl in return for Carl's transfer of title to Greenacre, which the corporation wants for a future plant site.

Paula, a shareholder, gave Fox, vice president of Dynamics, an "irrevocable" proxy to vote Paula's shares. When Paula later sought to revoke the proxy, Fox told her the proxy could not be revoked during Paula's lifetime or as long as Paula owned the Dynamics stock.

1. Discuss whether Ames and Bates are liable to Dynamics for any additional money in connection with the issuance of shares to them.
2. Discuss whether the declaration of the $2 cash dividend was proper.
3. Discuss whether the transaction with Carl was valid.
4. Discuss whether Paula has the right to vote her Dynamics stock.

Question 16

A, B, and C agreed to promote the formation of Z Corporation to engage in the manufacture of electronic equipment. A, without the knowledge of B and C, entered into a written agreement with X, whereby Z Corporation would, upon its formation, hire X as manager of research at a salary of $60,000 per year for five years.

A, B, and C executed articles of incorporation, and their attorney forwarded these articles to the secretary of state. However, the attorney failed to include the required filing fee, and for that reason the secretary of state refused to file the articles. The secretary of state sent notice of this failure to the attorney, but he had gone on vacation. This information was not brought to the attention of A, B, or C. A, B, and C elected themselves the first directors of Z Corporation, issued stock, and elected C its president.

B, in possession of certain equipment reasonably worth $50,000, conveyed it to Z Corporation for $100,000 worth of common stock, at par value. C contracted with Q to supply the corporation with materials valued under the contract at $20,000, signing the contract, "Z Corporation, by C, President." These materials were shipped and received by Z Corporation.

Because of a number of difficulties, Z Corporation's business never got a proper start. B and C then refused to hire X. The business is now insolvent and has filed for bankruptcy. Q has not been paid for his materials.

Discuss the rights and liabilities of the various parties.

Question 17

Banco is a banking corporation with 50,000 shareholders. It was formed under a law similar in all material respects to a general corporation law. Its board of directors voted unanimously to organize Combank, a corporation, to own and operate a bank in a low-income area. The resolution provided, among other things, that:

1. Combank would have two classes of stock, Class A and Class B, the shares of each having a par value of $10, with equal rights in all respects, except that Class B stock would be nonvoting.

2. Banco would purchase the entire issue of Class B stock of 100,000 shares for $1 million cash.

3. The 100,000 shares of Class A stock would be issued only to persons becoming depositors, at $10 per share.

4. For ten years, Banco would return its Class B dividends to Combank as a contribution to capital.

Before Combank's incorporation, O, an officer of Banco, negotiated a contract with Duc, a building contractor, to remodel a downtown building as offices for Combank. Work was to begin immediately and be completed within nine months. When Duc insisted that Banco's name be on the contract, O signed it, "Banco, by O, on behalf of Combank, a corporation to be formed."

One week later, Combank was duly incorporated. Banco purchased the entire authorized 100,000 shares of Class B stock and executed an assignment to Combank of all dividends on the Class B stock for a period of ten years. Three months after the Duc contract, Combank's officers and employees moved into the partially remodeled building. No action was taken by the Combank board of directors with respect to the Duc contract.

One month later, Combank's board voted 5 to 4, with director X voting with the majority, to hire Exco, a construction firm owned by X, to complete the remodeling in place of Duc. Pursuant to this action, Combank entered into a contract with Exco. At that time, Duc had performed satisfactorily and was on schedule.

1. Z, a Banco shareholder, brings a derivative action against the Banco directors for wasting corporate assets. Discuss whether the action will succeed.

2. Discuss whether Duc's contract is enforceable by Duc and, if so, against whom.

3. Discuss whether Exco can enforce its contract with Combank.

Question 18

Gasco is a State X corporation involved in the petroleum industry. Its stock is traded on the New York Stock Exchange. Its board of directors hired Media, a public relations firm, to campaign against the passage of a State X ballot proposition to use gasoline tax receipts for the development of a statewide public transit system. The contract provided that Gasco's financing of the campaign would not be made public by Gasco or Media.

A group of Gasco shareholders, calling themselves Citizens Against Pollution (CAP), learned of the contract. They submitted to Gasco management, for inclusion in the next proxy statement and for presentation to the Gasco shareholders at the next shareholders' meeting, proposals to:

1. Remove from the Gasco board those directors "who voted to authorize the Media contract or otherwise sought to prevent passage of the gasoline tax proposition."

2. Require the use of nonpolluting cleansing products in all company-owned gas stations.

CAP has complied with all SEC procedural requirements (including ownership requirements, word limitations, and limitations on the number of proposals per shareholder).

A State X statute requires public disclosure of all corporate expenditures "designed to influence the outcome of issues to be decided by public ballot."

Pursuant to a valid Gasco bylaw, only three of the nine Gasco directors are to be elected at the next shareholders' meeting. The Gasco charter provides that the board of directors may, by majority vote, remove a director for "sufficient cause."

Discuss and decide the following:

1. Is management required to present the CAP proposals to the shareholders and include them in the proxy statement?

2. If adopted at the shareholders' meeting, would the proposals be binding on the board of directors?

3. If a new Gasco board repudiates the Media contract, may Media nevertheless have it enforced?

Question 19

Jetco, a corporation whose stock is traded on a national stock exchange, has 200,000 shares of $25 par value common stock outstanding. It has a seven-person board of directors.

Dan, who owns 100 shares of Jetco stock, is a director of Jetco. Five months ago, Dan learned that Jetco had developed a secret new invention to convert organic waste to commercial fuel and that a public announcement of the invention was soon to be made.

Dan immediately wrote to three of Jetco's shareholders who, Dan knew, had previously announced their willingness to sell their shares for $22 per share, a price that was $3 a share above book value. Dan offered them $25 per share. They accepted his offer and sold a total of 4,200 shares to Dan. At this time, Dan also accepted, and immediately exercised, stock option rights to purchase 1,000 authorized, but previously unissued, shares from Jetco, for which he paid the option price of $21 per share.

Two months ago, Jetco's board chair, Wood, learned of the 4,200 shares that Dan had acquired from the three dissatisfied shareholders. When Dan refused Wood's demand that he resign as a director, the board, at its meeting two weeks later, declared Dan's board seat vacant, although his term of office would not expire for another six months.

A week later, the invention was announced, and the market value of Jetco stock rose substantially.

A few days ago, Dan sold, for $50 per share, the 4,200 shares he had acquired from the three dissatisfied shareholders.

1. Discuss whether Dan has the right to remain on the board for the balance of his unexpired term.
2. Discuss Dan's potential liabilities, and to whom, as a result of the above transactions.

Question 20

Art, Bob, and Carla were the three shareholders of Getco, a State X corporation, each owning one-third of the shares issued. They were also the three directors of the corporation. In a written shareholder agreement executed by all of them, they each granted a right of first refusal to the other two, equally, "should such shareholder seek to sell his or her shares to anyone other" than to Getco itself. This agreement also required a "90 percent majority vote for all shareholder or director action, including the election of directors," and required each shareholder to cast his or her vote for the election of the other shareholders as directors of Getco.

A State X statute provides as follows:

> Unless otherwise provided in the certificate of incorporation, if the directors of a corporation are equally divided respecting the management of its affairs, or if the votes of its shareholders are so divided that they cannot elect a board of directors, the holders of at least one-half of the shares of stock may present a verified petition for the involuntary dissolution of the corporation, as provided in this Chapter.

Carla died. Under the terms of her will, her shares of stock in Getco were bequeathed to Doris, her niece. Although Art and Bob claimed they had the right to purchase Carla's shares at her death, the probate court ruled that it had no jurisdiction to decide stockholder claims. The decree of distribution in the probate of Carla's estate distributed her shares in Getco to Doris.

Art and Bob have refused to elect Doris to the Getco board of directors, asserting that they are Getco's only valid shareholders. They have also held over in office as directors for two years since Carla's death, as no shareholder is able to muster a 90 percent vote to elect new directors. The board of directors has taken no action during the same period, and no dividends have been declared since Carla's death.

Doris seeks your advice as to how she can gain shareholder benefits and a voice in Getco's management or, in the alternative, have Getco dissolved and its assets distributed.

Discuss the advice you would give her.

Question 21

For several years, Willie Loman and Terry Malloy have been equal share-holders in Might Have Been, Inc. ("MHB"), a corporation specializing in memorabilia relating to depressing stage plays and movies. They also are the only members of the board of directors and have alternated years in the positions of president and secretary. It has never really mattered that much who held which position, as they always were in agreement. This year, notwithstanding MHB's extreme profitability, the two gentlemen just cannot seem to agree on anything, including whether their line of business should extend to works that are somewhat more uplifting, whether certain specific transactions relating to depressing stage plays and movies should be approved, and whether Terry must give up the job of president and let Willie take his turn. It may well be the case (although they have not yet discussed it) that they will not be able to agree to the election of themselves as directors.

Terry Malloy retains you to advise him, asking you to assume that Willie will continue to disagree with him about everything. He insists that you cover not only what his rights currently are with respect to resolving the various disputes and terminating his business association with Willie, but what they would have been if MHB had taken the form of either a limited liability partnership or limited liability company. He also would like to know how, under each scenario, things might have been different if a good friend of his, George Bailey (who he believes now would agree with him about everything), had been made a one-third owner at the time the relevant entity was created.

Question 22

Jax, Inc. (Jax), was incorporated almost seven years ago with authorization to issue 2,500 shares of common stock at a stated par value of $100 per share. Of these, 2,200 shares of Jax stock have been issued and are outstanding. For its initial five years, Jax incurred net operating losses totaling $80,000. Last year, however, the corporation had net earnings of $25,000. The Jax board of directors, consisting of A, B, and C, met on February 16 of this year and unanimously voted to declare a cash dividend of $10 per share on outstanding stock.

Pursuant to a bylaw authorizing the board to appoint officers and committees, A, B, and C also voted at the February meeting to create an executive committee composed of B, C, and W. W is not a director or officer of Jax, but he is a shareholder. The bylaw permitted, and the board resolution provided, that the committee would have powers similar to those of the board of directors.

On June 15 of this year, the board authorized the purchase by Jax of 220 shares of its stock then held by D, at a price of $95 per share. D had indicated she was ready to sell the shares at that price to a competitor of Jax.

On July 18 of this year, the executive committee directed Jax to issue 100 shares of previously unissued stock to E as "fully paid" shares, in return for E's promissory note to Jax in the sum of $7,500. The stock was issued to E for her note as described.

On August 31 of this year, A, Jax's president, wrote to F, a superintendent employed by the company who was retiring in one week, as follows: "In light of your many years of faithful service to this company, Jax will pay you a monthly pension of $300 for the rest of your life."

S, a Jax shareholder, asks you to advise him on the legality of the following:

1. The declaration of the cash dividend.

2. The creation of an executive committee.

3. The purchase of shares from D.

4. The issuance of the 100 shares to E.

5. The promise to pay F a monthly pension.

Discuss.

Question 23

Abby, chief executive officer of Oilco, was eating lunch with several Oilco executives when she saw her business school classmate, Barb, sit down at the next table. Abby was aware that Barb had become a prominent local stockbroker. In an unusually loud voice, Abby stated to her fellow executives, "I bet my former classmate would love to know that tomorrow we are going to announce a tender offer for ALT Corporation."

Barb overheard this remark and, when she returned to her office, bought 10,000 shares of ALT Corporation for her own account.

Barb also telephoned the Mutual Fund Complex (Mutual) and told its chief executive officer, "If you are smart, you will buy ALT Corporation stock this afternoon." Within one hour, Mutual placed an order to buy 50,000 shares of ALT, using Barb as the broker.

That afternoon, Barb visited Cora, a neighbor whom she had come to dislike intensely. Cora, at Barb's recommendation, had previously purchased 100 shares of ALT stock. Barb told Cora that ALT shares were about to decrease in value and that she was willing to buy the ALT shares from Cora at the stock's current price because Cora had bought the stock on her advice in the first place. Cora immediately sold Barb all of her ALT stock.

The following morning, Oilco announced a tender offer for ALT Corporation shares at a price 50 percent above its current market price. Approximately one month later, the tender offer was completed, with Barb and Mutual receiving profits of approximately 50 percent on their shares. Abby has not purchased ALT shares for more than three years.

1. Discuss whether Abby, Barb, or Mutual has violated SEC Rule 10b-5.

2. Discuss whether Barb has incurred any potential nonstatutory civil liability.

Question 24

X, LLC (X), is a member-managed limited liability company owned by Quentin (Q) and Ralph (R). Their ownership interests are equal, and each contributed $1,000 in start-up capital. X's relatively few assets were purchased primarily with borrowed money and are subject to security interests.

X is in the business of transporting toxic waste to various disposal sites owned and operated by unrelated entities. Q and R have been careful about maintaining the necessary license. One of the requirements for obtaining a license was to demonstrate "financial responsibility." This required either (1) a certification that X had equity capital in a certain amount or (2) proof of insurance against the consequences of negligent acts. Because X could not meet the equity capital test, Q and R were forced to obtain the necessary insurance.

One of the reasons that Q and R formed a limited liability company was because they did not want to bother observing corporate formalities. They are casual about keeping records and do not bother to keep X's scant funds in a separate account. Generally, whenever X is paid for a job, Q checks to see what maintenance is required for X's equipment and how much fuel is needed for its trucks. He then cashes the check and uses whatever is necessary for X's purposes. The remainder is split, 50-50, between Q and R. Q has a good head for figures, though, and makes sure that, when a debt payment is coming due, there is money to pay for it.

For the last year, X has provided hazardous waste transportation services to Y Medical Center (Y) pursuant to a contract calling for payments to X of $50,000 a year. There are no other hazardous waste transportation service providers in the area, and contracting with a service provider out of the vicinity probably would cost Y three times as much.

As the contract is about to expire, Y seeks to renew it. Counsel for Y prepares a new form of contract identical to the last. Without discussing the matter with Q, R signs the contract as X's president, just as he did the year before, then in the presence of Q. In fact, X does not have a president or any other officers. Last year, neither R nor Q considered this to be important enough to explain, and R continues to feel the same.

When R tells Q that he renewed the Y contract on the same terms, Q is furious, because he thought Y would have been willing to pay much more than it had been paying, simply to avoid having to go to the next cheapest provider. Q calls Y to say the deal is off.

Y sues X, Q, and R for the difference between the contract price and the amount it will cost to hire an out-of-vicinity service provider.

1. Discuss whether X will be liable to Y for any amount.
2. Discuss whether Q and/or R will be personally liable to Y.

Question 25

Adelphi, Inc., (Adelphi) is a corporation with two classes of stock outstanding. Its common stock is owned by ten record owners. Its preferred stock is owned by Peter (who owns 60 percent of the class), Paul (who owns 30 percent of the class), and Mary (who owns 10 percent of the class). None of the preferred holders also owns common stock. The preferred holders are entitled to a cumulative annual dividend of $100 per share, to be paid before any dividends are declared on the common stock. Adelphi's articles of incorporation provide that, if dividends on the preferred stock are not paid for more than two years, all voting rights vest exclusively in the preferred shareholders until all dividends in arrears have been paid.

Adelphi has not paid any dividends for over two years. Larry, Curly, and Moe, the members of the three-person board of directors of Adelphi, have explained that they felt it was essential to build up the corporation's reserves in light of volatile financial markets. Exercising their exclusive right to vote, Peter, Paul, and Mary elect themselves to replace Larry, Curly, and Moe. Without observing any particular formalities, they gather at a restaurant to come up with a plan of action. Paul and Mary are leaving on a cruise the next day, but tell Peter he has their proxies to carry out their plan.

The very next day, as soon as he waves good-bye from the dock, Peter types up and signs a board resolution recommending that the articles of incorporation be amended to provide that the common shares be made nonvoting and permanently vesting all voting rights in the preferred shareholders. He then signs, on behalf of himself, Paul, and Mary, a shareholders' action by unanimous written consent approving the amendment. The amendment is accepted for filing by the proper state authority. Peter then declares and causes to be paid all of the dividends in arrears on the preferred shares. Although, at the time Peter acts, it appears that Adelphi will be unable to pay off a bank loan coming due, Peter has reason to believe that he will be able to find other financing. In the nick of time, he does obtain another loan, one that will not come due for over a year.

Jethro is one of the holders of common shares. He is unhappy when he learns about the foregoing facts, particularly because no dividends have been declared on the common stock. He seeks your advice.

1. What are the possible claims to be made by him or by Adelphi against Larry, Curly, and/or Moe?

2. What are the possible claims to be made by him or by Adelphi against Peter, Paul, and/or Mary?

In answering, please ignore any issues relating to the standing of a shareholder to bring actions on behalf of a corporation or to the procedural requirements of asserting derivative claims.

Question 26

Limb, LLC (Limb), is a limited liability company properly formed under the laws of State M. The documents prepared and signed at the time of its formation do not describe the business to be carried on by Limb. They do state, however, that Limb is to be member managed and that the members have equal decision-making authority. It is the intention of Limb's two founding members, Holly and Cherry, to carry on a tree- and shrub-pruning business. In order to get the business up and running, they each contributed $5,000 to Limb's capital. Most of the money was used to purchase equipment and insurance; the remainder was used to place a few advertisements. After three months of operation, jobs are beginning to trickle in. Unfortunately, however, winter is setting in, and there will be little demand for Limb's services until spring.

One day while Holly is not around, Cherry gets a visit from Victor, the director of a local veterans aid society (Vets). Victor saw Limb's ad in the yellow pages, but evidently did not read it very carefully, as he is under the impression that Limb is in the business of supplying prosthetic devices. He has received a large donation earmarked for supplying artificial legs to amputee clients of Vets and is anxious to get the project started. He proposes to enter into a contract pursuant to which Limb would, for the period of one year, supply artificial legs to clients of Vets on an as-needed basis. He assures Cherry that there will be at least 20 clients requiring Limb's service. Cherry decides that there is no reason that she and Holly shouldn't branch out. She knows that she can find prosthetics on the Internet and doesn't see that fitting them should be all that hard. She tells Victor that Limb will provide and fit the devices for cost plus 15 percent. Victor, a busy man, knows that he might have been able to get a better deal elsewhere, but is happy to have the supply issue settled. They quickly jot down essential terms on a sheet of paper and sign it. The contract refers to Limb as the seller and provider of services, but Cherry signs only her own name; Victor, signing on behalf of Vets, asks for nothing more.

Cherry hits the Internet as soon as Victor leaves. Acting on behalf, and in the name, of Limb, she orders 20 "One size fits all—they're adjustable!" artificial legs. The terms she knowingly accepts when placing the order clearly state that all contracts are final. When Holly returns from a tree-trimming job, Cherry tells her what she has done. Holly is furious, saying that tree and shrub pruning was Limb's only purpose. She says that she will sue on behalf of Limb if any money is lost as a result of Cherry's actions.

Meanwhile, Victor happily reports to the benefactor who donated the money for artificial legs as to the terms of his contract with Limb. He is informed, in no uncertain terms, that the amount he has agreed to pay Limb is unreasonable and that he should search for a way to get Vets out of the contract. When he does so, he discovers that there is a State M statute providing that "none of the following professions may be conducted in the corporate form: medicine, law, . . . the fitting of artificial limbs, ..."

1. Is the contract Cherry and Victor signed enforceable against Limb?
2. Does Limb have any possible action against Cherry?

Do not discuss any issues having to do with Holly's standing to sue on behalf of Limb or any other issues having to do with the bringing of derivative litigation on behalf of an LLC.

Question 27

Harriet Hiss (H) is one of the four members of the board of directors of Story, Inc. (Story), a closely held corporation owned by H and various other members of the Hiss family. H is the only family member on the board. Story was formed by H's grandfather for the exclusive purpose of publishing literary fiction; its articles so provide, but are silent on the question of its powers.

H is getting on in years. Before she dies, she would like to see some sort of memorial to the Hiss family and its contribution to literature. She has no descendants and couldn't care less about leaving anything of value to the rest of her family. She proposes to the other members of the board that Story donate enough money (far in excess of the corporation's annual income) to construct and maintain a stunning new museum dedicated to literary fiction. The museum, which will be operated on a not-for-profit basis, will be known as the Hiss/Story Museum.

Story's board meets to discuss H's proposal. Three members of the board, including H, are present. The fourth, Gordon Genre (G), was not notified of the meeting, but happens to wander in during the discussion. Over G's strident opposition, the other members of the board approve the endowment of the Hiss/Story Museum. G's opposition is based on his perception that literary fiction is declining in popularity and that the corporation is less profitable every year. He believes it would be better to use the money to pursue new lines of business.

G is determined to attack the decision in any way he can and consults you.

1. Discuss whether G is likely to succeed in having the donation enjoined.
2. Discuss whether the directors who approved the donation can be held liable if it is made.

Essay Answers

Answer to Question 1

Important aspects
At the start of the answer to each essay question is a listing of the main ideas you should have in mind after you've read the question and begun to think about it. Please go back and read the question another time if there are big differences between these "important aspects" and your own initial reactions to the question.

Important aspects:
Duty of care (lack of skill), duty of care (lack of diligence), duty of care (lack of prudence), business judgment rule, provisions limiting monetary damages, duty of loyalty (self-dealing), duty of loyalty (lack of good faith).

1. *The duty of care*
One of the generally recognized fiduciary duties of the board of directors is the duty of care. The duty of care requires the skill, diligence and prudence of a reasonable person making decisions with respect to his or her own assets (or, in many jurisdictions, of a reasonable person in similar circumstances).

a. *Skill*
With regard to the skill question, a plaintiff might argue that Deanna did not have the requisite background to serve on a board engaging in intricate financial transactions. Although Deanna would point out that there is limited precedent on this matter, it is possible that a court influenced by recent events would rule to the contrary. On the other hand, if Deanna can make a convincing argument that such a requirement would lead to lack of diversity on boards, and that some constituents might go relatively unserved, she might carry the day. One counter is that every member of the board owes a duty to the corporation as a whole and should not be representing special interests or viewpoints.

b. *Diligence*
A second issue might be raised with respect to Deanna's lack of diligence. Most certainly, the members of board of corporations carrying on complex businesses must and do rely heavily on reports from committees and officers. Deanna probably would invoke these examples, as well as any statutory language that might appear (as in does in the Model Business Corporations Act) authorizing reliance. A plaintiff would respond that

reliance must be reasonable, and that reasonableness should be assessed by such factors as the significance of the transaction to corporate well-being. Although individual transactions might not have been enough to demand more inquiry by Deanna, the fact that Towncorp was engaging in so many that it ultimately brought disaster on the company might change the calculation.

c. Prudence
i. The hedging transactions

On the question of prudence, Deanna will want to raise her evidence about what other companies were doing and her argued ability to rely on advice from officers **as well as** to invoke the business judgment rule. This rule protects an informed business decision from assessment in hindsight; provided that the decision was within the realm of reasonableness when made, a court will not later second guess it, even if it turned out to be a disaster. An attempt by Deanna to invoke the rule might be rebutted insofar as the rule can only to be invoked to cover "informed" decisions. If Deanna's reliance on officer reports was not reasonable, her decision presumably will not be regarded as informed. Alternatively, the facts do not really make it clear whether the board ever formally approved the hedging transactions. If Deanna was never asked to make a decision, perhaps the business judgment rule should not be applied. If Deanna argues that delegation is a form of business decision, the discussion presumably would turn to the issue of whether delegation is within the realm of reasonableness, given the overall significance of the hedging transactions. The evidence of what other boards were contemporaneously doing presumably could be significant; even though failure to follow the crowd does not prevent application of the rule, "hiding in the herd" almost certainly would be of help.

ii. Money laundering

The board obviously did not make a conscious business decision about money laundering; thus, the business judgment rule is irrelevant. Arguments about lack of diligence might be quite apt. Still, monetary liability would very likely be limited by the provisions discussed immediately below.

d. Provisions limiting monetary liability for breach of the duty of care

Many jurisdictions mandate or permit election (in the articles of incorporation) of limits on monetary liability for breaches of the duty of care. In fact, in some jurisdictions, it is part of the plaintiff's initial burden to show that such limits do not exist.

2. *The Duty of Loyalty*

A plaintiff probably would try to characterize Deanna's actions as in breach of the duty of loyalty. The duty of loyalty requires the board to act in the corporation's best interests.

a. *Self-dealing*

One of the most usual applications of the duty of loyalty is in the context of self-dealing by officers or directors. The facts state that Deanna served on the boards of companies entering into hedge transactions with Timecorp, as well as on Timecorp's board. More facts are required to determine whether Deanna's connection with the other boards is sufficient to raise a viable self-dealing claim. If it reasonably can be argued that her interest as a board member for another company might have influenced her vote on the hedging transactions, either collectively or individually (perhaps because she feared loss of one or more lucrative board positions), a case for self-dealing would not appear to be frivolous. In such cases, the interested decision maker usually bears the burden of establishing that the transaction was fair (which in the case of the challenged hedges might be difficult owing to their complexity) unless approved by disinterested members of the board or shareholders after full disclosure. It does not appear that Deanna made full disclosure, so she probably would be required to show fairness.

b. *Lack of good faith*

Although the most familiar arguments about the duty of loyalty arise in the context of either self-dealing or usurpation of corporate opportunity, in this case there is a possible argument that failure to monitor constitutes a lack of good faith. Good faith recently has been recognized in Delaware as a component of the duty of loyalty. A plaintiff thus would allege that Deanna failed to adequately monitor Timecorp's financial department, leading both to the failed hedges and the money laundering operation. Deanna would respond that the Delaware courts have required "utter failure" to implement reporting or similar controls before imposing liability; she reviewed reports, and that should be enough. A plaintiff would respond that the fact that the officers reported did not mean that the board required it. A plaintiff also could invoke the second failure for which Delaware courts will impose liability: "conscious failure" to monitor operation of a reporting system once imposed. Given that the board apparently did not have in place any method of determining whether the company was engaged in illegal activity, and failed to follow up on the red flags raised by the dubious accounts, this seems to be a claim that Deanna should worry about—at least if Timecorp is incorporated in Delaware or a jurisdiction likely to follow Delaware precedent.

Answer to Question 2

Important aspects:
Limited liability, taxation, managerial rights, consideration for shares, right to employment, right to salary, returns of capital, rights on dissolution.

[Note: This question is not a traditional issue-spotter, but it is a very efficient way for your professor to see what you know about the differences between entities.]

Perhaps the easiest way to navigate the territory raised by the clients' situation is by stated goal:

1. *Limited liability*

Limited liability means that an entity's owners will not be responsible for the obligations of the entity. They can, however, still be liable on other grounds. For instance, if an owner of an entity guarantees its obligation, liability will accrue. If an owner of an entity is also its employee (not unusual in the small business setting), engaging in tortious conduct within the scope of employment will result in liability for the owner-agent, as well as for the entity.

All of the listed types of entities will achieve the goal of limited liability for at least *some* of the participants. Limited partnerships, however, provide limited liability only for limited partners; general partners are unprotected (although using a corporation as a general partner is a possibility, this seems too complex for what Antonio, Bottom and Claudius are trying to achieve). It is critical to note, with respect to all of the limited liability entities, that there can be no abuse of the entity by undercapitalization, siphoning of the assets, or the like, lest limited liability be lost by those perpetrating the abuse. Although "piercing the veil" of limited liability is best-known in the context of corporations, it nonetheless is clear that people may shoot themselves in the foot by misusing other entities as well.

2. *Pass-through (also known as conduit) taxation*

Pass-through, or conduit, taxation means that taxable income or loss calculating by the entity is allocated to the entity's owners on the basis of their various rights and reported by those owner's on their own tax returns in the year the income is earned or the loss is incurred by the entity. The competing alternative is two-tier taxation, pursuant to which an entity's income or loss is taxed to the entity in the year earned or incurred. When income is distributed to the entity's owners, it is taxed again.

The rule for unincorporated entities is that they may elect either pass-through or two-tier federal taxation unless they are publicly traded. This is known as "check-the-box" treatment.

As for corporations, the default rule is two-tier taxation. Still, an election under Subchapter S of the federal tax code will attain something close to the pass-through treatment available to unincorporated entities. To qualify for a Subchapter S election, a corporation (a) must (with some exceptions) have only shareholders who are natural persons, (b) must have no non-resident alien shareholders, (c) must have no more than 100 shareholders, (d) must have no more than one class of shareholders (although classes differing solely with respect to voting rights are permitted), and (e) must allocate profit and loss in accordance with interests in the business.

3. Equal management rights

This requirement easily will exclude the limited partnership and suggest that the limited liability limited partnership would be inappropriate for Antonio, Bottom, and Claudius. Limited partnerships typically are controlled by their general partners, and limited partners risk loss of their limited liability if (with extremely generous exceptions) they participate in management. Although under modern statutes (adopted in very few states) a limited liability limited partnership arguably could be created giving equal management rights to general and limited partners, it would seem somewhat pointless to do so: the primary reason the form is used is to limit management participation by at least some of the partners.

The default rule for limited liability partnerships (which may be viewed as an "improved" form of general partnership) is equal management rights. In some jurisdictions, this is also the default rule for limited liability companies; where it is not the default rule, it nonetheless can be voluntarily adopted.

Equal management rights frequently are attainable in the corporate context, but simply issuing all owners identical numbers of shares will seldom be a complete protection. Some sort of cumulative voting requirement or shareholder voting agreement probably would be necessary to assure that all owners assume seats on the board (which is where management presumptively occurs). Moreover, although modern statutes permit designation of such officers as may be desired, co-presidencies might be a bit confusing to those dealing with the corporation.

In some jurisdictions, an additional impediment will exist to using the corporate form. Where contribution of future services is not eligible consideration for the issuance of shares, Claudius's "eye for talent" probably cannot qualify as consideration for shares equal in value to the shares received by the others. Even if his "eye" is regarded as a promise not to work for others, its qualification is dubious. Nonetheless, with full disclosure to all (which seems to exist), the board probably could determine to issue shares to different shareholders at different prices, paid in qualifying consideration. Thus, Claudius would be required to put up at least some cash or property.

[Two minor points may be worthy of note, depending on the emphasis of your own professor. First, as the foregoing discussion suggests, Claudius is getting something for his services. Whatever it is worth will be taxable to him as income, and he should be made to realize that. Second, some jurisdictions still use par value as a measure in determining "watered" or "discounted" stock liability. These jurisdictions tend to also have limits on qualifying consideration for shares. Thus, in one of those jurisdictions, using the corporate form and electing a high par value would create additional problems for Claudius.]

4. Employment at a stated salary

None of the entities under consideration automatically give rise to a right to employment, much less at a stated salary. A specific agreement between the entity, when formed, and each of Antonio, Bottom, and Claudius would be advisable. It certainly is worth noting that work on behalf of a corporation might give rise to some sort of implied contract or recovery in *quantum meruit*. By contrast, the relevant statute specifies with respect to limited liability partnerships and (often) limited liability companies that there is no right to reimbursement for services rendered by partners (in limited liability partnerships) or members (in limited liability companies) unless otherwise agreed. California has, in highly sympathetic circumstances, implied agreements to the contrary, but this is a much criticized minority approach.

5. Imbalance in contribution for ownership interests

Antonio, Bottom, and Claudius have not asked you to evaluate the significance of the imbalance in "up front" consideration for their ownership interests. They should be made to understand that the default rule for limited liability partnerships and at least some limited liability companies is that return of capital is an obligation of the entity, which (although there is some uncertainty) probably must be satisfied by the owners in the event the entity is unable to do so. If Claudius is told to imagine that if the entity loses Antonio and Bottom's $1,000,000 in capital that he will be on the hook for one-third, he may be a bit perturbed. Although agreement to the contrary is certainly a possibility, fleshing out the agreement may raise some questions of its own.

Insofar as corporations are concerned, it is important to recognize that unless some sort of special agreement is unanimously entered in a state that permits it (as does the Model Business Corporations Act), equal share ownership entitles each holder to an equal distribution in the event of dissolution. This means that if Antonio and Bottom each pay $5,000,000 for their shares and the corporation is immediately dissolved, Claudius gets one-third.

6. *The punchline*
It is clear that neither a limited partnership nor a limited liability limited partnership would be appropriate for Antonio, Bottom, and Claudius. Otherwise, their goals can be achieved, with varying degrees of complexity and depending on jurisdictional variation, by any of the other forms. One of the variations that would be quite important is that the limited liability partnership form is not available everywhere. Limited liability companies are available everywhere; just how complex it would be to take advantage of this entity depends on the default rules of the state of formation. The corporate form is quite difficult to work with when there are rules about qualifying consideration and some parties are contributing future services. On the other hand, where there is no limitation on type of consideration and shareholder agreements about dissolution and other rights are possible, results can be obtained that are very similar to those attainable with a limited liability company. For many engaged in small business formation, the deciding factor may be federal taxation (with "check-the-box" being regarded as slightly preferable to the Subchapter S election). Still, for those contemplating fast growth and public ownership in the not-too-distant future, the corporate form may be the way to go.

Answer to Question 3

Important aspects:
Derivative v. individual rights, freeze-outs, removal for cause, withholding dividends, duties of controlling shareholders, validity of shareholder agreements, inspection of records.

1. *Motion for security for costs*
Apparently, in State X, security must be posted only for purposes of a derivative action.

A derivative action is one in which the harms complained about were done *primarily* to the corporation, rather than to the individual plaintiff. The defendants will contend that the refusal to distribute profits and the agreement to maintain Al (A) as the managing director impact upon all of the shareholders, rather than personally upon Paul (P). Thus, they would argue, the action is derivative in nature.

However, because P's basic assertion is that A and the other shareholders (via their appointed directors) are attempting to freeze him (personally) out of the corporation by (1) withholding dividends, (2) maintaining A as managing director, and (3) denying P inspection rights, P's lawsuit would probably be viewed as being primarily personal in nature.

Thus, the defendants' motion for security should be denied.

2. *P's requests for relief*
a. *Removal of A for misconduct*
A director may ordinarily be removed for good cause (fraud, gross incompetence, breach of the duty of loyalty, etc.). P could contend that A breached his duty of loyalty by putting his personal objective (i.e., the purchase of P's Durco stock) over his corporate duties (i.e., to avoid withholding dividends in bad faith when there are funds in excess of those necessary for operating expenses). Furthermore, because a controlling shareholder has a fiduciary duty to refrain from exercising his or her position in a manner that oppresses minority shareholders, if P could prove that A orchestrated an effort to hold back dividends for the sole purpose of inducing P to sell his Durco stock, P's request for dismissal of A should be successful.

Although A (as a 65 percent shareholder) could still presumably elect the new director who would be chosen to fill his vacancy, and, therefore, his removal might arguably be ineffectual, A's forced departure would nevertheless impress upon the other directors the importance of observing their fiduciary duties toward minority shareholders. Thus, A should be removed on the facts stated above.

b. Invalidation of the shareholders' agreement

Although shareholders' agreements (i.e., contracts whereby shareholders have agreed to vote their shares in a particular way) are ordinarily valid, one controlling the management of a corporation is permissible at common law only if (1) the agreement was made with respect to a close corporation, (2) the agreement involves only a minor encroachment upon the directors' managerial discretion, and (3) there is no complaining minority interest. Some jurisdictions will go further, permitting encroachments that are more than minor under the conditions discussed below. Moreover, there are statutes in many states permitting more far-reaching agreements if the agreements are unanimous or reflected in the articles of incorporation.

The agreement in question was to retain A as "managing director." The primary issue is whether the shareholders' agreement substantially limits the discretion of the **board**, not only the participants' discretion as shareholders. The discretion to choose who will run the business rests with the board of directors. Depending on the statutory law in State X, the shareholders' agreement to maintain A in office as the managing director could be considered interference with the board's ability to manage the business effectively, and P could argue that the board needs to be free to exercise its own business judgment without such limitations. In addition, there is the risk that A would try to instruct the other directors how to vote on matters pertaining to the management of the corporation. Allowing one director to dictate virtually all of management's decisions constitutes more than a "minor" encroachment upon the board. Decisions should be made only after a give-and-take discussion and majority vote of all of the directors present.

In a jurisdiction permitting more than a minor encroachment, the cases indicate that if the shareholders' agreement can meet three basic tests, it will ordinarily be upheld. To be found valid, the agreement must not (1) injure any minority shareholder, (2) injure creditors or the public, and (3) violate any express statutory provision. Although it is not clear from the facts whether State X has an express statutory provision addressing this situation (or a statute dealing with the rights of creditors and the public), it appears that the shareholders' agreement here cannot satisfy the first test. P is a minority shareholder who is not a party to the shareholders' agreement, and he arguably would be injured by the agreement to maintain A as managing director indefinitely, without regard to A's performance. Thus, again P should prevail.

c. Compulsion of directors to declare and pay a substantial cash dividend

If there is a surplus available, directors have a duty not to withhold dividends in bad faith. Although the defendants have asserted the business judgment rule (directors are not liable for corporate actions undertaken in good faith and with reasonable care) with respect to the nonpayment of dividends, this argument should fail. Their actions ***don't*** appear to have been undertaken in good faith (i.e., the objective seems to have been to "freeze out" P). If P can show that Durco's reserves are greater than necessary to continue its business operations, the excess funds should be distributed to shareholders.

d. Confirmation of P's rights to inspect Durco's records

The State X statute unqualifiedly authorizes shareholders to examine the books and records of their corporation. The defendants appear to contend it should be an ***implied*** provision of the statute that inspection of corporate records cannot be compelled when the shareholder's objective is improper (a "strike suit" would be such an instance, because its purpose is simply to make a bad-faith claim against the corporation). However, as P desires to review the documents for a legitimate purpose (i.e., to determine how much of the profits should be distributed as dividends), P should again prevail.

Answer to Question 4

Important aspects:
Changes to board and its composition, staggered boards, filling directorial vacancies, purpose of shareholder's meetings, motions to dismiss derivative action.

1a. *Legality of increasing the board's size to nine directors*
Stan (S) could argue that increasing the size of the board to nine members was illegal in that this action contravened both the articles of incorporation and the bylaws of Dixie. The directors of a corporation must ordinarily act in conformity with these documents.

The directors might argue in rebuttal that (1) the articles don't expressly limit the number of directors to five (they state only that the "initial" board shall consist of five directors), and (2) corporate bylaws are often viewed as being implicitly amended by resolutions that have been properly approved by the directors (except as to actions that impact significantly upon the business operations of the corporation, such as a sale of its assets).

However, S could respond that (1) the articles did intend the board to consist of only five members unless the document was amended (and this document can be altered only by shareholder action), and (2) in any event, enlarging the board is an action sufficiently significant to require shareholder approval (even if the directors could implicitly amend the bylaws) unless power is granted to the board either by the articles or by statute.

Many state statutes do permit boards of variable sizes and also permit the decision as to size to be made by either the shareholders or the directors. Nonetheless, the choice is to be made in either the articles or the bylaws, which would still allow S to make the arguments set out above.

1b. *Legality of staggered terms*
Because this action is contrary to the articles of incorporation (which provide for annual elections of directors), it is probably unlawful. While the board might contend that staggered terms still permit the annual election of *some* directors (probably three are elected each year), the ordinary meaning we would attach to the term "annual election" is that the *entire* board be elected at that time. Indeed, that is the meaning that *this* board attached to the phrase, as evidenced by the board's desire to change it.

1c. *Legality of refusal to call a special shareholders' meeting*
Although directors, officers, and (usually) 10 percent or more of the shareholders may notice a special meeting of shareholders, such a meeting will

only be compelled if it is for a proper purpose. Although S (as a 29 percent shareholder) is probably empowered to call for a special meeting of shareholders, the president can ordinarily be removed only by the board of directors (not by the shareholders). Thus, in this case, the board did not act improperly, and a court will not compel the holding of a special meeting. [Note that were the purpose of the meeting limited to an expression of shareholder opinion, the outcome might be different.]

1d. Legality of filling the newly created positions without a shareholder vote

Whether this action was proper or not depends, as an initial matter, on Dixie's articles of incorporation and bylaws. Ordinarily, the bylaws of a corporation provide that interim vacancies on the board may be filled by majority vote of the directors. However, statutes and courts frequently impose limits on the ability of the board to fill vacancies it has created by increasing its size, fearing that the board may take action to entrench itself. The facts of this question justify that fear. Thus, in the event that enlargement of the board was legal, the directors may well have acted unlawfully in filling the vacancies.

2. Should the court grant the board's motion to dismiss?

In some states, a derivative action cannot be maintained if a majority of the directors determines, in good faith, that the lawsuit is *not* in the corporation's best interests. However, where the derivative action asserts wrongdoing by a majority of the directors, director disapproval will ordinarily *not* preclude the lawsuit. In some jurisdictions, if the underlying complained-of action of the board protected by the business judgment rule, the outcome might be different; as discussed below, however, the business judgment rule does not seem to apply in this case.

The facts are silent as to whether the directors feared a takeover by a specific entity or whether that entity had a reputation for looting the corporations over which it gained control. If the board's action was not a reasonable reaction to a reasonably perceived threat of that sort, it appears to have been undertaken (1) for the self-interest of the members of the board (to protect their positions) and (2) to the detriment of the corporation (presumably, the additional directors are paid by Dixie). In addition, as discussed above, the board's actions probably were unlawful. If the board was acting in its own interest (breaching its duty of loyalty) or unlawfully, its members will not be protected by the business judgment rule.

In addition, although the new board members are experienced in business, their decisions have been highly questionable. The transactions approved by them were financially harmful to Dixie. The facts are insufficient to determine whether Dixie's financial setbacks resulted from unexpectedly changed economic conditions (in which case the members of the board would be protected from liability by the business judgment rule) or were due to faulty decision making by the board. Of course, if it could be shown that the board deliberately entered into unprofitable transactions to make Dixie a less attractive takeover candidate, it would *not* have acted in good faith and would be liable for losses to Dixie from those actions.

Although the board might contend that dismissal of some aspects of the derivative action was made by a "disinterested" body (the four *new* members), this argument should fail. The new members are close friends of the original directors and would (presumably) lose their positions if the derivative action were successful. This latter factor is particularly likely to justify a finding that they are *not* "disinterested."

Also, assuming S's derivative action alleges that *either* the business judgment rule does not apply *or* the directors' fiduciary duty to act in good faith was breached (as opposed to simply contending that increasing the number of directors and staggering their terms was unlawful), *none* of the directors is truly "disinterested." Thus, the court should *not* grant the board's motion to dismiss.

Answer to Question 5

Important aspects:
Fiduciary duty of minority shareholders, preemptive rights, mergers, fiduciary duty of majority shareholders, corporate opportunity, *ultra vires.*

1. Propriety of Andy's vote against the proposal to issue 100,000 shares of stock to Rich free of preemptive rights

It is well established that majority shareholders cannot exercise control in a manner that is injurious to the minority. Conversely, a minority shareholder is not permitted to act in a manner that promotes his or her interests to the detriment of other members of the corporation. Barb, Carla, and Dave could argue that by causing Corp to continue to pay an unusually high interest rate on the note, Andy has wrongfully exercised a "veto power" over Corp's attempt to preserve its assets.

Andy could contend in rebuttal, however, that he was not obliged to relinquish his preemptive rights, especially because Rich's acquisition of 100,000 shares would (under cumulative voting) cause Andy to lose the certainty of sitting on Corp's board of directors. Because an 80 percent vote is required to change the articles (which provide for preemptive rights), this document could ***not*** be amended without Andy's vote. Because endeavoring to retain a specific equity position within a corporation is a legitimate concern, Andy may have acted properly in voting against the sale of shares to Rich. However, the facts also indicate clearly that Andy did not want the note paid off because of its high interest rate. If, in fact, ***this*** factor compelled Andy to vote against Rich's proposal, then Andy would not have acted properly.

The facts are silent as to whether (1) the other three were willing to permit Andy to purchase 25,000 of the additional shares, and (2) Andy had the financial ability to purchase an additional 25,000 shares (thereby retaining his 25 percent interest in Corp). Andy had a duty of loyalty to Corp pursuant to which he is not to place his personal interests before those of the corporation. If both of these conditions could be satisfied, so that Andy could retain his equity position in Corp, presumably he would have to vote to approve the modified proposal or else face accusations of violating this duty of loyalty.

2. Injunction to prevent the Corp-Endrun merger

Mergers ordinarily require approval by the board ***and*** a specified proportion of both companies' shareholders. Some jurisdictions require that only a majority of shareholders approve a merger, while other states impose a higher proportion (ordinarily two-thirds). If the merger can be accomplished lawfully in accordance with Corp's presently existing articles and bylaws, Andy could contend that the majority shareholders are breaching their fiduciary duty by diluting his 25 percent ownership interest. However, if the other shareholders can show that their motivation was to preserve Corp's assets by terminating an excessive financial obligation, they would probably prevail.

If a merger requires Andy's authorization, the resolution of this issue depends on a consideration of the factors discussed above with respect to whether Andy breached his duty to place Corp's interests before his personal concerns.

If Andy prevailed on the issues of breach of duty, a court could restrain Corp and Endrun from consummating the merger.

3. Collection of interest payments on Corp's note

Directors are obligated to refrain from gaining any personal advantage to the detriment of their corporations. The other shareholders could contend that, pursuant to this duty, Andy should have advised the the board of the chance to acquire Lender's note for 90 percent of its face value (thereby saving $10,000 of principal and subsequent interest payments). Assuming Lender approached Andy with the intent of asking Corp (as opposed to Andy, individually) to purchase the note, Andy has probably usurped a corporate opportunity. Even if Lender had approached Andy in his individual capacity (i.e., as his friend, rather than as Corp's treasurer), many jurisdictions would still require Andy to disclose Lender's offer to the other directors before taking advantage of it himself.

Assuming Andy breached his duty of loyalty by not communicating Lender's offer to Corp's board, the other shareholders might, in some jurisdictions, be obliged to show that they could have raised the $90,000 demanded by Lender (i.e., obtained a loan or authorized and sold additional stock). If Corp could have purchased the note, it can probably now acquire the instrument from Andy for $90,000. In some jurisdictions, however, no showing of financial ability at the time of Lender's demand would be necessary.

Corp may also contend that the note is unenforceable under the ultra vires doctrine (the articles of incorporation prohibit incurring any single debt in excess of $75,000; the principal amount of the note was $100,000). In most jurisdictions, a corporation is precluded by statute from raising the ultra vires doctrine except in an action against a director or officer for breach of duty in approving the ultra vires transaction. Although a shareholder may raise the doctrine to enjoin a transaction, in this case all shareholders voted (as directors) to approve the debt and probably would be equitably stopped from pursuing the matter.

Answer to Question 6

Important aspects:
'34 Act registration, audit committee requirements, prohibited loans, shareholder votes on executive compensation (Dodd-Frank), shareholder votes on executive compensation (state law), shareholder votes on executive compensation (Rule 14a-8), duty of care, business judgment rule, provisions limiting monetary liability, duty of loyalty (failure to monitor), presidential authority.

1. Examco must register under the Securities Exchange Act of 1934.

A company must register a class of securities if either (a) the class is traded on a national exchange, or (b) the company has in excess of $10,000,000 of assets and the class is a single class of equity security in the hands of 500 or more holders. Although the facts do not state whether Examco is in compliance with the requirement that it register its common stock under the Securities Exchange Act of 1934 ("'34 Act"), they make it clear that it is obliged to do so. (Examco has $100,000,000 in assets and, counting Suellen, 500 holders of common stock.) Registration under the '34 Act triggers a number of other obligations. Although Examco may argue that since it did not register, it need not worry about compliance with these additional obligations, Suellen could make the policy argument that the Act is intended to protect those trading in the securities of a company with certain attributes, not just those trading in the securities of companies with management who are savvy enough to realize the Act applies.

2. Because Examco is required to register under the '34 Act, Sarbanes-Oxley obligations apply.

Among the obligations applying to companies required to register under the '34 Act are various requirements added by the Sarbanes-Oxley Act of 2002 ("SOX"). These include the following:

a. An independent audit committee

Examco is required to have an audit committee; that committee must be comprised entirely of independent directors. This means that the presence of Pablo and Choi on the board means that Examco cannot claim that its board of directors effectively functions as an audit committee. SOX also requires that there be at least one financial expert on the audit committee *or* that the company disclose why it does not think such an expert is required. This is a disclosure that would be difficult to make, at least on a truthful basis.

b. No loans to executive officers

Pablo's new employee benefit was specifically directed at executive recruitment and retention. This suggests that loans to executive officers are contemplated. This would be in direct violation of another one of the requirements of SOX.

3. Because Examco is required to register under the '34 Act, Dodd-Frank obligations apply.

Companies registering under the '34 Act also must comply with the various provisions of the Dodd-Frank Act of 2010. This means that its shareholders must be given an advisory vote on executive compensation, following full disclosure of all elements of that compensation. The solicitational materials regarding this vote must be prepared and circulated by management.

4. A shareholder vote limiting executive compensation is not valid under state law.

If Suellen were to seek to solicit votes to limit benefits for executives, she could most definitely expect Examco to raise the argument that her proposal relates to management of the business corporation—a matter committed by statute to the discretion of the board. Even if Suellen were content with persuading a few very large shareholders to agree with her, the shareholders still would be unable to act with any legal effect. The only exceptions that have been recognized have been in the close corporation context. Although Suellen might try to argue that Examco's possible non-compliance with the '34 Act means it should be treated as a closely held corporation, Examco would (properly) respond that this is a misreading of the close corporation cases, which look to whether there are only a few shareholders significantly overlapping with management. (Note that Suellen's argument here is so weak it would not be worth making if time is short.)

5. Under Rule 14a-8, Examco cannot be compelled to include Suellen's proposal in management's proxy materials.

Because Examco's common shares should be registered under the '34 Act, proxy solicitations are governed by Section 14(a) of that Act. Rule 14a-8 sets out circumstances in which shareholders can access management's proxy materials to transmit their own proposals to other shareholders. Critically, a shareholder's rights under Rule 14a-8 do not extend to proposals in violation of state law. Although the method around this is usually to state the proposal as advisory, rather than binding, this would get Suellen little, if anything, in addition to what Dodd-Frank already compels. Moreover, a shareholder's right under Rule 14a-8 does not extend to countering any proposal management itself is making. Since management presumably will be asking for the shareholders to give an advisory vote in favor of executive compensation (including benefit plans), Suellen's proposal could properly be excluded. There is also a strong argument that Suellen's proposal could be disregarded pursuant to a rule that proposals relating to management functions can be excluded. The Securities and Exchange Commission has taken an interesting variety of positions on this issue; in light of the Dodd-Frank requirement, resolution is no longer necessary.

6. The Board of Directors may be in violation of its fiduciary duties.
The generally recognized fiduciary duties of the board of directors are the duty of care and the duty of loyalty. The duty of care requires the skill, diligence, and prudence of a reasonable person making decisions with respect to his or her own assets (or, in many jurisdictions, of a reasonable person in similar circumstances). Without a doubt, modern boards of large corporations must and do rely heavily on reports from committees and officers. Moreover, it is not unusual for them to delegate various functions either to committees or officers. Presumably, Examco's board members would invoke these factual precedents, as well as any statutory language that might appear (as in does in the Model Business Corporations Act) authorizing reliance or delegation. Suellen would argue, however, that "whole hog" reliance and delegation of the type suggested by the facts is not reasonable.

Any director whose decisions are challenged as a violation of the duty of care will begin to think wistfully about the business judgment rule. This rule protects an informed business decision from assessment in hindsight; provided that the decision was within the realm of reasonableness when made, a court will not later second guess it, even if it turned out to be a disaster. An attempt by Examco's directors to invoke the rule might be rebutted in two ways. First, the rule can only to be invoked to cover "informed" decisions. Insofar as Examco's board actually approved anything, including the new employee benefit plan, questions could be raised about the extent of its inquiry. Second, what the rule covers must be a business decision. Suellen presumably would argue that the board did not actually make a decision about the benefit plan and that failures to decide should not be protected. If the board argues that delegation is a form of business decision, the discussion presumably would return to the issue of whether full delegation is within the realm of reasonableness. Particularly insofar as delegation evidently led to an illegal act by the company (loans to executive officers), application of the business judgment rule seems dubious.

It is worth noting that many jurisdictions mandate or permit election (in the articles of incorporation) of limits on monetary liability for breaches of the duty of care. In fact, in some jurisdictions, it is part of the plaintiff's initial burden to show that such limits do not exist.

Suellen, then, probably will be quite interested in characterizing the board's actions as a breach of their duty of loyalty. The duty of loyalty requires the board to act in the corporation's best interests. Although the most familiar arguments about loyalty have to do with self-dealing or corporate opportunity, there is a possible argument that failure to monitor constitutes a lack of good faith. Good faith recently has been recognized in Delaware as a component of the duty of loyalty. Suellen thus would allege that the Examco directors failed to monitor Pablo. The board would respond that the Delaware courts have required "utter failure" to implement reporting or similar controls before imposing liability; Pablo reported to the directors, and that should be enough. Suellen would respond that the fact that Pablo reported did not mean that the board required it. She also could invoke the second failure for which Delaware courts will impose liability: "conscious failure" to monitor operation of a reporting system once imposed. Given that the board apparently did not have in place any method of determining whether the company was engaged in illegal activity, Suellen's claim appears to be fairly strong (if she is in a jurisdiction willing to follow Delaware).

7. Pablo may have lacked authority to establish the new benefits plan

Even if the new benefits plan were limited to nonexecutives, it is arguable that its adoption was not authorized. Pablo would argue that the board's evident acquiescence in his "We can handle this at staff level" policy constituted a valid delegation of authority. Suellen would counter that such a broad grant could not be valid. Pablo's response would be that the grant should be considered relative to the act taken, not in the abstract, and that it would be reasonable for the board to allow him to design and implement an employee benefit plan. If Pablo's argument were to have any traction, he would need evidence about how usual such plans are and how much money was at stake.

Pablo might also base a claim that his act was approved by the board's failure to complain after receiving a report with a line about the new benefit. Would a reasonable person in Pablo's position really have understood that the board intended to approve the benefit, or would he just think that he had snuck something by? Did Pablo have any evidence that the board was actually reading the reports he submitted?

Finally, Pablo might also allege he had inherent authority to create and run the plan. The usual test for whether an act is within the president's inherent authority is whether it is in the ordinary course of business. This requires contemplation of such factors as how much future boards of directors will be constrained, how much money is involved relative to the size and health of the corporation, and how long the effect of the decision is likely to last. There simply are not enough facts to permit resolution of this issue.

Answer to Question 7

Important aspects:
Duty of loyalty, presidential authority, duty of care, business judgment rule, provisions limiting monetary liability.

1. Can Exco (E) rescind the transaction?
There are two independent theories under which E could attempt to rescind the transaction with Art's family (the Sellers).

a. Breach of duty of loyalty
When a director has a personal interest in a transaction the corporation is considering, he or she is ordinarily obliged to (1) disclose that interest to the entire board of directors, (2) refrain from voting on it, *and* (3) disclose any information indicating that the transaction may not be in the corporation's best interests. A transaction involving a director's immediate family would probably constitute a personal interest. While it is unclear from the facts whether Art believed the transaction was not in E's best interests, he clearly failed to meet the first two requirements.

Art *cannot* claim that the transaction was implicitly ratified by a majority of the board (i.e., when Bobbie, Curt, and Donna advised him that they approved of the transaction), because (1) there was never a formal vote on it, (2) he and Bobbie never disclosed to the other members of the board that the Sellers were members of Art's immediate family, and (3) there is no clear majority in favor of the purchase if Art's vote is discounted. Although some jurisdictions do permit the vote of an interested director to be counted, this does not address Art's failure to make full disclosure to the board.

b. Lack of authority
The president ordinarily oversees the day-to-day operations of a corporation. While this officer usually has the power to bind the corporation in routine transactions, a $5 million cash acquisition (constituting 10 percent of E's assets) would probably *not* be considered a routine or ordinary business transaction and, thus, would not be within this implied authority. Some jurisdictions might treat a board's informed acquiescence without complaint as a form of after-the-fact authorization; in this case, however, the board was not aware of all relevant facts.

2a. Can E recover for Yang's unprofitability from Art?

In addition to the theories described above, a derivative action against Art might also be sustained for breach of a director's duty of due care (i.e., a director must exercise the same due care with respect to corporate matters as he or she would with regard to his or her own assets or, in some jurisdictions, act with the prudence of a reasonable person in like position).

It is unclear from the facts whether Art investigated the transaction with the thoroughness a $5 million acquisition would require. Even if he did, his interest in the transaction would deprive him of the protection of the business judgment rule. Thus, if the price paid by E was excessive, E could probably recover (under the duty of due care *and* the other theories described above) from Art the diminishment in the value of Yang stock between the (1) time of purchase and (2) trial. In theory, this amount would be reduced to the extent, if any, that Art could show that Yang's decreased profitability was due to mismanagement by E. In practice, however, this would be difficult if E's mismanagement of Yang also rested on Art's shoulders as E's president.

In any event, note that many jurisdictions have statutes permitting or mandating limits on monetary liability for breach of the duty of care. Even if such a statute were in effect, it would not limit recovery for breach of the duty of loyalty.

2b. Can E recover for Yang's unprofitability from Bobbie?

The discussions above with respect to the duty of due care and (for the most part) a director's fiduciary duties would be applicable to Bobbie. Although Bobbie did not conduct the transaction, she was probably under a fiduciary obligation to disclose Art's conflict of interest to the entire board (even though Bobbie, in good faith, believed the transaction to be beneficial to E).

2c. Can E recover for Yang's unprofitability from Curt and Donna?

Curt and Donna are in a different position from Art or Bobbie because they never knew that the Yang shareholders were related to Art. As to the substance of the purchase agreement, without additional facts, it is difficult to establish that they did not use the requisite care in evaluating whether the purchase would be good for E. The facts do indicate that Art negotiated the purchase agreement and that he discussed the proposed acquisition with Curt, Donna, and Bobbie individually. It is quite possible that Art described the transaction to Curt and Donna in a manner that persuaded them of its benefit to E.

One could argue that, because the relationship between Art and the Yang shareholders could have been discovered by a review of Yang's corporate records, Curt and Donna had a duty to inquire into Yang's stockholder list. To evaluate this argument, we need to know whether reasonably prudent directors generally inquire into the stockholders of companies to be acquired. If not, or if Curt and Donna acted reasonably in relying on Art and the other directors, then their liability is tenuous, at best.

Answer to Question 8

Important aspects:
Demand requirement, demand futility, duty of care, duty of loyalty, provisions limiting monetary liability, corporation's ability to redeem stock, dissolution.

1. Freda's derivative action against XYZ

Before he or she can bring a derivative suit, a shareholder must ordinarily make a demand on the directors to undo an improper action. In some jurisdictions, this requirement is absolute. In many states, however, demand is excused when it is likely to be futile. Because all of the directors voted for the contract with XYZ and would, therefore, be personally liable for damages (i.e., the difference between the contract price and the market rate for such services), Freda could assert that any demand would have been futile and was, therefore, unnecessary. The directors could contend in rebuttal that the allegedly improper agreement was entered into only six months ago, and, therefore, they could have corrected their actions in a relatively inexpensive manner. Freda should prevail on this issue (although, in some jurisdictions, if the vote on the contract by some of the directors was protected by the business judgment rule, the outcome might be different).

Some jurisdictions require that a demand be made on disinterested shareholders prior to commencing a derivative action. If a majority of shareholders fails to ratify the lawsuit, it cannot be commenced. In addition, some states require that a security bond for expenses be posted. However, there is nothing to indicate that either requirement is present in this instance.

In summary, Freda's derivative action can probably proceed.

a. Duty of due care

Directors must make a reasonable effort to learn the facts necessary for making a proper decision. Freda would contend that Carla and Dan failed to undertake any such effort in approving a contract for services that was at double the market rate. Although Carla and Dan could assert that they reasonably assumed Al and Bob would offer only a contract competitive with market conditions, this contention should fail. Without any reasonable effort to learn the relevant facts, Carla and Dan should not be able to claim the protection of the business judgment rule.

Thus, Freda should be successful in asserting that Carla and Dan breached their duty of care in approving the service agreement with XYZ. An argument based on the duty of care also should succeed against Al and Bob, because they did not, on behalf of Etco, exercise reasonable business judgment.

b. Duty of loyalty

Directors owe a duty of utmost good faith to their corporations. If a director has a direct financial interest in a transaction, he or she is ordinarily obliged to make full disclosure and refrain from voting on that matter. Although Al and Bob did disclose their ownership of XYZ, they failed to reveal that the contract with Etco was at double the normal market rate. They also should not have voted for the agreement (if Carla and Dan still approved it after knowing *all* of the relevant information, it would have passed, 2 to 0, even without their votes).

Presumably, had Al and Bob informed Carla and Dan that the cost of XYZ's services was twice the market rate, Carla and Dan would *not* have approved the contract. Thus, Al and Bob breached their duty of loyalty to Etco.

c. Remedies

Based on the foregoing, Freda's derivative suit should result in (1) rescission of the Etco-XYZ contract and (2) a judgment that Etco's directors are jointly and severally liable for the intervening overpayments. This sum would be paid to Etco, but Freda should be able to recover her attorneys' fees and legal expenses. It is important to note, however, that many jurisdictions have statutes permitting or mandating limits on monetary liability for breach of the duty of care. Even if such a statute were in effect, it would not limit recovery for breach of the duty of loyalty.

2. Etco's redemption of Carla's stock

The directors could initially contend that Freda cannot bring an individual lawsuit for their redemption of Carla's stock. A derivative action is appropriate when the conduct at issue *primarily* injures the corporation, not the individual shareholder. A depletion of corporate assets is ordinarily the subject of a derivative action. Thus, the directors could have this aspect of Freda's suit dismissed. However, another potential issue must be discussed in the event that this conclusion is incorrect.

First, Freda could contend that redemption of shares must be provided for in the corporation's articles of incorporation. Because Etco had no such provision, this action would be invalid. The board's unanimous approval of this action would *not* constitute an amendment of the articles, because changes to this document ordinarily require shareholder approval following recommendation by the board.

In the alternative, Etco could contend that the redemption is actually a repurchase of shares by Etco. Because corporations have an inherent right to repurchase shares from their shareholders, assuming the repurchase will not harm creditors or other shareholders, Freda's first contention would probably be rejected unless she could show harm to the corporation.

Assuming the redemption/repurchase question is decided against Freda, she could then argue that a distribution to shareholders to reacquire shares is subject to statutory limitations (as is explicitly the case in many jurisdictions). These limitations often provide that (1) such distributions can be made only so long as the remaining corporate assets will exceed its liabilities, and (2) the distribution cannot result in corporate insolvency. Although Etco does not appear to be approaching insolvency, its lack of retained earnings suggests that its assets might not exceed its liabilities after the repurchase takes place.

Freda might also argue that the directors breached their duty of care in approving the repurchase. Although the decision would seem to be protected by the business judgment rule, in most jurisdictions, the rule will not protect against waste. Other than assisting Carla with a familial emergency, there appears to be *no* corporate purpose that benefits Etco.

A court is likely to rescind the redemption of Carla's stock. However, an order requiring repurchase of Freda's shares would be unlikely. (It should be noted, however, that, in some jurisdictions, Freda might have a cause of action for failure to afford her an equal opportunity to have her shares repurchased. This action would lie against a controlling shareholder for breach of a duty akin to that of a partner; in light of the board's decision, Carla might be regarded as controlling or being part of a control group. This clearly would be Freda's individual right, rather than a derivative right.)

A court would be very unlikely to dissolve Etco under these circumstances. The corporation apparently made money in the preceding year, and, in general, only if the ends of corporate existence (i.e., making a profit) are not being attained will dissolution be ordered.

Answer to Question 9

Important aspects:
Derivative standing, demand requirement, demand futility, self-dealing, preemptive rights, insider trading (Rule 10b-5), insider trading (Rule 16(b)), insider trading ("special facts" doctrine).

The first and third demands by Emma (E) relate to claims primarily by Deco, rather than by E personally. Thus, in determining how the directors (DIRS) should respond, it must initially be determined if E could successfully assert a *derivative* action.

The DIRS might contend that E was not a shareholder at the time of the alleged wrongs (she did not inherit the stock until later) and, therefore, *cannot* bring a derivative action. However, because E inherited stock from someone who *was* a shareholder (Paula) at the time of the alleged wrongs, E can be said to stand in Paula's shoes, and she may prosecute a derivative action if Paula could.

Because all the DIRS are alleged to have participated in the wrongful actions, any demand made upon them would presumably be futile (and probably, therefore, would be excused). In some jurisdictions, however, demand is absolutely required; in others, a claim that all directors are wrongdoers is subject to scrutiny to assure that it is merely pro forma for the purpose of excusing demand. Moreover, in some states, a majority of the disinterested shareholders must concur in bringing the derivative action (assuming the purported wrongs could be ratified by the shareholders). For purposes of this discussion, we'll assume none of these variations applies.

Thus, a derivative action by E is possible.

1. Could the DIRS set aside the purchase of the Savco stores?
Because Tom was a director of Savco at the time of the purchase, he was "interested" with respect to Deco's purchase of the four Savco stores.

As a matter of common law, a transaction involving interested directors can ordinarily be set aside, unless (1) the transaction was shown by the interested directors to be fair, or (2) it was approved by a majority of the disinterested directors or shareholders after full disclosure. Even in the case of disinterested approval, it may be set aside if shown by the plaintiff to be unfair. The only point that could be put in issue is Tom's failure to disclose his interest (assuming it was not known by the other DIRS). However, because the purchase was fair at that time, nothing would have been gained from such a disclosure by Tom. In addition, two years have passed since the transaction, and it would be impractical to attempt to unwind it now.

Thus, the DIRS should reject E's first demand.

2. Will E be permitted to assert preemptive rights with respect to the 25,000 shares issued to Smith?

As a matter of common law, a shareholder often has the right to buy newly issued shares in a proportion equal to his or her existing stock ownership. However, this right sometimes does *not* extend to previously authorized shares, even though they have never been sold. In addition, preemptive rights often do not apply to situations where, as here with Greenacre, stock is exchanged for assets, because it is a logistical nightmare for shareholders to participate proportionately in such transactions. More important, modern statutes address the existence of preemptive rights, often stating that no such rights exist unless provided for in the articles of incorporation.

Thus, this demand should also be rejected by the DIRS.

3. Can Deco recover the $300,000 saving by Tom?

There are three theories under which the DIRS could assert that Deco is entitled to recover the $300,000 loss avoided by Tom.

SEC Rule 10b-5

Under SEC Rule 10b-5, a corporate insider who fails to disclose a material fact with respect to the purchase or sale of stock may be liable to the buyer for the difference between the sales price and the value of the stock after the nondisclosed information becomes known. However, because Deco did not buy the shares, Deco would not have an SEC Rule 10b-5 cause of action in this instance. Thus, the DIRS should reject E's demand on this ground.

SEC Rule 16(b)

Under SEC Rule 16(b), the short-swing profit made through a sale and purchase, or purchase and sale, of stock by a corporate director or officer (or a shareholder who owns at least 10 percent of a class of stock) within a six-month period can be recovered by the corporation. The corporation must be listed on a national securities exchange or have (1) assets of at least $10 million and (2) at least 500 shareholders of one class of equity security.

Even assuming the latter requisite is satisfied, Deco would have *no* cause of action under SEC Rule 16(b) because the facts state only that Tom sold his Deco stock. There is no indication that Tom had purchased the shares within the prior six months. (The fact that Tom resigned prior to his sale of Deco stock would *not* be relevant, because he presumably purchased the stock while a director of Deco.) Thus, in the absence of additional facts, the DIRS should refuse E's demand to commence a lawsuit against Tom on this ground.

Special-facts doctrine

Under the common law special-facts doctrine, when a corporate insider fails to disclose special facts (i.e., those of unusual or extraordinary significance) with respect to a sale or purchase of stock to an existing shareholder, the latter can recover the difference between the price paid and the value of the stock when those special facts become known. A few courts (e.g., *Diamond v. Oreamuno*, 248 N.E.2d 910 (N.Y. 1969)) have held that the corporation involved can recover the gain made or loss avoided by the insider, if the aggrieved shareholder fails to seek recovery. In this instance, however, there is no indication that Tom sold his stock to persons who were Deco shareholders.

Thus, the DIRS should refuse E's demand to sue Tom under this doctrine, too.

(This is another place where we'll note that, although the outcome of the analysis in Part 3 above seems obvious, the discussion should be included. In fact, it must be included, given the call of the question.)

Answer to Question 10

Important aspects:
Piercing the corporate veil (undercapitalization), pre-filing transactions (corporation *de facto*), pre-filing transactions (corporation by estoppel), pre-filing transactions (statutory liability), watered stock liability, consideration for shares, corporate opportunity, derivative v. individual claims, misrepresentation.

1. Liabilities of A, B, C, D, and E to Z Corp's creditors
a. Undercapitalization
Shareholders of a corporation are ordinarily **not** personally liable for its obligations (beyond their investment in the corporation). The corporate veil may be pierced, however, when the entity is originally organized without adequate capital to meet debts that can reasonably be expected to arise in its type of business. While the $40,000 in cash that Z Corp (Z) raised from the sale of its stock seems to be a respectable amount of capital, if the electronic devices in question are ordinarily expensive to create and market or foreseeably lead to large amounts of liability, and, in fact, the $40,000 would be insufficient, Z's shareholders could be personally liable to its creditors. Note, however, that, in a majority of jurisdictions, inadequate capitalization is merely one factor to be considered along with affirmative fraud or wrongdoing, a failure to follow formalities, and/or other factors.

It should be noted that some jurisdictions hold a shareholder liable only if he or she participated in the **management** of the corporation. In those states, D and E, being only investors, could probably avoid personal liability to Z's creditors despite undercapitalization.

b. Liabilities of A and B prior to the filing of Z's articles of incorporation
Assuming the undercapitalization argument described above is unsuccessful, creditors could assert that prior to filing the articles, no corporation existed, and, thus, A and B would be personally liable to them.

Under the common law, a de facto corporation exists when there has been (1) a good-faith attempt to comply with the applicable organizational requirements and (2) some use of the corporate structure. Because A and B signed the articles of incorporation, held a shareholders' meeting (the facts indicate that they established themselves as a two-person board), and (apparently) conducted business under the Z Corp name, a de facto corporation would probably be found to have existed.

A and B could also contend that the corporation-by-estoppel doctrine should apply (i.e., because contract creditors presumably believed they were dealing with a corporation, they should not now be permitted to question its existence). Assuming it could be shown that creditors of Z believed, or reasonably should have believed, that they were transacting business with a corporate entity, they might be barred from recovering against A and B personally for debts incurred prior to the time the articles were filed.

In summary, under the common law, assuming *no* undercapitalization, A and B probably have no personal liability. Modern statutes, however, often provide that no corporation exists before the receipt of evidence that the articles of incorporation have been accepted by the relevant filing authority. This would change the outcome. On the other hand, some such statutes also provide that those who purport to act on behalf of a corporation, knowing it has not been formed, incur personal liability. This would suggest, by negative implication, that A and B should not be held liable because their failure to file was inadvertent.

c. C's possible liability for receiving watered stock

Usually, stock must be fully paid for at the time of issuance. Most states permit stock to be issued in payment for valuable services *previously* rendered to the corporation. Thus, the ten shares issued to C for his previous services are valid.

Because the $5,000 promissory note was exchanged for equipment independently appraised at $6,500, the stock received by C for the note is probably *not* watered. (The fact that C had obtained the office equipment for $1,000 is irrelevant, because he was not obliged to pass his bargain on to Z.)

Depending on the laws of the state in which Z incorporated, the 40 shares received by C for *future* services might, however, be deemed watered, because Z received no contemporaneous value for these shares.

Assuming a portion of C's shares were watered, whether the difference between the par value and the watered value can be recovered by Z's creditors would depend on the applicability of a theory based on misrepresentation, statutory obligation, or a trust fund. In "misrepresentation" states, only unknowing creditors whose obligations accrued *after* the watered stock transaction can recover (i.e., they are presumed to have relied on the corporation's stated capital in deciding to transact business with the corporation). The "statutory obligation" states interpret the general corporation statute as implicitly providing creditors with the right to sue shareholders who have received watered stock. Those states have a statute giving the **corporation** the right to sue a shareholder for the unpaid portion of his or her shares. Courts have sometimes interpreted this to mean that, if the corporation is insolvent, creditors may sue the shareholder in the same manner as the corporation would be able to do. In a "trust fund" jurisdiction, any creditor (regardless of when the obligation was incurred) may recover up to the watered amount. Note that some jurisdictions also expressly provide by statute for actions by creditors in these circumstances.

d. Corporate opportunity

If C learned of the developmental opportunity by reason of his corporate position, then the corporate opportunity doctrine would certainly be applied. Even if C learned of the opportunity in his individual capacity, many jurisdictions would still have required that he disclose the opportunity if it was in a field directly related to Z Corp's activities.

Assuming that this issue is resolved against C, D may still contend that he does not owe any fiduciary responsibilities to Z Corp because he is not a director, officer, or controlling shareholder. Considering that D acted with C, a director, and that there are only five shareholders in the corporation, chances are that D would be held liable.

If an individual uses information gained from a corporate position for personal gain, the value of that opportunity can be recovered by the corporation (unless, in some jurisdictions, the corporation could **not** have exploited the opportunity). C and D will contend that, because Z was unable to take advantage of the developmental opportunity, no damage to the corporation occurred, but they probably would be obliged to show that a diligent effort to obtain the necessary funds for the corporation would **not** have been successful.

The underlying premise to this defense is not quite so simple, and it has caused the courts some difficulty. If accepted on its face, the person who has the high corporate position that enabled him or her to learn of the opportunity will not have any incentive to assist the corporation to overcome its difficulties. Furthermore, because of the person's inside position, the corporation's inability to take advantage of the opportunity is a fact that outsiders will have difficulty disproving because they are outsiders and not privy to knowledge about the corporation.

There are two types of corporate inability that are generally received well by the courts, and one that is not. The two theories that may pass judicial muster are (1) the corporation's **legal** inability (e.g., because of antitrust restraints) and (2) the *refusal* by the person making the offering to deal with the corporation. The third theory, which is not always well received by the courts, is the corporation's *financial* inability to take advantage of the opportunity. The courts reason that, if the opportunity is a good one, there will be some way to persuade an entity or a person to lend the corporation money.

The courts are not in agreement about whether and when to accept the defense of corporate inability. Some courts have adopted a very strict position that the insider must make full disclosure to the corporation and offer it the opportunity. If the insider fails to do this, he or she will simply not be allowed to argue that the corporation could not have taken advantage of the opportunity in any event. Some courts have adopted more lenient views, such as inquiring whether the opportunity was one that the corporation could have undertaken financially, but the stricter position represents the general trend.

If this state is one in which the courts take a very strict view, C and D would not be allowed to defend themselves on the grounds of corporate inability, because the facts indicate that they did *not* advise the other directors of the opportunity. If, however, this state has adopted a more lenient position, then C and D would probably not be liable, because the facts state clearly that Z's financial difficulties had become generally known.

Assuming a corporate opportunity was taken by C and D, only a few jurisdictions permit the corporation's creditors to recover the value of the lost opportunity. Some, however, permit creditors to assert any rights the corporation had against the culpable individuals *if the corporation is bankrupt.*

Finally, the corporate opportunity must be valued. The damages in this instance would probably be the developmental opportunity's present fair market value, less the cost of exploiting that opportunity. While C and D would contend that this figure should be reduced by an amount equal to their proportionate interest in the corporation, the fair market value calculation is probably a more accurate indication of the harm suffered by Z.

2. *Possible liabilities of A, B, C, and D to E*

The possible grounds of recovery by E are (1) corporate mismanagement (against A, B, and C if their actions caused Z to fail, and their decisions were *not* within the business judgment rule), (2) the corporate opportunity taken by C and D, and (3) the watered stock issued to C.

However, these harms primarily affected the corporation (rather than E individually). Although E may be able to assert a derivative action against the culpable parties, there may be little incentive for her to do so, because any proceeds recovered would be paid to Z (which, in turn, would distribute the recovery to Z's creditors).

On the other hand, the most likely thrust of E's cross-complaint is to set herself apart from A, B, C, and D and to relieve herself of any liability to the creditors (in effect saying, "*They* committed these acts; I was merely a passive investor, and, therefore, I should not be held culpable"). On this basis, E might still find enough incentive to continue the action.

The only individual action E could assert against A, B, and C, personally, would be for misrepresenting the assets of the corporation (i.e., as a consequence of C's watered stock, E was fraudulently induced to purchase Z stock). However, it is unlikely that E could prove that Z would *not* have become insolvent if C had paid $10,000, rather than the $7,500 in value that C did deliver to Z ($1,000 in past services and $6,500 worth of office equipment).

It therefore appears that E could not, as a practical matter, successfully sue the other shareholders.

Answer to Question 11

Important aspects:
Inadvertent partnership, dissolution, right to salary, management authority, obligations to third parties, returns of capital.

1. Was Edam a partner?
a. Actual partnership

Whether Edam was a partner in Asiago, Brie & More is an issue that is logically prior to several of the others. Nothwithstanding the intent of the parties *not* to form a partnership, if they intend to form a relationship that is an association of two or more persons carrying on as co-owners a business for profit, a partnership exists. As a general rule, entitlement to a share of profits as interest on a loan does not creates a presumption of partnership, but neither does characterizing an arrangement as a loan mean that a partnership does not exist. The dispositive question will be whether the parties understand that the putative partner will have the rights and obligations of co-ownership. Here, Edam has retained a veto power over certain uses of capital. This alone probably is not sufficient to establish that he is a co-owner. He does not appear to have any right to bind the partnership by his own acts, nor does he have any right to initiate a decision-making process. Edam and/or Asiago might argue that his "vote" on the boursin means that the parties understood he had a right to vote; Brie would respond that, unless otherwise agreed, the consent of all partners to the admission of a new partner is required. Given her obvious disagreement with Asiago and Edam's judgment, the fact that she did not immediately object to Edam's arguable assertion of an ownership right should not be taken as her consent to recognize him as a partner.

b. Apparent partnership or partnership by estoppel

Even if Edam is not an actual partner, CheezRUs might argue that his constant presence in the cheese shop, coupled with the shop's name, would lead a reasonable third party to believe that he was a partner. If Colby overheard Edam's remark about his "vote" this could also cut in Colby's favor. There seems to be some possibility, then, that Asiago and Brie "held out" Edam as their partner.

2. Getting out of the partnership

Brie agreed with Asiago to carry on a partnership for a term of two years. If Asiago does not agree to dissolution, this means that Brie's dissolution of the partnership would be wrongful. Still, even though Brie may not have the *right* to dissolve, she still has the *power*. If she causes a dissolution, she will be liable for damages. It is not, however, obvious what those damages would be.

Analysis of the issue changes a bit if Edam is actually a partner (but not if he were only apparently a partner). Under the 1914 version of the Uniform Partnership Act, a single partner can bring about dissolution. Under the 1997 version, a single partner can dissociate, but that does not mean that the whole partnership can be forced to dissolve. If the dissociation is in breach of the partnership agreement, the disassociating partner will be liable for damages.

3. Brie's Right to a Salary

Partnership statutes generally provide that, absent an agreement by the partners, no partner has the right to remuneration for working in the business. In circumstances in which a "working grunt" partner is called upon to contribute to another partner's return of capital (which, as discussed below, may be the case here), courts have occasionally implied an agreement to value labor as equivalent to capital, effectively creating a right to salary. Brie would attempt to invoke this rule; Asiago would respond that this approach is a distinct and much criticized minority rule. Because the criticism (that the implied agreement amounts to an end-run around the statutory attempt to keep this matter out of court) seems well taken, it is unlikely that Brie would prevail on a salary claim.

4. Who is Liable to CheezRUs?
a. Brie's Liability

At a minimum, Brie should expect some liability to CheezRUs. It will be as an individual, if her order is not regarded as on behalf of the partnership. If her act is on behalf of the partnership she will be jointly and, in most jurisdictions, severally liable (as would the other partner(s)).

b. Asiago, Brie & More's Liability (and the Liability of Asiago)

The rule is that, absent an agreement by the partners, they have equal rights to make decisions within the scope of the partnership business; in case of a dispute, the majority rules. If there are only two partners, there can be no majority, so either will have equal right to bind. This raises two issues.

i. Was there an agreement to the contrary?

Was there arguably an agreement that decisions about cheese were to be left to Brie? After all, they specified that she was going to perform all labor. Asiago would argue that just meant she had to do the physical labor, not that she got to make all the decisions. Given the lack of clarity, this seems a stronger interpretation. A finder of fact probably would not believe that Asiago would contribute so much money and give up all decision-making authority so casually. Note, however, that even without an agreement allocating decision-making authority to Brie, she has just as much right to order the cheese as Asiago has not to order it. Liability is established by Colby's response.

ii. Was Edam actually a partner?

This issue was analyzed above, with the conclusion that Edam probably was not actually a partner but arguably was held out as an apparent partner. If he were an actual partner, Asiago's phone call, seconded by Edam, should have the effect of preventing Brie's order from binding the partnership. Thus, Asiago would have no liability. This would be true whether or not Edam also was an apparent partner. If Edam is only an apparent partner, however, Brie would still have as much actual right to make the cheese decision as Asiago, and the partnership would be bound. Thus, Asiago would have liability in addition to Brie.

c. Edam's liability

If Edam is neither actually or apparently a partner, he will have no liability. If he actually was a partner, the partnership was not bound, and Edam would have no liability. If he only apparently is a partner, he will be liable to those who entered into contracts with the partnership in reliance on the appearance. Colby will argue both that an appearance of partnership was created and that he relied on it. Edam will argue (but probably unsuccessfully) that this is a perverse result, given that Colby (probably) knew that two out of three apparent partners objected to the transaction. Colby might buttress his side by responding that he had no idea how many partners there were, especially given the name of the partnership.

5. Rights and obligations vis a vis Asiago and Edam for leaving the partnership

Brie's rights and obligations *vis à vis* Asiago and Edam are determined by which version of the Uniform Partnership Act applies. Under the 1914 version, Brie's can force the winding up of the partnership and the application of its property. Alternatively, she can claim as a creditor against the continuing business. In the latter scenario, the amount owed to her is the fair market value of her interest in the partnership at the time she ceases to be associated with it. The interest she will be entitled to will be calculated either as a statutory percentage or as a profit share determined by her original percentage. She will be allowed to elect which form of compensation she prefers. Under the 1997 version, Brie's only alternative is to claim as a creditor with interest calculated at a statutory rate.

The most important thing for Brie to understand if the partnership is dissolved is that repayment of its debts is required. These include debts to third parties **as well as** the obligation of the partnership to return capital contributions. Thus, the total of $600,000 owed to Edam and Asiago will have to be paid by the partnership, and the partners will have to contribute in the same proportion that they generally share losses. Although they have not specifically addressed losses, the default rule is that losses are shared in the same percentage as profits. If there are only two partners (Asiago and Brie), Brie will be responsible for $300,000 (note, however, that if Edam chose to sue Brie severally, he would be able to do so in most jurisdictions and the allocation of a portion of the debt to Asiago would be left for Brie to pursue). If Edam is a partner, each will be responsible for $200,000.

6. What if the entity were an LLP?

If Asiago, Brie & More were a limited liability partnership ("LLP"), most of the same issues would be presented and solved in the same ways, including the question of whether Edam is a partner. There would, however, be two differences.

a. Liability to CheezRUs and Edam

If Asiago, Brie & More were an LLP, its partners would have no liability to third party for entity obligations (other than those based on their own wrongdoing). Thus, if Brie created a partnership liability by ordering the boursin, no partner would be individually liable for it. Similarly, if Edam is a lender, the obligation to repay his $300,000 loan cannot be visited on the individual partners.

b. Obligations to return capital in the event of dissolution

Statutes enabling the creation of LLPs generally do not state whether the "no individual liability for obligations to the LLP" rule applies to the LLP's obligation to return capital to the partners. Certainly, Brie would want to argue that the language of the statutes does not make an exception for obligations with respect to capital. Asiago (and Edam, if he is a partner) would definitely want to point out that the few cases thus far considering the issue have found an exception—thus having the stronger side of the argument.

Answer to Question 12

Important aspects:
Corporate opportunity, duty of loyalty, duty of care, preemptive rights, insider trading ("special facts" doctrine), insider trading (Rule 10b-5).

1. Babb's option

Under the "corporate opportunity" doctrine, a director or officer cannot use information acquired as a consequence of his or her corporate position for personal gain, unless (1) after full disclosure to the noninterested directors, the corporation declines to pursue the opportunity, or (2) depending on the jurisdiction, the corporation is clearly unable to exploit it. Because no facts given suggest that Ajax could not exploit the opportunity (particularly in light of the amount allocated for site acquisition), neither alternative seems to excuse what Babb has done. Assuming, however, that some such facts exist, it is relevant to discuss the defense of corporate inability.

The underlying premise to the corporate inability defense has caused the courts some concern. If carried to its limits, the director or officer will not have any incentive to assist the corporation to overcome its financial difficulties. Furthermore, because of the person's position as an insider, the corporation's alleged inability to take advantage of the opportunity is a fact that outsiders will have difficulty disproving simply because they are outsiders.

There are two types of corporate inability that are generally received well by the courts, and one that is not. The two theories that may pass judicial muster are (1) the corporation's *legal* inability (e.g., because of antitrust restraints) and (2) a *refusal* to deal with the corporation by the person making the offer. The theory that is not always well received by the courts is the corporation's *financial* inability to take advantage of the opportunity. The courts reason that, if the opportunity is a good one, there will be some way to persuade an entity or a person to lend the corporation money.

The courts are not in agreement about whether and when to accept the defense of corporate inability. Some courts have adopted a very strict position that the insider must not prejudge the corporation's ability, but must make full disclosure to the corporation and offer it the opportunity in any case. If the insider fails to do both of these things, he or she will simply not be allowed to argue that the corporation could not have taken advantage of the opportunity. Some courts have adopted more lenient views, such as inquiring whether the opportunity was one that the corporation could have undertaken financially, but the stricter position represents the general trend.

Because (1) Babb learned of Ajax's interest in the land at a board meeting, and (2) the property was one of the parcels Ajax had targeted for possible purchase, the corporate opportunity doctrine appears applicable.

Although Babb might contend that Ajax's interest in the parcel was too remote, because no final decision to purchase the land had been made, the fact that Babb (presumably) acquired the option solely for the purpose of reselling the land to Ajax should result in Ajax's prevailing on this issue.

When a corporate opportunity has been usurped, the corporation can assert whatever equitable or legal remedy is available to make the culpable party disgorge his or her advantage. Because the best means of negating Babb's actions is to compel her to assign the option to Ajax, this remedy seems appropriate here.

2. Ajax's purchase of Whiteacre

A corporation is **not** precluded from conducting business with its directors. However, in most jurisdictions, a director's duty of loyalty requires the director to disclose his or her interest in the transaction and to refrain from voting on the matter. In addition, the transaction must be approved by a majority of disinterested board members. If this is done, the transaction generally may be set aside only after a showing that the transaction is unfair to the corporation. If, however, these steps are not taken, the transaction will be upheld only if the defendant shows that the transaction was fair.

The facts seem to indicate that the board knew it was buying Whiteacre from Carl. Even if Carl had not explicitly disclosed this, the other directors may have been aware that Carl was the owner of Whiteacre via the title records. In addition, the purchase would have been authorized even without his vote. Assuming (1) the other directors of Ajax knew that Carl owned Whiteacre, and (2) the purchase was approved by a disinterested majority of the board, the transaction could **not** be rescinded by Ajax.

Possibly, it could be asserted that the directors violated the director's duty of due care by paying $50,000 for land originally acquired by the seller for $10,000. Under the doctrine of due care, directors must exercise the same degree of care and skill with respect to corporate matters as would a reasonably prudent person with respect to his or her own affairs (or, in some jurisdictions, a reasonably prudent person in like position). However, there is nothing in the facts to indicate how long Carl had owned Whiteacre or whether Whiteacre had appreciated in value to the purchase price. Assuming the $50,000 purchase price represented the approximate present fair market value of Whiteacre, the business judgment rule would protect the action of the directors.

Finally, it might be asserted that Carl breached his duty of loyalty if he failed to disclose the price for which he had purchased Whiteacre. Perhaps this information might have indicated that the price being paid by Ajax was too high. Nevertheless, if Whiteacre is presently worth $50,000, lack of this disclosure would probably *not* be an adequate basis for avoiding the purchase.

3. The sale of treasury stock to Dale

A shareholder ordinarily has preemptive rights to acquire shares authorized subsequent to the shares he or she initially purchased, in proportion to his or her original interest in the corporation. However, this right usually does *not* extend to treasury stock. The resale of treasury shares does *not* constitute a dilution of the shareholder's interest in the corporation.

In addition, stock issued for services is frequently not subject to preemptive rights. Because Dale insisted upon purchasing the shares as a condition to employment, the stock was arguably an inducement for her services to the corporation.

Thus, Earl will probably *not* be able to enjoin the sale of treasury stock to Dale.

Finally, the sales price charged to Dale for the shares is probably *not* subject to attack, because $71 per share exceeds the par value ($50) and book value ($70.50) of the stock. If, however, it could be shown that the fair market value of Ajax stock clearly exceeded $71 per share, a breach of the duty of due care may have occurred.

4. The sale of Greenacre

Although Greenacre is being sold at a $20,000 loss, the sales price alone is *not* sufficient to demonstrate breach of the duty of due care by Ajax's directors, and the facts are silent as to why the land depreciated over the five years. Assuming the fair market value of Greenacre is presently about $50,000 and the directors believed in good faith that overall corporate purposes were best served by disposing of this land, the directors would be protected by the business judgment rule, and the sale could not be successfully attacked.

5. Fox's purchase of Gert's shares

Under the special-facts doctrine, a corporate insider who obtains nonpublic information about material facts affecting the value of stock has a duty to disclose such information to an existing shareholder in connection with a purchase or sale of the corporation's shares. Where this duty is breached, the aggrieved party can recover any damages resulting from the defendant's fraudulent conduct.

If a sufficient period of time had elapsed between the time the financial report was distributed to Gert and Fox's purchase of Gert's shares, the fact that Ajax's stock had a book value of $70.50 would be considered *public* information. Therefore, no disclosure would be necessary, and there would be no breach of a duty to disclose.

Under SEC Rule 10b-5, it is unlawful for an insider, via an instrumentality of interstate commerce, to withhold nonpublic, material information in the context of a purchase or sale of his or her corporation's stock. Again, however, assuming Gert received the financial report from Ajax with sufficient time to have read it, the information was "public." Thus, Fox would have no SEC Rule 10b-5 liability.

Answer to Question 13

Important aspects:
Demand requirement, demand futility, duty of loyalty, duty of care, corporate waste, right to indemnification, executive compensation, restrictions on transfer of shares.

1. Derivative action

When an alleged harm is done primarily to the corporation, rather than to an individual shareholder, a derivative action is the exclusive remedy. While the directors' actions in events (1) through (3) stated in the facts arguably diminished the value of Pat's stock, thereby causing her a personal loss, their conduct would probably be viewed as impacting *primarily* on the corporation. Therefore, Pat (P) must commence a derivative action, and any recovery would accrue to Ajax (although P can recover her attorneys' fees and court costs if the lawsuit is successful).

The directors' vote approving all the actions was unanimous, making a demand on the board futile; therefore, in many states, it would probably not be required as a prerequisite to bringing a derivative suit. In some states, however, demand on the directors is absolutely required. In others, a claim of futility is subject to scrutiny to make sure that it is not pro forma (*i.e.*, by asking if the board's complained-of action would be protected by the business judgment rule) for purposes of excusing demand. In some states, it is also necessary to give disinterested shareholders an opportunity to approve the directors' actions (provided the board's conduct was not illegal or ultra vires). Assume that this is not one of the states taking one of the variant approaches described.

a. Ajax's repurchase of its shares at $80 per share

Directors owe a duty of loyalty to act for the corporate good, rather than to further their personal interests. The facts are silent as to why the directors sought to prevent the minority shareholder from acquiring control of Ajax. However, if there was reason to believe that this shareholder would loot or otherwise have a detrimental effect upon Ajax, no breach of the duty of loyalty would have occurred. On the other hand, if the board's motivation was to protect their directorships, using corporate funds to repurchase stock for this purpose would be improper.

Under the director's duty of due care, directors must exercise the same degree of skill and care with respect to corporate matters as would a reasonably prudent person with respect to his or her own affairs (or, in some jurisdictions, a reasonably prudent person in like position). Arguably, paying $80 per share for stock that has a market value of $75 per share would constitute a breach of this standard. However, given the fact that Ajax's shares had a book value of $92 per share and the sellers demanded $80 per share, the price paid by the directors probably would be considered reasonable, and, thus, they would be protected by the business judgment rule. Thus, assuming (1) an adequate justification for preventing the minority shareholder from acquiring control of Ajax and (2) the availability of sufficient surplus to acquire the shares in question, an action against the directors for paying shareholders $80 per share would probably fail.

In any event, note that many jurisdictions have statutes permitting or mandating limits on monetary liability for breach of the duty of care. Even if such a statute were in effect, it would not limit recovery for breach of the duty of loyalty.

b. The agreement with Bob

Traditionally, retirement benefits for *past* services were invalid. These benefits have often been viewed as a "waste" of corporate assets, because no value accrues to the corporation from such an arrangement.

However, recent statutes and case law permit this type of compensation as a reasonable exercise of the business judgment rule (e.g., the morale of other employees is enhanced by the recognition that loyal employees are treated appropriately). The current version of the Model Business Corporations Act (MBCA) permits such payments to former employees.

Because Bob was Ajax's "longtime" treasurer, a $5,000 per year lifetime retirement bonus is probably reasonable. Thus, whether Ajax's agreement with Bob can be annulled depends on the applicable rule in this jurisdiction.

c. Indemnification payments to Curt

Most jurisdictions permit indemnification for an officer when he or she reasonably believed his or her actions were in the corporation's best interests and the conduct was *not* illegal. However, when the indemnity is given in connection with a derivative action, there is a division of authority. Although some states permit *no* indemnity in this situation, most jurisdictions (and the MBCA) permit indemnification of legal fees and costs if the action is dismissed or settled *prior to* the director's being adjudged liable to the corporation.

The facts are unclear as to whether Curt reasonably believed that the contributions were proper and as to the legality of the contributions. Assuming there is a problem with the propriety of the contributions, an agreement by Ajax to indemnify Curt *regardless* of whether he is adjudged liable is, as described above, invalid in most jurisdictions.

d. The stock option plan

Directors and officers are entitled to reasonable compensation for the services they render to their corporations. Stock options are a form of compensation that is ordinarily acceptable, because it gives the recipients an inducement to remain with the corporation and operate it in a profitable manner.

The facts are silent as to the present value of the stock options and the extent of the responsibilities assumed by the recipients. Assuming the options do *not* result in clearly excessive compensation, taking these factors into account, the stock option plan is probably valid.

2. P's right to have the Ajax shares registered in her name

Because this action affects P individually (as opposed to the corporation), she could bring a personal claim in this instance.

A transferee of corporate stock is ordinarily *not* bound by restrictions that are absent from the face of the certificate, unless she otherwise had actual notice of them. Therefore, unless P was somehow aware of the restriction, it would *not* be binding upon her. Thus, P can probably compel Ajax's secretary to transfer the shares to her. It should also be noted that, if the restriction is unreasonable, it is invalid (even if P had knowledge of it).

Answer to Question 14

Important aspects:
Derivative v. individual claims, demand requirement, demand futility, improper declaration of dividends, duty of care (trucks), duty of care (ad campaign), business judgment rule, duties of controlling shareholder, improper withholding of dividends, duty of loyalty (purchase of debentures), duty of care (purchase of debentures).

1. Agee's claims against the directors of Freightco (F)
Agee arguably has two claims against F's directors: (1) improperly declaring a dividend and (2) breach of the duty of due care by (a) failing to allocate available capital to the purchase of new trucks and (b) investing $1 million in an advertising campaign.

a. Type of action
Because the alleged harms were done primarily to the corporation (rather than to Agee, individually), Agee is obliged to bring a ***derivative*** action against F's board of directors.

It is assumed that Agee was a shareholder at the time the described events occurred. If he wasn't, a derivative action could not be asserted. The directors are the alleged wrongdoers. Therefore, a demand on the board would be futile and would probably not be required as a prerequisite to bringing a derivative suit, although there are states that absolutely require such a demand, impose a level of scrutiny to make sure the allegation that all directors are wrongdoers is not pro forma, or require demand on the disinterested shareholders.

b. Improperly declaring a dividend
A decision to declare dividends from earned surplus ordinarily rests with the good-faith business judgment of the directors. However, dividends are ***never*** proper where these payments would result in the corporation's becoming insolvent.

The facts are unclear as to whether the $500,000 in dividends paid by F so depleted the corporation as to cause its bankruptcy. Because F raised $1 million from the sale of debentures, it will probably be difficult for Agee to prove that the dividend caused F's insolvency.

c. Failing to purchase the trucks
Under the director's duty of due care, directors are required to exercise the same degree of skill and care with respect to corporate matters as they

would with regard to their own affairs (in a number of jurisdictions, the standard is that of a reasonably prudent person in like position). If they do, they are protected by the business judgment rule, which means that the fact that their decisions subsequently result in losses to their corporation is not a basis for attack.

Agee could argue that the failure (1) by ten directors even to read the report of the management consulting firm and (2) of the entire board to implement the corrective action (i.e., the purchase of new trucks) necessary to avoid bankruptcy constituted a breach of their duty of care.

The directors could possibly argue in rebuttal that (1) the report of a consulting firm need not be accepted by the board, and (2) in their reasonable judgment, F's overall financial interests were best served by a large-scale advertising campaign (which, in fact, was undertaken).

Nevertheless, if Agee can show that F's bankruptcy was primarily due to its failure to purchase new trucks, the business judgment rule would probably not afford protection. The directors should have at least read and seriously discussed a specially prepared report that predicted bankruptcy unless a *particular* course of action was undertaken promptly.

d. Advertising campaign

Lastly, Agee could assert that undertaking a $1 million advertising campaign (which was obviously unsuccessful) breached the duty of due care. He would contend that, by incurring such a large, speculative indebtedness, F's ability to pay its ordinary corporate obligations was undermined. However, the directors might have reasonably believed that the advertising campaign would generate sufficient revenues to satisfy F's present and subsequent obligations.

Assuming F's directors could show some basis for believing the advertising campaign would be successful, they probably have *no* liability to their shareholders on this basis.

Summary

Assuming Agee can show that F's bankruptcy is attributable to its failure to acquire new trucks (rather than general market conditions), the directors would be liable for the corporation's losses. The five directors who did read the report are *not* absolved from liability, because they apparently failed to (1) insist on consideration of the report or (2) argue for the purchase of new trucks.

2. Claims against F based on the conduct of the directors of Landco (L)

Because F dominated the board of L, it is important to note that F generally would be regarded as owing to L's minority shareholders all of the duties of L's board. Thus, F would be liable for any of the possible breaches by L's board discussed below. This liability, of course, may be moot in light of F's bankruptcy.

3. Agee's claims against the directors of L
a. Failure to declare dividends

Because dividends are paid directly to stockholders, a shareholder must bring an action in his or her individual capacity to compel directors to undertake this type of action.

As noted above, the payment of dividends is ordinarily within the good-faith business discretion of the board. However, dividends cannot be withheld arbitrarily or in bad faith. If L's directors repudiated the staff recommendation to declare a $1 million dividend for the purpose of supporting the parent corporation (via purchase of the debentures), the bad-faith element would probably be satisfied.

b. Purchase of F's debentures above market price

Agee could alternatively assert a derivative action against L's directors for (1) breach of the duty of loyalty and (2) breach of the duty of due care in purchasing F's debentures.

i. Breach of the duty of loyalty

Directors are ordinarily obliged to disclose any personal interest in a corporate transaction and refrain from voting on these matters. However, L's directors could argue that (1) given the close relationship between F and L, each of them was already aware that the others were also members of F's board, and (2) L's articles and bylaws explicitly permitted them to vote in these instances.

Nevertheless, directors must still exercise good faith (i.e., act in a manner that is fair to all of the shareholders). There appears to be no reason for the purchase of debentures at a price in excess of their open market value, other than to bestow a "gift" on that entity. Here, L's directors voted to purchase F's debentures for much more than their market value. Thus, the L directors should at least be liable for this aspect of the transaction.

ii. Breach of the duty of due care

Agee could also assert that the debenture purchase violated the directors' duty of due care, because L's directors were aware of the relatively speculative manner in which the proceeds from the debenture sale were to be used by F. As a consequence, L's directors should have realized that F might become bankrupt and, therefore, be unable to repay the debentures. There is no argument that the directors' decision is protected by the business judgment rule, owing to the self-interest of F, the shareholder controlling the board. Thus, Agee can probably recover the $1 million purchase price, plus interest (which L presumably lost as a result of F's bankruptcy), from L's directors in a derivative action. Note, however, that many jurisdictions have statutes permitting or mandating limits on monetary liability for breach of the duty of care. Also, it seems from the facts that L's directors almost assuredly breached the duty of due care by (apparently) failing to ascertain the price of F's debentures on the open market prior to purchasing those securities.

Answer to Question 15

Important aspects:
Discount stock, watered stock, improper declaration of dividends, pre-emptive rights, irrevocability of proxies.

1. Liability of Ames and Bates to Dynamics
a. Liability of Ames

Shares issued *for cash* less than the stated par value are called "discount shares." Some states hold that, if shares are marked "fully paid" by a corporation, no action can be taken against the person who receives the stock. If this is such a jurisdiction, Dynamics *cannot* recover the discounted amount from Ames.

Another view, however, holds that a corporation may recover the discounted amount or at least rescind the transaction to the extent of the discounted shares. However, in at least some of these states, a corporation can contend that its directors may sell stated par value stock for a discounted amount if there is a good-faith business justification for such action. This appears to be the case here, because (1) Ames could have repudiated her stock subscription agreement prior to the time Dynamics was formed, and (2) her contribution was (apparently) needed for operating capital. In quite a few states, moreover, there is no requirement that shares be issued at par or above. The only requirement there is that shareholders pay the consideration established by the directors, which Ames did.

Finally, it should be noted that, because the total discount below par on the shares is only $1,000 (20 shares × $50), it may be impractical to pursue this relatively small amount from Ames.

b. Liability of Bates

A share issued for services or property representing a value that is less than the stated par value is called "watered stock." The facts are silent as to the value of Blackacre at the time Bates was issued shares with a par value of $100,000.

Although Bates had purchased Blackacre one year earlier for $55,000, it is possible that Bates paid less than its fair market value or that its fair market value had increased to $100,000. Only one year later, the board of Dynamics valued Blackacre at $160,000, so there appears to have been a pattern of appreciation in real estate in that area. If Blackacre was worth approximately $100,000 when Bates received his shares, the stock was *not* watered. If, however, Blackacre was not worth exactly $100,000 when Bates transferred title to this property to Dynamics, Bates could alternatively argue that, in most states, if the board in its good-faith business judgment determines that certain property is important to the corporation, it may issue watered stock in exchange for that asset. If Blackacre was worth less than $100,000, but, in the good-faith business judgment of Dynamics's board, Blackacre was important to the corporation's future success, the transaction would be valid. In addition, in those states not requiring sales at par, the issue would be moot.

In summary, it appears that Bates probably has *no* liability to Dynamics.

2. Declaration of $2 dividend

Although the determination to declare dividends ordinarily is subject to the good-faith discretion of the directors, in some states, there must be an adequate surplus from which these distributions will be made; in others, the corporation's assets must exceed its liabilities after giving effect to the distributions.

Because Dynamics experienced a net operating loss of $50,000 during its first fiscal year of operation, no dividend could be paid from earned surplus (the usual source of corporate dividends). In addition, there is no indication in the facts of a paid-in surplus (i.e., value received by a corporation for its stock in excess of the par value of those shares).

The only possible source of paying dividends in this situation is revaluation surplus (i.e., when assets of a corporation are revalued upward to reflect their current fair market value). However, not all jurisdictions permit dividends to be paid from revaluation surplus. In addition, even if this jurisdiction did permit revaluation surplus, Dynamics's surplus would be only $10,000 (revaluation surplus of $60,000, less the $50,000 of operating losses). Because the dividend would require Dynamics to pay out $15,000 (7,500×$2 per share), there is still a $5,000 shortfall.

In summary, in states permitting dividends only out of some sort of surplus, the dividend appears to be improper. The directors could be restrained from paying the dividend, or, if it has already been made, the directors are liable to Dynamics for the $15,000 paid out, along with any other losses suffered by the corporation as a result of the dividend payments. As noted above, however, there are a number of states that permit dividends to be paid (as long as the corporation will not be made insolvent) to the extent that (fairly valued) assets exceed liabilities. In these states, the dividend could be proper.

3. Transaction with Carl

Although existing shareholders may have preemptive rights to maintain their proportionate interests in the corporation when new shares are issued, this doctrine is ordinarily inapplicable to shares that have already been authorized. Because Dynamics was authorized to issue 10,000 shares, and only 7,500 were outstanding at the time of the transaction with Carl, preemptive rights of existing shareholders would *not* attach to this transaction.

It should also be noted that, in many jurisdictions, preemptive rights do not apply where shares are issued as consideration for assets or services. Finally, the modern trend (by statute) is to recognize preemptive rights only if the articles of incorporation expressly provide for them.

Determining whether Carl's stock was watered depends on whether Greenacre was worth approximately $50,000 when the shares were issued to him. Because the board apparently had a good-faith business rationale for obtaining Greenacre (i.e., the site of a future plant), the transaction could probably *not* be successfully attacked, unless the price for Greenacre was clearly excessive. Note, too, that some states have eliminated any requirement that shares be sold at par or above.

4. Paula's right to vote her Dynamics stock

Unless coupled with an interest, a proxy is ordinarily revocable. Although the interest of an officer in a corporation may be sufficient, the usual instance in which this has been recognized involves the grant of a proxy in order to induce the officer to take (or stay in) the job. Assuming Paula gave her proxy to Fox merely because it was too inconvenient for her to attend the annual shareholders' meetings, Paula probably could revoke her proxy. This would be the case even if the proxy were in writing and purported to be effective for Paula's lifetime (particularly in a state with a statutory limit on the period of irrevocability).

Paula may revoke the proxy either by notifying the corporate secretary that the proxy given to Fox has been revoked or by her attending the shareholders' meeting and personally voting her shares.

Answer to Question 16

Important aspects:
Ratification, promoter's liability, partnership liability, *de facto* corporation, corporation by estoppel, statutory liability for pre-incorporation transactions, piercing the corporate veil, watered stock.

1. X's rights

a. Against Z Corporation

A corporation ordinarily has no liability under a preincorporation contract, unless the agreement is approved or otherwise adopted after the corporation is formed. First, there is a question as to whether Z Corporation ever attained a corporate status (discussed below).

However, even if Z Corporation did attain corporate status, the agreement between X and A was never expressly or implicitly adopted by Z Corporation. In fact, B and C, two-thirds of the board, did not know of the original agreement and later refused to hire X. This refusal is probably tantamount to a rejection by the board of Z Corporation.

Thus, X has no rights against Z Corporation.

b. Against A

Unless he or she has explicitly disclaimed liability, a promoter ordinarily has liability for his or her preincorporation contracts. Although the agreement provided that Z Corporation would, upon its formation, hire X, X arguably assumed that someone would be bound by the contract. Thus, while it was obvious to X that A was acting on behalf of a ***prospective*** corporate entity (rather than in his personal capacity), A is probably personally liable to X.

c. Against B and C

At the time of the agreement with X, A, B, and C probably were partners. B and C, thus, would be jointly and severally liable for obligations incurred within the scope of the partnership's business. Even given B and C's response when they learned of the contract with X, it seems as though the reaction might be personal as to X and that the contract might have been within the scope of the partnership's business. There are, however, not enough facts to reach a satisfactory conclusion.

2. *Personal liability of A, B, and C to Q*

Ordinarily, shareholders are not personally liable for corporate debts. However, if the corporate status is ***not*** established, the business relationship of A, B, and C may be deemed a partnership. As such, each of them would be jointly and severally liable for the debts of the entity incurred within the scope of the partnership's business. This is not the approach taken in all jurisdictions, especially with respect to passive investors, but the facts do not establish that any of A, B, or C were passive.

Because the articles of incorporation were never filed with the secretary of state, it is unlikely that the shareholders could claim that a de jure corporation existed.

However, under the common law, a de facto corporation exists when (1) there has been a good-faith attempt to comply with the requisites for corporate formation, and (2) the persons involved have made use of the corporate form. A, B, and C made a good-faith effort to comply with corporate formalities by executing articles of incorporation and retaining an attorney to make the appropriate filings. They also acted in accordance with a corporate form by issuing stock, electing directors and a president, and entering into transactions on behalf of the corporation (e.g., the contract with Q was signed, "Z Corporation, by C, President"). It is, therefore, possible that a de facto corporation existed, in which case A, B, and C would not be personally liable to Q. Nonetheless, there are jurisdictions where it is thought that the de facto corporation doctrine has been eliminated by statute. There, evidence that the articles of incorporation have been accepted for filing is conclusive evidence of the formation of a corporation. In the absence of such evidence, no corporation has been formed. Some of those jurisdictions, however, also have statutes that provide that anyone purporting to act on behalf of a corporation, knowing that it has not yet been formed, is liable for the acts taken. This suggests, by negative implication, that, if persons such as A, B, and C acted without knowledge of the defective incorporation, they will not be liable.

Next, under the common law doctrine of corporation by estoppel, a plaintiff who deals with a party under the belief that it is a corporation may be estopped from disputing the corporation's status for purposes of that transaction. Because Q was aware that C signed the agreement, "Z Corporation, by C, President," the corporation-by-estoppel doctrine may be applicable with regard to the transaction with Q. Under that doctrine, A, B, and C would have no personal liability to Q. Finally, the facts are silent as to whether the initial capitalization of Z Corporation was adequate. If it was not, the corporate veil could be pierced, and A, B, and C would each be personally liable for Z Corporation's debts. Note, however, that, in a majority of jurisdictions, inadequate capitalization is merely a factor to be considered along with affirmative fraud or wrongdoing or a failure to follow formalities.

3. Liability to other creditors of Z Corporation

As discussed above, if a de facto corporation exists and Z Corporation was adequately capitalized, the shareholders have no personal liability to **any** of the corporation's creditors. The corporation-by-estoppel doctrine might also apply, depending on the facts surrounding each creditor's transaction.

4. Liability of B

Once a corporation marks shares "fully paid," it is usually estopped from claiming that the shares have not been paid for. However, its creditors may be able to recover any "watered" portion of that stock from the recipients of the shares. Shares issued for services or assets the value of which is less than the par value constitute "watered stock."

Because the equipment conveyed by B to Z Corporation was worth $50,000 less than the par value of the stock received in exchange, B may be liable to creditors of Z Corporation to the extent of $50,000. Recovery by these creditors may depend on which of three theories—the trust fund, misrepresentation, or statutory obligation theory—is applicable. In a jurisdiction that has abolished by statute the requirement that shares be sold at par or above, none of these three theories would apply.

Under the trust fund theory, a corporation's capital is considered to be a trust fund for **all** creditors. Thus, a shareholder who receives watered stock is liable to corporate creditors, whether or not (1) acquisition of the shares occurred before the debt to the creditor was incurred or (2) the creditor relied on financial information provided by the corporation.

Under the misrepresentation theory, the issuance of stock is an implied representation to creditors that the corporation has received consideration at least equal to the par value of its outstanding shares. A shareholder who receives watered shares has participated in a misrepresentation to persons who **subsequently** extend credit to the corporation. Under this theory, only persons who became creditors of Z Corporation **after** the transaction with B could recover the watered amount from him.

Under the statutory obligation theory, the general corporation statute has been interpreted by some states as implicitly providing creditors the right to sue shareholders who have received watered stock. This is based on the corporation's right to sue a shareholder for the difference due on those shares. If the corporation is insolvent, the courts, in essence, have allowed the creditors to bring the action that the corporation might have brought.

It should be mentioned that, for a creditor to recover for watered stock, it must first obtain a judgment against the corporation. After an attempt to satisfy the judgment from corporate assets fails, the creditor may proceed against the shareholder.

The trustee-in-bankruptcy of Z Corporation might also attempt to recover from B under a breach of fiduciary obligation theory. Where a potential conflict of interest exists, a director is ordinarily obliged to (1) disclose his or her interests and any material information pertaining to the transaction and (2) refrain from voting on the matter. If it could be shown that B was aware that (1) the equipment was worth only one-half of the par value of the stock, and (2) A and C thought the equipment was approximately equal in value to the par value of the stock B received, B breached his fiduciary obligation to Z Corporation by not disclosing this disparity. If B violated his fiduciary responsibilities, Z Corporation's trustee-in-bankruptcy could either rescind the transaction or recover the losses Z incurred as a result of B's conduct.

Answer to Question 17

Important aspects:
Demand requirement, demand futility, duty of care, business judgment rule, corporate waste, authority of officers, implied ratification, *quantum meruit*, promoter liability, duty of loyalty, estoppel.

1. *Z's derivative action*

We will assume that Z was a shareholder when Banco formed Combank (the plaintiff must ordinarily be a stockholder at the time of the alleged wrong to commence a derivative action).

Ordinarily, a plaintiff must make a demand on the directors of a corporation prior to commencing a derivative action. However, in some jurisdictions, this demand is excused where it would obviously be futile. Because (1) Z's action would demand return of $1 million (the amount Banco paid for the Class B stock), plus interest, from the directors, and (2) the directors **unanimously** voted to organize Combank, it is highly unlikely that a demand upon the directors would be successful. Note, however, that some jurisdictions impose an absolute requirement of demand on the directors, some impose scrutiny with respect to whether the allegation of directorial wrongdoing is pro forma for purposes of establishing the futility of demand, and some impose a requirement of demand on the disinterested shareholders of the corporation. Assuming that none of the variant requirements described were in effect, Z's failure to make a demand upon Banco's directors would probably **not** prevent him from commencing a derivative action.

Z is apparently contending that the board of Banco wasted corporate assets by expending $1 million to create a competitor (i.e., Combank is also a bank), without any immediate possibility of realizing a return on this investment (i.e., dividends are to be returned to Combank as additional capital for ten years). In addition, because Banco's Class B stock is nonvoting, Banco would have no input in matters involving Combank's operations. Under these circumstances, Banco's directors have arguably made a "gift" of their corporation's assets to Combank.

Under the director's duty of due care, directors must exercise the same degree of care with respect to corporate matters as they would with regard to their own affairs (or, in a number of jurisdictions, the care of a reasonably prudent person in like position). Because Banco is apparently a substantial corporation (e.g., it has 50,000 shareholders and the ability to commit $1 million to Combank), its directors might argue that this action is justified by the goodwill and attendant favorable publicity that will accrue to it by the creation of Combank. They could contend that the investments in Combank might induce new customers to deposit their funds in Banco.

In addition, they could contend that the original $1 million investment remains an asset of Banco, and the agreement to return dividends for a period of ten years was necessary to assure adequate capitalization of Combank during its initial phase of operations.

Although questionable, the investment in Combank can arguably be expected to benefit Banco. Under these circumstances, the business judgment rule should protect Banco's board, depending on how thoroughly Banco's board examined the potential benefits and costs. Thus, Z's derivative action very well might fail.

2. Duc's contract
a. Banco's liability

If Duc attempts to enforce the contract entered into with O, Banco could assert that O did not have authority to bind it. Although the facts state that O was an officer of Banco, there's no indication whether (1) O was expressly authorized to enter into the contract with Duc, or (2) O held an office that would normally have the authority to commit Banco to such a costly contract.

If, however, O did have express authority or the inherent authority of office to bind Banco, Banco would be liable under the agreement regardless of whether it was subsequently approved by Combank.

Without additional information about O's status, it is not clear whether or not Banco has liability to Duc.

b. Combank's liability

Although it is not clear from the facts at what point Combank's board knew of the Duc contract, Duc could argue that Combank implicitly approved the contract by failing to object to it for at least one month after Combank's officers and employees moved into the building while remodeling was in progress. Combank could contend in rebuttal that it took them a month to recognize that Duc's work had not been authorized by Combank's board and that the resolution to retain Exco constituted a rejection of the O-Duc contract.

It is possible that Combank should have inquired more promptly into Duc's authorization to perform the remodeling, and, thus, it may have implicitly adopted the O-Duc agreement.

In any event, Duc could probably recover the reasonable value of the benefit bestowed upon Combank under a *quantum meruit* theory. The work done by Duc prior to retention of Exco presumably reduced the work required of Exco.

c. Personal liability of O

O would probably be deemed a corporate promoter. Although she specifically indicated that the contract was for a corporation "to be formed," in most states O would be personally liable to Duc if the contract was not performed.

3. The contract with Exco

If directors have a personal interest in a transaction, they are ordinarily obliged to (1) disclose that interest to the other directors and (2) refrain from voting on the matter. Here, Combank director X owned Exco, but there is no indication in the facts that director X disclosed this information. Further, he did vote on the Exco matter.

Because (1) director X voted in favor of the contract, (2) his vote was necessary for its passage, and (3) any approval by the disinterested directors does not appear to have been fully informed, the contract with Exco can probably be rescinded unless it is affirmatively shown to be fair to Combank. Ordering Duc to discontinue the remodeling of Combank's premises might be a material breach of the agreement with Duc and needlessly expose Combank to an action by Duc for contractual damages, thus suggesting that entry into the agreement with Exco created problems to Combank that arguably were unfair.

Finally, although Exco might have an action for breach of contract if Combank repudiates their agreement, because director X (1) was (or should have been) aware of the preexisting relationship with Duc and (2) nevertheless voted for the agreement, Exco would probably be *estopped* from bringing an action against Combank.

Answer to Question 18

Important aspects:
Rule 14a-8 (election to office), Rule 14a-8 (proper subject), Rule 14a-8 (ordinary business matter), Rule 14a-8 (personal grievance), binding effect of shareholder vote, filling board vacancies, *ultra vires, in pari delicto.*

1. Management's obligation to present the CAP proposals to shareholders and include them in the proxy statement

Because Gasco's stock is traded on a national exchange (the NYSE), it is subject to the proxy rules promulgated under Section 14 of the Securities Exchange Act of 1934. Under SEC Rule 14a-8(a), a shareholder is ordinarily entitled to submit, for inclusion in management's proxy solicitation, proposals he or she intends to present at the upcoming shareholders' meeting. However, there are many exceptions to management's obligation to include such materials, some of which may apply to these facts.

a. Proposal to remove those directors who authorized the Media contract and sought to impede the gas tax proposition

Most important, management may refuse to include a proposal if it relates to an election to office. The Securities Exchange Commission has taken the position that proposals relating to the removal of individuals from office are within this exception. This would seem to dispose of this issue.

If, however, the SEC were to reverse itself on the question of removals, another exception might apply. Management may refuse to include a proposal if, under the laws of the corporation's domicile, it is *not* a proper subject for shareholder action. It is unclear from the facts whether stockholders can remove a director in this state. We are advised only that Gasco's charter provides that the **board** may remove a director for sufficient cause. In most jurisdictions, there is a common law right of shareholders to remove directors for cause. Furthermore, the majority of modern statutes have expanded the rights of shareholders to remove directors. These statutes most often permit directors to be removed with or without cause, unless the articles of incorporation provide differently. Here, there is no indication in the facts that Gasco's articles contain language addressing this issue.

"Cause" typically exists if a director has committed fraud or waste or otherwise overtly misused his position. This standard is arguably satisfied by the directors' **deliberate** effort to circumvent the State X statute requiring disclosure of corporate expenditures made for the purpose of influencing public ballot measures. However, the directors could contend in rebuttal that, unless this law provides for significant criminal penalties in the event it is violated, removal is **not** proper. They were only attempting to promote corporate objectives by preventing action that would presumably make Gasco's business less profitable.

Although a close question, unless the directors' actions were criminal in nature, their removal is probably **not** a proper subject for shareholder action if removals are permitted only for cause.

b. Proposal to require only nonpolluting products in company-owned gas stations

As noted above, management may refuse to include a proposal that is not a proper subject for shareholder actions. In a publicly held corporation, management decisions are the exclusive province of the directors unless there is something to the contrary in the articles. The choice of cleansing products would certainly seem to be a management decision.

Here, however, it is important to examine the language used in the proposal. A shareholder proposal stating that management be required or ordered to do something will always be excludable under this theory (that it is not a proper subject for shareholders) if the action proposed is something shareholders do not have the right to vote on under the corporation's state law. However, the majority of states do permit shareholders to make recommendations or requests, and, therefore, the proposal would then not be excludable as improper under state law if it used this type of language.

Even if phrased as a recommendation, it is possible that the proposal could be excluded as relating to the corporation's ordinary business matters. Although the SEC has viewed this exclusion differently from time to time, it currently takes the position that it does not authorize exclusion of proposals relating to significant policy issues, even if ordinary business matters also are implicated. The proposal seems to relate to a matter of social significance and probably could not be excluded on this basis.

Finally, management may refuse to include a proposal if it appears clearly to have been submitted primarily to redress a personal grievance. It could be argued that this proposal is a grievance stirred by the pro-environmental lobby, reflecting the personal views of the complaining shareholders.

The stockholders could respond that, even if the proposal emanates from the desire to have an environment free of pollutants, it nevertheless relates to an aspect of Gasco's general business policy. The use of nonpollutants in company-owned gas stations would place Gasco on the cutting edge of environmentally conscious energy companies, which would arguably constitute a unique advertising appeal to its consumers.

This proposal probably would not be characterized as a personal grievance, and the directors, therefore, probably must include it, provided it is properly phrased as a recommendation or request.

2. Binding effect of proposals

Assuming that the shareholder proposal to remove some of the directors is approved at the meeting, whether or not it is included in management's proxy statement, the question of whether it is binding is one discussed above—is this a proper matter for a shareholder vote? As already discussed, unless there has been a serious criminal violation, involvement of the directors in the Media contract is probably *not* sufficient "cause" for dismissal. In addition, a director must ordinarily have an opportunity to defend his or her actions and obtain judicial review of an unfavorable decision on a "for cause" removal. If, however, the shareholders can remove directors without cause, they will prevail.

It might be argued that, because only three of the nine directors are to be elected at the shareholders' meeting, removing all of the directors (assuming the decision to enter into the contract with Media was approved unanimously) would result in there being no management of Gasco. However, articles of incorporation ordinarily provide for interim appointments or elections if a director is removed. Even in the absence of such a provision, either the directors or the shareholders would have such a right as a matter of common law or statute.

The second proposal, if pertaining to the operation of Gasco's business, would *not* be binding upon the board. As noted above, management decisions are the exclusive province of the directors.

3. The contract with Media

Two arguments can be made that this agreement is unenforceable.

First, it might be asserted that the contract is ultra vires, because it requires Gasco to do something that is contrary to State X's law (i.e., refrain from disclosing corporate spending designed to influence public ballot issues). The ultra vires defense is not one that can be raised by the corporation itself; if raised by the shareholders, however, in an attempt to enjoin performance, it could be successful. The determination, however, will be based on the equities of the situation, and a court might simply strike the illegal provision and permit the balance of the contract to stand. This remedy seems more appropriate as the provision, having become known, has ceased to have any effectiveness.

Second, Gasco might argue that it and Media are in *pari delicto* with regard to an illegal provision, and, therefore, the contract is unenforceable. However, because the provision was presumably inserted at Gasco's insistence, a court would probably not permit Gasco to evade its contractual responsibilities under these circumstances.

Thus, Media can probably enforce the contract.

Answer to Question 19

Important aspects:
Removal of directors by board, removal for cause, insider trading ("special facts" doctrine), insider trading (Rule 10b-5), insider trading (Rule 16(b)).

1. Dan's right to remain on the board of directors
Unless expressly authorized to do so by the articles of incorporation or bylaws, directors cannot ordinarily remove another board member. Even when the directors are authorized to remove another board member, it can only be for cause (e.g., fraud upon the corporation, gross incompetency, misuse of corporate assets, etc.). Making a profit by using inside information to acquire shares, which results in no diminution of corporate assets, arguably would not satisfy this standard. However, given recent case law and legislation aimed at discouraging such conduct, as well as the negative publicity to a corporation that results from insider trading, Dan's actions might constitute sufficient cause for dismissal.

2. Dan's potential liabilities
a. Liability to shareholders
There are several theories under which Dan could be liable to the three shareholders from whom he purchased stock.

i. Special-facts doctrine
Under the special-facts doctrine, a corporate insider is obliged to disclose unusual or extraordinary nonpublic information to an existing shareholder from whom he or she is buying stock.

The secret invention in this instance is certainly extraordinary, as evidenced by the fact that the market value of the Jetco stock more than doubled after news of the invention became public.

The shareholders can either (1) rescind their transactions with Dan (i.e., tender to Dan the purchase price of their stock and receive in return the shares sold to him) or (2) recover the difference between the present market value of Jetco stock and the purchase price to Dan.

ii. SEC Rule 10b-5
Under SEC Rule 10b-5, deceitful practices involving the purchase or sale of securities are prohibited. These include the failure of corporate insiders to disclose nonpublic, material information.

Although an instrumentality of interstate commerce must be used in connection with the purchase or sale of securities to activate this provision, this element would be satisfied by Dan's use of the mail (i.e., Dan wrote to the shareholders).

The remedies available to aggrieved shareholders under the special-facts doctrine are also applicable pursuant to SEC Rule 10b-5.

b. Liability to Jetco
i. SEC Rule 10b-5
Unless the grantors of Dan's stock options (presumably the other board members) know about the invention, Dan's acceptance and exercise of his stock option would also constitute a "purchase" of Jetco shares using inside information; *SEC v. Texas Gulf Sulphur Co.*, 401 F.2d 833 (2d Cir. 1968). Thus, with regard to the 1,000 shares Dan purchased from Jetco, the corporation can either recover the profit made by Dan or rescind the transaction.

ii. SEC Rule 16(b)
Under SEC Rule 16(b), a corporation such as Jetco, which is traded on a national exchange, can recover short-swing trading profits made, or losses avoided, by a director with respect to the purchase and sale, or sale and purchase, of securities within any six-month period. If the culpable party is a director, he or she would need to have occupied that position only at *either* the purchase date *or* the sale date.

Because Dan purchased and sold the shares obtained from the former stockholders within a six-month period, Jetco can recover Dan's profit.

When calculating the profit earned for purposes of SEC Rule 16(b), the lowest purchase price is matched against the highest sale in order to maximize the profits. Stock certificate numbers are not matched to determine the profits produced by the sale of particular shares. Dan sold 4,200 shares for $50 per share. Because Dan had purchased 1,000 shares at $21 per share within the previous six months, he realized a $29 per share profit on 1,000 of the 4,200 shares (1,000 shares × $29 per share = $29,000). His profit on the remaining 3,200 shares was $25 per share because he had, within the previous six months, purchased 4,200 shares for $25 per share (3,200 shares × $25 per share = $80,000). Therefore, Dan's total profit under SEC Rule 16(b) was **$109,000.** (Note that, if profits had been calculated by matching the particular shares sold and bought, they would have amounted to $105,000 (4,200 shares × $25 per share), because the 1,000 shares acquired for $21 per share would not have entered into the calculation.)

iii. Special-facts doctrine

In jurisdictions that recognize *Diamond v. Oreamuno*, 248 N.E.2d 910 (N.Y. 1969), Jetco also has an action against Dan under the special-facts doctrine for the 4,200 shares that he acquired from the former stockholders (assuming the aggrieved parties failed to commence suit against Dan). Under the holding of this case, when former shareholders who have an action under the special-facts doctrine refrain from asserting their rights, *the corporation* can recover the profit made or loss avoided by the insider.

It is also conceivable that the profit made by Dan from his purchase of the 1,000 shares of Jetco stock could be recovered by the corporation under this theory. However, if Jetco was legally obliged to sell the shares to Dan despite his disclosure of the inside information, this theory would probably fail.

c. Other liability

Under the Insiders Trading Sanctions Act of 1984, an insider may be obliged to disgorge his or her profits to the SEC and is subject to treble damages for any profits gained or losses avoided. In addition, there is a potential criminal penalty for each willful violation of SEC Rule 10b-5.

Answer to Question 20

Important aspects:
Restrictions on transfer of shares, improper withholding of dividends, successor-in-interest, enforceability of shareholder agreements, invalid constraint on directors, cumulative voting, right to dissolution (statutory), right to dissolution (common law).

1. Doris's right to obtain shareholder benefits
a. Right to receive stock
Courts ordinarily construe provisions that restrict the transfer of shares in a narrow manner. The language in the shareholder agreement addresses the situation in which a shareholder "seeks to sell" his or her shares. Here, however, Carla did not "sell" her Getco stock; she devised the shares under her will. Under these circumstances, no right of first refusal could exist, because no offer involving the shares in question was made.

In addition, if Art, Bob, and Carla had intended the provision to be operative upon death, their contract could have easily provided that, upon the death of any shareholder, the remaining stockholders were entitled to purchase the decedent's shares for their fair market or book value.

Thus, a court would probably determine that the shareholder agreement does *not* apply to testamentary transfers. Therefore, upon surrender of Carla's shares, Doris would be entitled to a decree of specific performance, requiring Getco's secretary to issue an equal amount of stock in her name.

b. Right to dividends
The payment of dividends ordinarily rests within the discretion of the board of directors. However, when the directors' refusal to make dividend distributions constitutes bad faith or an abuse of their discretion, they can be compelled to make the payments to the shareholders.

If it can be shown that Art and Bob have withheld dividends for the purpose of "freezing out" Doris (i.e., persuading her to terminate her ownership interest in Getco), Doris can compel them to make a reasonable distribution of the available corporate surplus.

2. Voice in Getco's management
Doris could first contend that, as Carla's successor-in-interest, she steps into Carla's position under the shareholder agreement. Under that contract, each shareholder is required to vote for the election of the other stockholders as directors of Getco. Thus, Doris could probably obtain a court order compelling Art and Bob to comply with the shareholder agreement.

In the alternative, assuming Doris could vote Carla's stock, she could assert that the provision requiring shareholders to vote for the other stockholders is not binding upon her, because she did not sign the shareholder agreement. However, it would be difficult for Doris to assert both that she stands in Carla's shoes under the shareholder agreement and that the provision in question does not bind her because she never signed the agreement.

In addition, Doris could assert that the provision for directorial voting is invalid, because application of this clause might preclude election of the most capable individuals available and otherwise prevent directors from using their independent judgment on behalf of the corporation. However, it should be noted that not all shareholder agreements of this sort are invalid; on the contrary, many such shareholders' voting agreements are valid if they are unanimous. Still, in some jurisdictions, such agreements are unenforceable if they attempt to control matters that are appropriately left to the discretion of the board of directors and the trespass is more than minor.

Assuming the argument that she is not bound by the shareholder agreement is successful, Doris could elect herself (or another person of her choosing) a director, if cumulative voting is in effect. Under "straight" voting, each shareholder casts his or her votes for *each* potential director. Under cumulative voting, which is sometimes required by the articles of incorporation, bylaws, or applicable statutory law, each shareholder has votes equal to the number of directors to be elected, multiplied by the number of his or her shares, to be distributed among no more candidates than the number of open seats. Thus, under cumulative voting, Doris could elect one of the three directors.

3. Dissolution of Getco
a. Pursuant to the statute
The statute provides for two situations in which a corporation may be dissolved:

(1) there is an equal division among directors with respect to management of the corporation, or

(2) the votes of shareholders are so divided that a board of directors cannot be elected.

The first situation does not apply, because two-thirds of the directors are in agreement about Getco's management.

The second situation is arguably operative, because a full board (presumably three persons) has not been elected for two years. However, the failure to elect a board emanates from Art's and Bob's insistence that Doris does not qualify as a shareholder, rather than because of fractionalized shareholder voting.

However, in either event, Doris possesses only one-third—not the requisite one-half—of Getco shares needed to act. Thus, Doris probably **cannot** dissolve Getco under the State X statute.

b. Pursuant to common law
Because there is no indication that the statute in question was meant to supplant common law principles, Doris could assert any grounds for dissolution that exist under general corporate law.

There are four typical grounds for dissolution: (1) the directors are deadlocked in the management of the corporation; (2) the directors or those in control have acted in an illegal, oppressive, or fraudulent manner; (3) the shareholders are deadlocked in voting and have failed to elect successor directors for at least the last two consecutive annual meetings; or (4) the corporation's assets are being wasted or misapplied.

If Doris can show that (1) Art and Bob have acted, and are likely to continue to act, for the purpose of suppressing her legal rights with respect to Getco, and (2) there is no other reasonable means of safeguarding her position, some states will permit the court to dissolve a corporation (i.e., sell off the corporate assets and distribute the proceeds to shareholders). Because Art and Bob have (1) continually refused to recognize Doris's ownership interest in Getco and (2) failed to declare dividends, Doris can argue for dissolution.

Further, Doris can assert that Getco should be dissolved because of Art's and Bob's incompetency. As shareholder-directors, they have (presumably) breached the articles of incorporation by failing to hold shareholders' and directors' meetings. In addition, their failure to take **any** action during a two-year period arguably demonstrates a lack of responsibility.

Confronted with the probability of an adverse court determination, Art and Bob would presumably recognize Doris's ownership and dividend rights. If Doris receives the shares previously owned by Carla and is permitted to vote this stock, it is unlikely that Getco would be dissolved at this point. Assuming the corporation has operated profitably, there is probably an insufficient basis for dissolution. However, if Art and Bob continue to exploit their majority position to oppress Doris, dissolution of Getco could be ordered.

Answer to Question 21

Important aspects:
Corporate analysis: deadlock on scope, specific transactions and elections, rights to dissolution, court-ordered buy-out, effect of third shareholder; *limited liability partnership analysis:* deadlock on scope, specific transactions and elections, rights to dissolution, effect of third partner.

1. Terry's rights given the formation of a corporation
a. Disagreements as to the scope of the business

Most corporations are formed under statutes that provide that if the articles of incorporation are silent, the purpose of the corporation is to carry on any lawful business. The articles should be inspected to see if they say anything about depressing movies, but assuming they are silent, determining the line or lines of corporate business generally would be a matter for agreement by the board of directors. If the directors are deadlocked, the *status quo* would prevail.

b. Disagreements with respect to specific transactions within the previously authorized scope of the corporation's business

A distinction must be drawn between specific transactions that are within the corporation's scope and within the ordinary course of business and those that are within its scope but outside the ordinary course. The distinction would primarily have to do with the significance of the transaction. For instance, the acquisition of another corporation carrying on a similar business in depressing movie memorabilia might be so significant that it could only be authorized by the board of directors. The acquisition of particular depressing-movie-memorabilia items might be within the scope of authority of one or more of the officers. Since Terry appears to be holding over in the position of president (see below), he would argue that the position of president carries with it the inherent authority to enter into transactions in the ordinary course of business, whereas the office of secretary does not. Willie would argue (if he is forced to concede the holding-over point) that the board has through a consistent course of conduct granted the same authority to the secretary that is possessed by the president. If this argument were accepted, as it very well might be, either Terry or Willie would be able to bind the corporation to "ordinary course" transactions, and neither would be able to veto the other's contracts.

c. Disagreement as to the election of the president

Willie almost certainly will argue that the reasonable understanding of the parties, based on past conduct, is that election to office is for a period of one year. There is no provision for holding over as officers and as there is for directors; thus, the office of president is vacant. If so, it will stay vacant, because deadlock at the board level evidently will preclude election of a new president (or secretary, for that matter). Terry will argue that unless the term is explicitly one year, it should be regarded as indefinite. To do otherwise would expose the corporation to the possibility that it would have no authorized agents. As a result, third parties would refuse to deal with it and its business would grind to a halt. Given the judicial response to the need of corporations for certainty in such matter, Terry probably has the stronger side. Thus, he probably will occupy the position of president until there is a vote to remove him. Given the deadlock, this is not likely to occur.

In general, on the issue of deadlock, it should be noted that gamesmanship about quorums and attendance at meetings is extremely unlikely to be of any avail in a corporation with only two directors. Unless the corporation's formative documents provide for action by precisely one-half of the directors, rather than a majority, one person's attempt to act in the absence of another cannot succeed.

d. Disagreement as to the election of directors
Whether or not Willie and Terry have the right to cumulate their votes for directors, there will always be a deadlock. Statutes generally provide that if successors cannot be elected, the incumbents will hold over, so it appears that both Willie and Terry will remain on the board.

e. The prospect of dissolution, assuming failure to agree on the matter
Although Willie and Terry could act as directors to recommend, and as shareholders to approve, dissolution of MHB, Terry assumes they cannot agree to do so. Statutes generally provide that shareholders may seek court-ordered dissolution upon satisfaction of various tests. One common test is the inability of the shareholders to elect directors for two years. This would suggest that Terry could get a court-ordered dissolution in two years. The fly in the ointment, which we should assume Willie would introduce, is that courts sometimes read the statutes as saying "shareholders may seek, but that doesn't mean courts must decree" dissolution. They then proceed to apply additional common law tests, including whether or not the corporation is profitable and/or whether or not it can be carried on for the mutual advantage of the shareholders. Thus, Terry probably cannot be assured of the effectiveness of a suit to dissolve so long as MHB is profitable.

f. The prospect of a buy-out

It light of the assumption that Willie will not agree to anything Terry proposes, it appears that no voluntarily negotiated buy-out of interests is likely. Various types of court-ordered buyouts may be authorized by statute or recognized as a matter of common law, but this is an area in which the law lacks predictability. It also is not clear whether Terry desires such a result.

g. What if there were a third shareholder?

If there were a third shareholder, a third director's position might or might not have been established. If there were one, and voting were cumulative, each of the shareholders could elect a director. Voting at the board level then would be 2:1. If voting were not cumulative, George and Terry could vote together to elect the entire board. In either event, George and Terry's dominance would appear to give rise to the ability to decide issues related to scope of business, authority of officers with respect to specific transactions, and election of officers. (Which probably also means that Terry would not desire dissolution). If there are only two directors, the two-thirds owners should be able to fill both seats, with the same results.

2. Terry's rights given the formation of a Limited Liability Partnership (LLP)

a. Disagreements as to the scope of the business

Unless otherwise agreed up front, the scope of a partnership cannot be expanded without the agreement of the partners; deadlock would mean that no expansion is legally possible.

b. Disagreements with respect to specific transactions within the previously authorized scope of the LLP's business

The default rule is that the partners have an equal ability to bind the partnership within the scope of the business, although if there is a disagreement, the majority rules. This would mean that Terry and Willie would have equal rights to bind MHB since neither one would be a majority.

c. Disagreements with respect to the election of directors and officers

An LLP does not need as a matter of law, and a two-person LLP would be unlikely to have, either centralized management or officers. Accordingly the issue of disagreement in this area would be unlikely to arise.

d. The prospect of dissolution, assuming failure to agree on the matter

In general, any partner in an LLP can dissociate unless there is an agreement to the contrary. This would give Terry the right to claim as a creditor against the continuing business, if Willie chose to continue it. The amount owed to Terry would be the fair market value of his interest in the partnership at the time he ceased to be associated with it. The interest he would be entitled to would be calculated as a statutory percentage of the amount owed him. This is essentially the equivalent of a court-ordered buy-out.

f. What if there were a third partner?

A third partner would not change the rule that the scope of the partnership is determined by all the partners, unless they have agreed to some other arrangement. A third partner would, however, mean that two partners, voting together, could control the ability to resolve management issues within the scope of the partnership's business. Thus, Terry and George could cut off Willie's ability to enter contracts with which they disagreed. The analysis with respect to election of directors and officers (that is, that there probably wouldn't be any to worry about) would not change. Terry's right to dissociate would continue. In addition, Terry and George could, if they chose, vote together to force a winding up of the entire business.

If there is a third partner, it also is possible that the partnership agreement might provide for an expulsion vote. If so, Terry and George could expel Willie and carry on without him.

3. Terry's rights given the formation of a Limited Liability Company (LLC)

This analysis is tricky and, in fact, impossible to conduct without more information about the default rules of the jurisdiction in which the LLC is formed. It is possible that the analysis would be identical to the LLP analysis. In the alternative, it might be quite similar to the corporate analysis.

Answer to Question 22

Important aspects:
Ability to pay dividends, delegation, ability to repurchase shares, consideration for shares, presidential authority, duty of care, business judgment rule, corporate waste.

1. Declaration of cash dividend

Ordinarily, dividends are paid from earned surplus (assets in excess of paid-in capital and liabilities). Because Jax has a deficit of $55,000 ($80,000 in losses over its initial five years, less the $25,000 in net earnings for the prior year), no dividends should be forthcoming.

In some states, however, nimble dividends may be paid. Under this theory, dividends may be paid from the prior and current year's operating profits, taken as a whole. Assuming that the applicable law recognizes this view, an aggregate dividend of $22,000 ($10 × 2,200 outstanding shares) is proper, in view of Jax's $25,000 operating surplus for the prior year.

In addition, some states permit dividends to the extent that total assets exceed liabilities. Because Jax's capitalization was $220,000, dividends are probably permissible under this theory.

2. Appointment of executive and finance committee

Corporations are ordinarily permitted to create committees and delegate powers to these bodies. One such committee is the executive committee. An executive committee generally has powers equal to the powers of the board and is to exercise them when the board is unable to meet. These committees are often prohibited, however, from performing certain acts, such as authorizing the issuance of shares. MBCA §8.25(e). Thus, the action of the executive committee in issuing stock was probably illegal. Moreover, it is arguable that the committee had an illegal member—W, who was not a director. If illegally composed, the committee's actions probably would be invalidated.

3. Purchase of shares from D

A corporation may ordinarily repurchase its shares, provided (1) there are adequate funds available, (2) the price is reasonable, and (3) the motivation of the directors is proper.

In many jurisdictions, the right to repurchase outstanding shares is subject to the same conditions applicable to declaring dividends. If this is the rule in this state, the discussion in Part 1 above would also be relevant.

The price of $95 per share—$5 under the par value—appears to be reasonable, unless there is some reason to believe that the fair market value of Jax shares is below this figure.

Finally, if a 10 percent shareholder (which the competitor would become by reason of acquiring 220 shares) is able to obtain information about Jax that could be used to the corporation's detriment, the board's motivation probably would be proper.

In summary, the repurchase of 220 Jax shares by the board to preclude their sale to a competitor appears to be valid.

4. *Issuance of 100 shares to E*
In some states, there is legislation that requires that shares be issued only for money paid, services rendered, or property actually transferred to the corporation. In these states, a promissory note (unless adequately secured) is usually *not* sufficient value for the original issuance of shares. If E's promissory note was *not* secured, the sale to E would have been improper and can be rescinded by Jax.

In some states, a corporation *cannot* issue stated par value shares for an amount below the prescribed figure. However, if (1) the board, in its good-faith judgment, believes the purchase price is fair in light of the current market value of the shares, and (2) there is an immediate need for cash, a fewstates permit the sale of stock for a price below the stated par value. Here, more facts are needed to determine whether these two preconditions are satisfied.

Finally, it should be noted that, in a few states, when discounted shares have been marked "fully paid," the corporation is estopped from rescinding the transaction or requiring the purchaser to pay the difference between the amount paid and the par value. Moreover, in many states, par value no longer constitutes a limit on offering price. Shares (even those with par value) can be issued for any consideration deemed adequate by the board.

5. *Promise to pay a pension to F*
The promise by A to pay F a pension could be unenforceable for two reasons.

First, the determination to authorize a lifelong pension is arguably something that is extraordinary and requires board action. Thus, while A is the president of Jax and may determine the salary of day-to-day employees, whether he can bestow lengthy pensions is a question of whether such a promise would be extraordinary. Case law in at least some jurisdictions holds that it would not be extraordinary.

Second, bonuses gratuitously given at the termination of an employee's career are sometimes viewed as a "waste" of corporate assets and, therefore, unenforceable.

Nevertheless, many jurisdictions permit pensions to be bestowed at the conclusion of an employee's career. These states view these payments as a reasonable exercise of business judgment, because pensions arguably enhance loyalty to the corporation and make it a more attractive place to work.

Thus, the pension is probably enforceable.

Answer to Question 23

Important aspects:
Insider trading (tipper/tippee liability under Rule 10b-5), insider trading (liability under Rule 10b-5 for face-to-face trading), insider trading ("special facts" doctrine).

1a. Did Abby violate SEC Rule 10b-5?

A tipper is liable under SEC Rule 10b-5 when (1) he or she either is an insider of the corporation whose shares have been traded or has fraudulently misappropriated (secretly taken) the information from someone to whom he or she owes a duty of confidentiality, (2) he or she receives a benefit from disclosing the information or intends to make a pecuniary gift to the tippee, and (3) the tippee knew (or should have known) that the tipper was breaching a fiduciary or similar duty.

Abby was not an "insider" of ALT. Rather, she was the chief executive officer of an entity that intended to make a public tender offer for ALT stock. Whether she misappropriated the information from her own employer depends on whether her remarks in front of other Oilco executives constitute notice of what she is doing. (Note that she would, in any event, have liability under SEC Rule 13e-3, but that is not what the question asks.)

Assuming that the first condition for tipper liability is satisfied, other potential issues must also be discussed.

A "tip" probably occurred by reason of Abby's recognition of Barb as a prominent stockbroker and her mention of the impending tender offer in an unusually loud voice. The lack of a direct statement to Barb is not likely to be significant.

As to the second condition, it does ***not*** appear that Abby obtained any direct personal gain from disclosing the impending tender offer to Barb. Possibly, she merely wanted to impress Barb with her special knowledge of an imminent, large-scale transaction.

It is difficult to determine from the facts whether Abby intended to bestow a pecuniary benefit upon Barb. Because they were business school classmates and Abby was aware that Barb was a stockbroker, Abby arguably should have known that Barb would use this information for financial gain. On the other hand, if they were mere classmates (rather than close friends), intent by Abby to bestow a gift upon Barb is less likely.

The third condition appears to be satisfied because Barb, as a business school graduate and prominent stockbroker, presumably realized that the information was nonpublic and, therefore, that Abby was breaching a fiduciary duty.

Considering all these factors, it may well be that Abby has incurred "tipper" liability.

1b. Did Barb violate SEC Rule 10b-5?

Barb has potential liability under SEC Rule 10b-5 as a tippee (by purchasing ALT shares for her own account), as a tipper (for advising Mutual to purchase ALT stock), and for her misrepresentation to Cora in connection with her purchase of Cora's shares.

Tippee liability (information from Abby)

A tippee violates SEC Rule 10b-5 if (1) the information is received in breach of the tipper's obligation to refrain from disclosing the information, (2) the tippee recognizes that a breach of that relationship has occurred, and (3) the tipper (Abby) receives some benefit from the disclosure or intends to bestow a pecuniary gift upon the tippee. These requirements were discussed in Part 1a above.

In light of the conclusions reached above regarding the probability that Abby would incur liability as a tipper, Barb probably would be liable as Abby's tippee.

Tipper liability (information to Mutual)

If a tippee would be liable for trading, she also will be liable for the trades of persons to whom she passes the same information under circumstances in which it is foreseeable the recipient will trade. If, however, the recipient would not be liable as a tippee, this might change the outcome.

There is nothing to suggest that Mutual knew, or had reason to know, that Barb received her information improperly. It might be contended that (1) the pointedness of Barb's statement ("If you are smart") and (2) the urgency with which she imparted this to Mutual (that afternoon) should have suggested to Mutual that Barb was using improperly obtained information. On the other hand, Barb's urging could be viewed as merely vigorous business advice. It thus is not clear whether Barb would be liable under SEC Rule 10b-5 for Mutual's purchase.

Liability for transaction with Cora

SEC Rule 10b-5 requires that the defendant used an instrumentality of interstate commerce. Because Barb personally visited Cora and apparently purchased the shares from her at that time, Barb's possible fraud upon Cora would *not* be within the jurisdictional purview of SEC Rule 10b-5. If use of an instrumentality of interstate commerce (i.e., the telephone) is foreseeable before the transaction is consummated, this conclusion would change. Barb clearly committed fraud in connection with the purchase of a security.

1c. Did Mutual violate SEC Rule 10b-5?

As discussed above, if Mutual had no reason to suspect that Barb obtained her information improperly, Mutual would have no SEC Rule 10b-5 culpability (despite the fact that it acted upon Barb's information).

2. Has Barb incurred any nonstatutory civil liability?

Under the special-facts doctrine, when a corporate *insider* enters into a stock transaction with an existing shareholder, the insider has a fiduciary duty to disclose any unusual or extraordinary nonpublic, material facts to the shareholder.

Although Barb was *not* an insider of ALT Corporation and, therefore, arguably owed no special duty of disclosure to Cora on that basis, a court might find that Barb, as Cora's stockbroker, had a common law fiduciary duty of disclosure to Cora. More important, Barb affirmatively misled Cora and, therefore, most likely would be liable under common law fraud principles. If so, Cora could either (1) rescind the transaction (i.e., cause Barb to reconvey the stock to her for the purchase price) or (2) recover the enhanced value of the stock.

Answer to Question 24

Important aspects:
Authority of members of an LLC, piercing the veil of an LLC, liability for misrepresentation of authority.

1. X's liability to Y

A limited liability company (LLC) will be bound to a contract that is entered into by an agent who is either actually or apparently authorized to do so. Here, the contract was entered into by one of the members of a member-managed LLC who purported to be its president.

To know what R's actual authority as a member is, we would need to know whether there is anything in the relevant LLC statute or in X's formative documents that would limit his ability to make decisions on behalf of the LLC. Assuming that there is not, the authority of a member of a member-managed LLC is basically that of a partner in a general partnership. Each member has equal rights to make management decisions within the scope of the LLC's business; in the event of a dispute, a majority rules. In a two-member LLC, however, there can be no majority. Thus, R would have the actual authority to enter into contracts in the ordinary course of X's business. The facts do not indicate whether the contract with Y is extraordinary; we do know, however, that an identical contract was entered into last year, so it probably is not extraordinary. On the other hand, it is large in light of X's described size.

Whether or not the contract was extraordinary also would be relevant to determining if R had apparent authority to enter into it acting as X's president. Apparent authority is based on a third party's reasonable understanding derived from acts attributable to the principal—in this case, the LLC. An LLC may or may not have officers; if it has them, their titles and authority will be determined either in the formative documents or by action of the members. It seems fairly clear that, because R signed last year as president while in the presence of Q, the only other member of the LLC, Y would reasonably believe from Q's acquiescence that R was president of X, with all the authority inherent in the position. A corporation's president generally has the inherent authority to enter into contracts in the ordinary course of business, and there is no reason to think that the rule would apply differently in the case of an LLC.

Thus, assuming that the contract is not extraordinary, Y probably can enforce it against X, either on the basis of R's actual authority as a member or R's apparent authority as president.

2. Q and R's liability as a result of piercing the veil of limited liability

Even if X is liable on the contract, it is quite likely that it will not be able to satisfy its obligation. Q and R's conduct has given a significant basis for argument that the LLC's veil should be pierced and liability imposed on its members. Typically, courts are willing to pierce the veil of a corporation when injustice is shown and a certain set of factors is shown. There is no policy reason that the same willingness would not exist in the case of an LLC. The typical corporate factors include undercapitalization, siphoning of funds, lack of record keeping, and (to a lesser extent) lack of corporate formality. Because LLCs generally are managed with less formality than corporations, lack of formality should not be considered as a factor here. It is clear from the facts that Q and R are lax about record keeping. There are interesting subissues presented relating to injustice, undercapitalization, and siphoning.

a. Injustice

Because it does appear that Y is getting a very good deal on the contract terms and because it does not seem that it has yet relied on or changed its position, a court might not feel that it is really "unjust" to deny it a full contractual recovery. There is also an argument that, because Y knew it was dealing with a limited liability entity, it could have asked to see X's balance sheet; if it chose not to do so, it is not "unjust" to refuse to allow Y to look through X. This argument has not, however, been very successful in the corporate arena.

b. Undercapitalization

It certainly appears that Q and R have not endowed X with sufficient capital to meet its foreseeable obligations. The only argument to the contrary would be based on its satisfaction of the "financial responsibility" requirement for licensing purposes. There is a line of corporate cases giving deference to regulatory assessments on this issue. Still, because the insurance required to be maintained relates only to negligence and the loss to Y is contractual, these cases are not on all fours. A court probably would find X to be undercapitalized.

c. Siphoning

The concept of "siphoning" corporate funds basically refers to diverting corporate monies to the private purposes of the shareholders without satisfaction of the statutory tests intended to assure that corporations remain solvent. Although distributions by member-managed LLCs, like those of general partnerships, may not be subject to the same statutory tests, the idea that the members should not be taking funds that should be applied for LLC purposes still seems relevant. Here, the facts state that maintenance, fuel, and debt service needs are attended to before "distributions" are made. There is no mention of what other needs X may have; nonetheless, it seems unreasonable for Q and R to leave so little for it.

3. R's liability for misrepresenting authority

Because R misrepresented his position (and, therefore, its inherent authority) to Y, he arguably would be liable for foreseeable damage. Because his actual authority as a member would seem to be the same as his apparent authority as president, however, liability seems unlikely.

Answer to Question 25

Important aspects:
Improper withholding of dividends, duty of care, duty of loyalty, improper declaration of dividends, validity of amendment to articles (duty of loyalty), validity of amendment to articles (irregularities in board action), validity of amendment to articles (irregularities in shareholder action).

1. Liability of the old board

Jethro evidently would like to claim that Larry, Curly, and Moe have breached some duty to the common shareholders by failing to pay dividends. The traditional rule with respect to the payment of dividends is that, if surplus is available, dividends cannot be withheld in bad faith. In modern terms, the concept of available surplus should be replaced with the concept of lawful payment. In some jurisdictions, this remains the question of whether surplus is available, coupled with an inquiry into whether payment would result in corporate insolvency. In others, it has become the question of whether payment would either result in corporate insolvency or result in a situation in which liabilities exceed assets.

It is not at all clear to what extent dividends lawfully could have been declared by the old board. It is clear, however, that no dividends could have been declared on the common shares until the dividend preferences of the preferred holders were satisfied. This might have left very little for lawful distribution. In any event, even if amounts were available, there would be no liability for failure to declare a dividend on the common shares unless the failure were in bad faith. Bad faith, in this context, essentially demands motivation to act other than in the interests of the corporation, and there is no evidence that Larry, Curly, and Moe were so motivated.

2. Liability of the new board
a. Liability of Paul and Mary for breach of the duty of care

Directors owe corporations a duty of care, which certainly includes attention to corporate affairs. There is no concept of directorial proxy. Although some matters are delegable to committees, the significant matters on which Peter took action are nondelegable. Even when matters can be delegated, a delegating director is not excused from acting reasonably with respect to oversight of the delegated matter. It thus could be argued that Paul and Mary breached their duty of care when they left for their cruise, leaving only Peter to make decisions about amending the articles and declaring dividends. The counter to this claim is that Paul and Mary did give the matters sufficient attention. We do not know the amount of study they gave the affairs of the corporation before meeting at the restaurant, or what was said there. It is quite possible that all the necessary decisions were made before they left.

Even if Paul and Mary breached their duty of care, liability is a different issue. The articles of incorporation might provide that there will be no monetary damages for such a breach of duty. Moreover, proving that a breach of the duty of care by Paul and Mary caused any damage to Jethro would be problematic.

b. Liability of Peter, Paul, and Mary for breach of the duty of loyalty in amending the articles

Although elected by a single class of shares, members of the board of directors owe a duty of loyalty to the corporate entity. This means that they cannot prefer the interests of the class that elected them. This duty is sometimes hard to navigate in the context of such decisions as when to redeem a particular class and leave another outstanding. It is not hard to navigate in a case such as this one, in which there does not appear to be any good reason for transferring voting rights from the common to the preferred on a permanent basis.

The structure of the argument should go as follows. First, Jethro must show that the board of directors has acted in a fashion to confer a benefit on the class of shares that they themselves hold and that this benefit is not equally shared by the common holders. This should be easily done. Then, the board of directors will have the burden of showing that they acted fairly. It does not appear that they will be able to sustain this burden. Thus, the amendment of the articles of incorporation probably will be set aside.

c. Liability of Peter, Paul, and Mary for unlawful declaration of dividends on the preferred stock

As discussed above, in some jurisdictions, a distribution to shareholders can be made only out of available surplus and only to the extent it does not result in corporate insolvency. In others, a distribution to shareholders may not be made if it would render the corporation insolvent or if the assets of the corporation would not, after the distribution is made, exceed its liabilities. We do not have enough information to tell if there is a surplus or if assets would exceed liabilities after the distribution. The insolvency test, however, does not seem to have been violated, because Adelphi was able to obtain a new bank loan. We would need to know, however, whether it is reasonable to believe that Adelphi will be able make the required payment next year.

d. Liability of Peter, Paul, and Mary for failure to declare dividends on the common stock

This issue basically is a repeat of the possible liability of the old board to declare dividends. There are, however, more facts suggesting that Adelphi's legal ability to pay dividends is limited (cutting against liability), as well as more facts to suggest that the board generally is engaging in self-preferring conduct that might be construed as bad faith (cutting in favor of liability). Because the company does appear to be short on cash and because dividends on the common stock cannot lawfully be declared until the arrears on the preferred stock are satisfied, Peter, Paul, and Mary probably will not be liable on this count.

3. Validity of amendment to articles of incorporation

There are three reasons that the amendment to the articles of incorporation might be invalid. The first was described above: the act of the directors in recommending the amendment was self-interested and apparently unfair.

The second reason the amendment might be invalid has to do with irregularities in its adoption. Amendments to a corporation's articles of incorporation must be recommended by the board of directors and approved by the shareholders before filing with the proper state authority. It is arguable that neither of these requirements was satisfied.

Jethro might claim that Peter acted alone in adopting the board's recommendation. If so, the requisite of either an action by unanimous written consent or a duly noticed meeting attended by a quorum was not satisfied. A counter that Peter exercised a proxy for Paul and Mary would fail, as directors generally cannot act through proxies. An argument that the meeting requirement was satisfied at the restaurant could be more successful. Even though no notice was given, all of the directors attended, evidently without raising the notice issue. If they actually agreed to recommend the amendment, the fact that the resolution was not typed up until the next day should not matter.

Jethro might also argue that, if shareholders are to act by unanimous written consent, all must sign the relevant document. However, Paul and Mary said they were giving their proxies to Peter, and proxy voting for shareholders is well recognized; it seems a short step to permitting proxy signatures for purposes of unanimous written consent. Moreover, there is no reason that signature by an agent should be against public policy; after all, many shareholders are entities that can sign only through an agent's hand. It seems likely that a court would overlook this irregularity.

A court, however, could not overlook the fact that the common shareholders were not given a chance to vote on the amendment. Although the articles of incorporation stated that the preferred class was entitled to exercise all voting rights until the dividends in arrears were paid, this provision could not overcome the usual statutory requirement that any amendment to the articles of incorporation affecting the rights of a class in a way unique to the class (such as the permanent loss of the common stock's ability to vote) must be approved by a vote of the class. Thus, the amendment to the articles should be struck down.

Answer to Question 26

Important aspects:
Non-enforcement of illegal contracts, lack of authority, *ultra vires*, breach of fiduciary duty.

1. Is the contract between Vets and Limb enforceable?
a. Illegal contract
If Victor wants to avoid the contract on behalf of Vets, he might argue that it called for an illegal act by Limb. The facts state that a State M statute provides that corporations cannot fit artificial limbs. The statute says nothing about limited liability companies. There are, in fact, many state statutes and state constitutional provisions specifically mentioning partnerships and/or corporations, but, because they predated the recognition of limited liability companies (LLCs), fail to mention them. Courts must, in these situations, attempt to determine the purpose of the legislative or constitutional drafters and then invoke that purpose in deciding how to treat LLCs. It appears that the drafters of the State M statute wished to permit the fitting of artificial limbs only if individuals were to be personally responsible for the activity. Because LLCs, like corporations, confer limited liability on the owners of the business, a court probably would hold that they could not engage in the business of fitting artificial limbs. Thus, Victor might well prevail on this issue.

b. Lack of authorization
If, for some reason, Victor wants to enforce the contract with Limb, but Limb wishes to avoid it (probably not the case, given that it is about to be in possession of 20 artificial legs), Limb would argue that, although the members had equal decision-making authority within the scope of its business, Cherry did not have authority to bind the LLC in a matter outside that scope. Although Limb's formation documents did nothing to define that scope, that has often been the case with partnerships as well. It is clear in the partnership context that scope is defined by the consent of the partners; this should be the case with LLCs as well. It seems quite clear that fitting artificial limbs is a different business from trimming trees and shrubs, so Limb should prevail. Victor might argue that he acted reasonably in relying on the representation of a member as to what business the LLC is in, but it is well established in the area of partnership that this is not the case; there is no reason to expect a different outcome in the context of an LLC.

The fact that Cherry signed the contract with Vets without reference to her agency capacity does not affect the enforceability of the agreement against

Limb. If Cherry had the authority to enter into it (which she probably did not), she could bind even an undisclosed principal. The method of signature might suggest an intent to be personally bound, but the question does not ask about Cherry's personal liability. If it did, it also would be relevant to note that Cherry might well be liable for misrepresentation of authority, if Vets incurs any damage as a result.

2. Limb's rights against Cherry
a. The doctrine of ultra vires

The first possible basis for suing Cherry is the argument that she caused the LLC to commit an ultra vires act. The doctrine historically has been applied to invalidate actions taken by **corporations** that are beyond their corporate purposes or powers. Modern statutes, however, have limited the doctrine, providing that the issue can only be raised in actions by shareholders to enjoin an action, by the corporation in a suit against directors or officers causing it to take an ultra vires act, or by the state in a *quo warranto* proceeding. These statutes do not address LLCs, but Holly might argue that she is in something like the second situation; a great deal of legal argument about LLCs requires **analogy** to corporate and/or partnership precedents. The analogy probably would fail, because the ultra vires doctrine itself generally has fallen out of favor, as it is linked with outdated ideas about the need to strictly limit corporate conduct to activities contemplated by their state charters. By contrast, LLCs were developed to maximize flexible business planning, and there generally have been no requirements that an LLC's purposes and powers be limited by chartering documents or otherwise.

If an analogy were accepted, however, the doctrine would only apply if the act indeed were beyond the LLC's purposes or powers. Because the question stipulates that Limb's formative documents are silent on these matters, the only real limit presumably would be that the LLC engage in activities that are legal. This would suggest that entering into the contract with Victor would be ultra vires, because that contract (as discussed above) very arguably called for an illegal act. By contrast, there does not seem to be anything illegal about owning artificial legs, so the contract Cherry entered into on the Internet probably would not be ultra vires.

b. Breach of fiduciary duty

Although the state statutes permitting the creation of LLCs vary in their description of the duties owed by members, it is clear that those members are in a fiduciary relationship with respect to the entity and each other.

The duties inherent in a fiduciary relationship include duties of due care and loyalty (a component of which may be good faith). Cherry acted heedlessly, failing to investigate the requirements for entering into the business of fitting artificial limbs and, as a result, causing the LLC to enter into two agreements that appear to be extremely imprudent, and one of which very well may be illegal. If the agreement with Vets is not enforceable, yet Limb is required to pay for the artificial legs Cherry ordered, there is a very good chance that Cherry will be liable to Limb. (Although the question did not ask for a discussion of the enforceability of Cherry's Internet contract for the legs, it is worth noting that it would be subject to the same defenses having to do with lack of authorization as the contract with Vets. Thus, there may be no significant damage to Limb.)

Answer to Question 27

Important aspects:
Ultra vires, irregularity of directors' meetings (notice), irregularity of directors' meetings (quorum and voting requirements), duty of care, business judgment rule, corporate waste, statutory provisions limiting liability, duty of loyalty, standing to sue, demand requirement, demand futility.

1. Can the donation be enjoined?
a. The doctrine of ultra vires
The first possible basis for enjoining the donation is the argument that it is ultra vires. The doctrine is applied to invalidate actions taken by corporations that are beyond their corporate purposes or powers. Modern statutes, however, provide that the issue can only be raised in actions by shareholders to enjoin an action, by the corporation in a suit against directors or officers causing it to take an ultra vires act, and by the state in a *quo warranto* proceeding.

The first issue, then, is whether the endowment of the Hiss/Story Museum is outside the corporation's purposes or powers. Although Story's articles are silent as to its powers, most state statutes provide that a corporation has all the powers of an individual to engage in acts necessary or convenient to its business (sometimes the language refers to "in furtherance" of its business), including the making of charitable contributions. Should this be taken to include the power to make an unusually large contribution, something an individual certainly could do? If the language relating to "necessary or convenient" or "in furtherance" is to have any meaning, some restriction on the size of a gift presumably does exist. Thus, a for-profit corporation could not give away all of its assets. A gift well short of substantially all the corporation's assets also may be suspect. Some courts approving corporate charitable contributions have been heavily influenced by the deductibility of the gift; the fact that Story's gift would exceed its annual income (and, therefore, probably wouldn't be tax deductible) certainly would be troubling to such a court. It seems quite likely that *a shareholder* could have the donation enjoined. G, however, is a director. G presumably could alert the shareholders other than H as to what is going on and encourage one of them to seek an injunction. There have been cases in which a corporation with regrets about a contract has conspired with a shareholder to seek an injunction; the issues raised in such cases having to do with whether the shareholder is acting as the corporation's agent would not seem to be presented on these facts.

b. Procedural irregularities
i. Lack of notice

The second basis for enjoining the donation is the procedural irregularity of the meeting at which it was approved. A director's meeting must be preceded by valid notice to all members. Because G was not sent a notice, the meeting could not be validly held in his absence. G, however, did attend. Although one can attend a meeting solely for the purpose of raising lack of notice, this does not appear to be what happened. It therefore appears that G waived the ability to raise lack of notice.

ii. Failure to satisfy the quorum and voting requirements

A quorum of the directors must be present in order for a meeting to be validly held. In the absence of specification to the contrary, this would require a majority of the directors to be present. A quorum of a four-member board is three (two is not a majority). The usual vote of directors required for a motion to carry is, in the absence of specification to the contrary, a majority of those directors present and voting.

G might try to characterize H as "interested" in the transaction, because she is personally enthusiastic about the idea and does not seem to be motivated by the best interests of the corporation and its shareholders. At one time, interested directors could not be counted for purposes of satisfying quorum or voting requirements. The modern approach, however, is to permit interested directors to be counted for both purposes. Note that, given satisfaction of the usual quorum and voting requirements, a majority of the "disinterested" directors (two out of three) voted for the donation.

2. Will the approving directors be liable for approving the donation?
a. Standing

G might contend that it is up to the board to decide when to commence litigation on the corporation's behalf and then go on to argue that, because the other board members would be deciding whether to sue themselves, the decision should be left to him alone. Although this is a matter the board might be able to delegate to a committee, there is little likelihood that the other board members would agree to do so. If G then argues that he may make the decision alone simply because of the other board members' self-interest, he probably will fail. A decision to bring litigation out of the ordinary course of business is a decision to be made by the board like any other. Thus, quorum and voting requirements would need to be satisfied, which would be impossible in this situation, as long as the membership on the board does not change.

In any event, the most usual method of imposing liability on the directors of a corporation is by a derivative action instituted by one of its shareholders. G is not a shareholder; G might, however, succeed in interesting a shareholder to bring suit. Before bringing a derivative suit, a shareholder must ordinarily make a demand on the directors. In some jurisdictions, this requirement is absolute. In many states, however, demand is excused when it is likely to be futile. Because the majority of Story's directors voted in favor of the donation, a shareholder could assert that any demand would be futile and was, therefore, unnecessary. A shareholder might well prevail on this issue (although, in some jurisdictions, if the vote on the contract by some of the directors was protected by the business judgment rule, the outcome would be different).

Some jurisdictions require that a demand be made on disinterested shareholders prior to commencing a derivative action. If a majority of shareholders fails to ratify the lawsuit, it cannot be commenced. In addition, some states require that a security bond for expenses be posted. However, there is nothing to indicate that either requirement is present in this instance.

b. Violation of the duty of care

Directors owe a duty to act in a manner reasonably calculated to be in the corporation's best interests; the business judgment rule precludes the application of hindsight to that determination. This does not mean, however, that there is absolutely no judicial second-guessing on the subject of reasonableness. A typical formulation might state that, short of waste of corporate assets, the business judgment of the directors will not be questioned. The facts given clearly do suggest the issue of waste. The plaintiff will have the burden, however, of demonstrating that the directors have done something that is manifestly unreasonable. Only if the directors were self-interested (see below), shown to be acting in bad faith, or the like would they not be entitled to a presumption of reasonableness. In support of the reasonableness of their decision, the directors who approved the donation presumably would argue that making the donation would result in excellent publicity and goodwill, keeping the Story name in the public eye, even as literary fiction declines. They might also argue that conserving funds to enter new lines of business would not be legitimate, given the articles' restriction of purpose, although there does not seem to be any reason to suppose that an amendment to the articles could not be recommended to the shareholders.

Separately, causing a corporation to engage in an ultra vires act (as the donation may be) very probably is a breach of the duty of care or a demonstrated lack of good faith. Certainly, the statutes dealing with ultra vires invite lawsuits by corporations against those causing them to act ultra vires; although the theory is not specified, it is presumably breach of one or more fiduciary duties.

In is worth noting that many jurisdictions have statutes permitting or mandating limits on monetary liability for breach of the duty of care.

c. Complications added by the duty of loyalty/duty to act in good faith

Directors also owe corporations a duty of loyalty, which includes refraining from dealing with the corporation in a manner that constitutes unfair self-dealing. The duty to act in good faith in assessing the interests of the corporation is sometimes described as a component of the duty of loyalty.

It would not be frivolous to assert that H is "interested" in the establishment of the Hiss/Story Museum, in light of her stated interest in seeing her family's contribution to literature recognized. That argument might be countered with one to the effect that the benefit would be one that would be shared with all the other shareholders, all of whom are members of the Hiss family. If she were regarded as "interested" and she were the only decision maker, it is plausible that a court would require her to justify the fairness of the gift. Failing such a justification, the usual remedy would be avoidance (effectively the same as an injunction in this case). She was not the only decision maker, however, and it appears that the approval of the "disinterested" directors could shift the burden with respect to fairness back to the plaintiff—provided that the donation is not deemed waste, as discussed above.

Multiple-Choice Questions

1. In return for an unsecured promissory note in the amount of $5,000, ABC Corp. issued 500 shares of $100 par value stock to Bill. Upon receipt of Bill's note, ABC's secretary marked the shares as "fully paid" on its books. A short time later, the board of ABC seeks to repudiate the transaction and, after tendering the $5,000 note back to Bill, requests return of its shares. However, Bill refuses to give up his shares. (You may assume that ABC is solvent.)

   Based on the foregoing, which of the following statements is most likely correct?

   A. In at least some jurisdictions, ABC may rescind the transaction.

   B. Judgment creditors of ABC can enforce the note.

   C. The shareholders of ABC can demand payment of the note from Bill.

   D. None of the above statements is correct.

2. One year ago, in exchange for property, the board of ABC Corp. issued stock to Jackie with a stated par value of $12,000. The board reasonably believed, in good faith, that the property was worth $12,000. However, shareholders of ABC now have an expert who is willing to testify that the property's fair market value is presently only $10,000. The shares are designated as "fully paid" on the corporation's books.

   Based on the foregoing, which of the following statements is most likely correct?

   A. ABC Corp. can rescind the transaction or recover $2,000 from Jackie.

   B. Persons who became judgment creditors of ABC Corp. after the transaction with Jackie can recover $2,000 from her.

   C. The shareholders of ABC Corp. at the time of the transaction can recover $2,000 from Jackie.

   D. The transaction cannot be rescinded, nor can any sum be recovered from Jackie.

3. In exchange for property worth $10,000, ABC Corp. issues stock to Jackie with a stated par value of $12,000. (You may assume the directors were aware that the stock was issued for property worth less than the par value of the shares.) The shares are designated as "fully paid" on the books of the corporation. Subsequently, Jackie transfers the shares to Moe for $15,000. ABC recently became insolvent.

Based on the foregoing, which of the following statements is most likely correct?

A. Judgment creditors of ABC Corp. can recover $2,000 from Jackie.

B. Shareholders of ABC Corp. at the time of the transaction can recover $2,000 from Jackie.

C. Shareholders of ABC Corp. at the time of the transaction can recover $5,000 from Jackie.

D. No sum can be recovered from Jackie by creditors and/or shareholders.

4. A and B sign an agreement with Carl, a promoter for X Corporation, whereby A and B each agree to purchase 500 shares of $10 per share par value stock. This contract is made prior to the time X Corporation is formed. After X Corporation is formed, but before the subscription agreement is affirmed by the board, A advises X's directors that she is repudiating the subscription agreement.

Assuming there is no legislation that makes subscription agreements irrevocable for a prescribed period of time, which of the following statements is most likely correct?

A. A is not liable because she revoked prior to acceptance of the contract by the corporation.

B. A is liable because the corporation was formed prior to her attempted repudiation.

C. A is liable because B failed to join her in repudiating the subscription agreement.

D. A is liable *if* she failed to notify Carl of her repudiation.

5. A and B sign a subscription agreement. Subsequently, the corporation is formed and accepts the contract via a properly adopted board resolution. However, prior to any tender of the shares A promised to buy, the corporation goes bankrupt. Creditors of the corporation (via the trustee-in-bankruptcy) now seek to enforce the subscription agreement against A and B.

Based on the foregoing, which of the following statements is most likely correct?

A. A is not liable because the stock was never delivered to her prior to the corporation's bankruptcy.

B. A is not liable because the corporation is bankrupt, and, therefore, the shares she would receive are worthless.

C. A is liable because the corporation was formed and had accepted the contract.

D. A is liable only to the corporation, but *not* to its judgment creditors.

6. Zeek, a promoter for Amco Corporation, entered into a contract with Paula to purchase widgets. Zeek signed the agreement, "Zeek, on behalf of Amco, a corporation to be formed." Amco is subsequently formed, but refuses to ratify the contract.

   Based on the foregoing, which of the following statements is most likely correct?

   A. Zeek is personally liable under the agreement.

   B. Zeek is not personally liable under the agreement.

   C. Zeek and Amco are jointly and severally liable.

   D. None of the above.

7. Zeek entered into a contract with Paula to purchase widgets. Zeek signed the agreement, "Zeek, on behalf of Amco, a corporation to be formed." Subsequently, Amco is formed, and the contract is ratified unanimously at a properly called board of directors meeting.

   Based on the foregoing, which of the following statements is most likely correct?

   A. Only Zeek is liable under the agreement.

   B. Only Amco is liable under the agreement.

   C. Both Zeek and Amco are liable under the agreement.

   D. None of the above.

8. John, a promoter, enters into a contract with Alice, whereby Alice will serve as a consultant to Exco Corporation for $2,000 per month for one year. John signs the agreement as follows: "John, on behalf of Exco, a corporation to be formed, but not for himself personally." Subsequently, Exco is formed, and a board of directors of seven persons is appointed. Although John does not initially advise the Exco board about the contract with Alice, most of the board's members observe Alice working at Exco's premises on behalf of the corporation. However, when the contract is considered at the monthly board meeting five months after incorporation, it is unanimously rejected.

   Based on the foregoing, which of the following statements is most likely correct?

A. John is liable under the contract with Alice.

B. Exco is liable to Alice.

C. Neither John nor Exco is liable to Alice.

D. None of the above.

Questions 9-11 are based on the following facts:

A, B, and C decide to form Exco Corporation, which will manufacture and sell widgets. They agree that A will be the president and that they will each be directors. They communicate this information to Len, a lawyer, and request that Len perform the necessary requisites for corporate formation. Len agrees to perform this function, but advises A, B, and C that it normally takes several weeks to incorporate. Len sends the articles of incorporation to the secretary of state. However, he inadvertently omits the necessary filing fee. Due to a backlog at the secretary of state's office, the rejected articles are not returned to Len for almost two months.

Three weeks after deciding to form Exco, A contracts with Billie to purchase $20,000 worth of widget components, to be delivered in four months. A, assuming the articles would be filed, stock issued, and officers elected within four months, signs the agreement: "A, future president of Exco Corporation."

One week after this transaction, B accidentally collides with Chuck while driving her personal vehicle to pick up office materials for Exco's future operations.

9. Based on the foregoing, which of the following statements is most likely correct as of the time of B's accident with Chuck?

   A. Exco is a de jure corporation.

   B. Exco is a de facto corporation.

   C. No corporate structure exists.

   D. Exco is a corporation by estoppel for purposes of the accident with Chuck.

10. Exco is subsequently properly formed. If Billie commences an action against A, personally, for the $20,000 owed under the contract, A's strongest argument to avoid or minimize personal liability would most likely be that:

   A. Exco was a de jure corporation.

   B. Exco was a de facto corporation.

   C. The corporation-by-estoppel doctrine is applicable.

   D. He is liable only for one-third of the debts incurred on behalf of Exco.

11. Exco is subsequently properly formed. (You may assume that, in the collision between B and Chuck, B was at fault.) If Chuck sues A,

no corp at time of accident

personally, for the injuries sustained in his accident with B, it is most likely that A:

A. Has no liability for the accident.

B. Is personally liable for Chuck's damages.

C. Is liable for only one-half of Chuck's damages.

D. Is liable for only one-third of Chuck's damages.

12. X works in the mailroom at ABC Corporation. One day, while delivering mail to the corporation's executives, X overhears a geologist advise the president of ABC that the corporation has just discovered oil. That day, June 1, X purchased, via a telephone call to his broker, 200 shares of ABC stock at $25 per share. On June 15, the oil discovery was made public, and ABC stock increased to $50 per share. X sold his 200 shares on June 16, at $50 per share. ABC shares are traded on the New York Stock Exchange. Prior to overhearing the conversation, X had **not** owned any ABC shares.

Based on the foregoing, which of the following statements is most likely correct?

A. X is liable to the corporation under SEC Rule 16(b).

B. X is liable to the sellers of the shares under SEC Rule 10b-5.

C. X has violated SEC Rule 10b-5, but is not liable to the sellers of the shares under that rule.

D. X has **no** liability for the transaction described.

13. X is the treasurer at ABC Corporation, which is traded on the New York Stock Exchange. On June 1, X purchases 200 shares at $30 per share of her corporation's stock over the New York Stock Exchange. Two weeks later, on June 15, ABC discovers oil. X had no idea this event might occur when she purchased the ABC stock. On June 30, the oil discovery becomes publicly known, and ABC's stock increases to $50 per share. On September 20, X sells her ABC stock for $48 per share.

Based on the foregoing, which of the following statements is most likely correct?

A. X is liable to the corporation under SEC Rule 16(b).

B. X is liable to the corporation under SEC Rule 10b-5.

C. X is liable to persons who sold her the ABC shares under SEC Rule 10b-5.

D. X is likely to be liable to the corporation under common law principles.

14. X is the vice president of ABC Corporation, which is traded on the New York Stock Exchange. X learns, via a conversation with Obie, the president of ABC, that the corporation had recently made an unexpected discovery of a large oil field on property it owns. That night, X visits Bob, a friend of hers who owns 200 shares of ABC stock, and X purchases these shares for $25 each, their fair market value. This transaction is concluded at Bob's apartment, with X giving Bob a check for $5,000 and Bob tendering the stock certificate pertaining to the shares with an appropriate endorsement to change the name of the stockholder on ABC's records. Two weeks later, the oil find becomes publicly known, and ABC stock dramatically appreciates in value.

    Based on the foregoing, which of the following statements is most likely correct?

    A. X is liable to ABC under SEC Rule 16(b).

    B. X is liable to ABC under SEC Rule 10b-5.

    C. X is liable to Bob under SEC Rule 10b-5.

    D. X may be liable to ABC under the "special facts" doctrine.

15. ABC Corporation's shares are traded on the New York Stock Exchange. Ossie purchased 100 shares of ABC's common stock on January 4 for $60 per share. These shares represented less than 1 percent of ABC's outstanding common shares. Three months later, Ossie became a director and, the next day, sold these shares for $50 per share. One month after his sale of the ABC stock, Ossie bought 100 additional shares for $10 per share.

    Based on the foregoing, which of the following statements is most likely correct?

    A. Ossie has no liability under SEC Rule 16(b).

    B. Ossie has liability of $1,000 under SEC Rule 16(b).

    C. Ossie has liability of $4,000 under SEC Rule 16(b).

    D. Ossie has liability of $5,000 under SEC Rule 16(b).

16. ABC Corp. stock is traded on the New York Stock Exchange. Ossie, who is *not* an officer or director, purchased 100 shares of ABC's common stock on January 8, paying $40 per share. These shares represented 3 percent of ABC's outstanding common shares. Three months later, Ossie became a director and, two months after this event, sold the 100 shares for $70 per share.

Based on the foregoing, which of the following statements is most likely correct?

A. Ossie has no liability under SEC Rule 16(b).

B. Ossie has liability to the purchaser(s) of his shares under SEC Rule 10b-5.

C. Ossie is liable to ABC for $3,000.

D. Ossie is liable to the seller of the ABC shares for $3,000.

17. ABC Corp. retained Smith & Smith, a prominent, established accounting firm, to prepare its financial statement for presentation to the shareholders at the annual meeting. In preparing the statement, the accountant negligently omitted a material item of negative financial information. This resulted in ABC's financial statement appearing much more positive than warranted. No one at ABC was aware of this error. Joan purchased 100 shares of ABC stock on the basis of this information. Immediately after the erroneous information became public, ABC stock fell in value by $10 per share.

Based on the foregoing, which of the following statements is most likely correct?

A. Smith & Smith is liable to Joan under SEC Rule 10b-5.

B. ABC is liable to Joan under SEC Rule 10b-5.

C. Smith & Smith and/or ABC is liable to Joan under the special-facts doctrine.

D. Neither Smith & Smith nor ABC has liability to Joan under SEC Rule 10b-5 or the special-facts doctrine.

18. Amy was about to sell her shares of ABC Corporation stock. Paul, who had once met Amy at a party and disliked her, told Amy that ABC shares would soon increase in value because the company had discovered a new process for extracting nicotine from cigarettes. In fact, Paul had heard from a friend who worked at ABC that the company was laying off employees. On the basis of Paul's statement, Amy kept her ABC stock. However, it soon decreased in value by $5 per share after ABC's true financial condition became known. (You may assume that Paul does **not** work for ABC.)

Based on the foregoing, which of the following statements is most likely correct?

A. Amy could successfully sue Paul under SEC Rule 10b-5.

B. Amy could successfully sue Paul under SEC Rule 16(b).

C. Amy could successfully sue Paul under the special-facts doctrine.

D. Amy cannot successfully sue Paul under any of the foregoing doctrines. *She kept her stock, no trading*

Questions 19-21 are based on the following facts:

Arlo, a director of ABC Corporation (a publicly traded entity), is informed that the annual financial statement, soon to be made public, will show that the corporation has suffered losses during the previous fiscal year. While purchasing some food in the corporation's cafeteria, Arlo mentions to Mark, one of the food servers, that the corporation "had lost a lot of money" during the year. Arlo did this because Mark had asked her why she looked so "down." Gale, who was visiting a business school friend at ABC and was in the food line behind Arlo, overheard this information.

19. The next day, Arlo sold her ABC shares for $20 per share. When ABC's losses became known three months later, its stock slipped to $12 per share.

    Based on the foregoing, which of the following statements is most likely correct?

    A. Arlo is liable under SEC Rule 16(b) *if* she had purchased her shares for an amount less than $20 within the six months preceding her sale of ABC stock.

    B. Arlo has no liability under SEC Rule 10b-5 *if* she made no express statement in connection with her sale of the ABC shares.

    C. Arlo has no liability under SEC Rule 10b-5 *if* she had originally purchased the stock for less than $20 per share.

    D. Arlo is liable under SEC Rule 10b-5, but under no circumstances is she liable under SEC Rule 16(b).

20. The next day, Gale sells her ABC stock, which she had purchased one year ago for $18 per share, for $20 per share.

    Based on the foregoing, which of the following statements is most likely correct?

    A. Gale has liability under SEC Rule 16(b).

    B. Gale has liability under SEC Rule 10b-5.

    C. Gale has liability under the special-facts doctrine.

    D. Gale has no liability.

21. The next day, Mark sells his ABC stock (all of which he had purchased one month ago) to avoid any losses. Prior to this sale, Mark held an 11 percent interest in ABC.
    Mark is technically an employee of the corp

Based on the foregoing, which of the following statements is most likely correct?

A. Mark is liable under SEC Rule 16(b).

B. Mark is liable under SEC Rule 10b-5.

C. Mark is liable under the special-facts doctrine.

D. Mark has no liability.

22. M owns 20 percent of Zeta Corporation's common stock. There are 10,000 shares outstanding. Zeta Corporation is traded on a national stock exchange. M is *not* an officer or director of Zeta. M engages in the following transactions, all during the last calendar year:

Date	Transaction	Sales price
1/1	Buys 500 shares of Zeta common stock	$7
4/5	Buys 200 shares of Zeta common stock	$6
5/5	Sells 600 shares of Zeta common stock	$8

Which of the following is M's liability, if any, to Zeta Corporation under SEC Rule 16(b)?

A. No liability.

B. $400.

C. $600.

D. $800.

24. Martin, the president and a director of Aardvark, Inc., owns 60 percent of Aardvark's common stock. The remaining 40 percent is owned by 125 other shareholders. On April 1, Martin, as a consequence of his control of the Aardvark board, persuaded a majority of the directors to reject an offer by Ant Corporation to merge Aardvark into Ant Corporation. The vote to accept Ant's offer lost, 5 to 4. Ant Corporation had offered consideration worth $35 per share of Aardvark stock. The fair market value of Aardvark stock is approximately $30 per share. On April 15, Martin sold his controlling interest in Aardvark to Zoo Company, which was previously a competitor of Aardvark, for $50 per share. Martin and Zoo had been negotiating the price for his stock for about one month.

Based on the foregoing, which of the following statements is most likely *not* correct?

A. Aardvark may have a cause of action against Martin for breach of his duty of loyalty.

B. The minority shareholders of Aardvark may have individual actions against Martin for breach of the majority shareholders' duty to minority shareholders.

C. The minority shareholders may bring a derivative action against Martin for breach of his duty of loyalty.

D. The minority shareholders may have individual actions for damages against Martin under SEC Rule 10b-5.

Questions 24-32 are based on the following facts:

Fox Corp. issued and has outstanding 1,000 shares of common stock that are owned by a husband, wife, their son (Jr. Fox), and an employee (Jones) as follows:

Mr. Fox .... 250 shares (25%)

Mrs. Fox.................................... 250 shares (25%)

Jr. Fox....................................... 250 shares (25%)

Jones .... 250 shares (25%)

For its first two years of operation, Fox Corp. had the following balance sheets:

FIRST YEAR

ASSETS

Cash .... $ 50,000

Accounts receivable 125,000

Inventory 55,000

Nevada real estate 400,000

Equipment 80,000

TOTAL ASSETS $710,000

LIABILITIES

Accounts payable $250,000

Note payable to Bank X 115,000

Note payable to Bank Y 250,000

TOTAL LIABILITIES $615,000

SHAREHOLDERS' EQUITY

1,000 shares of $1 par value
common stock ....$ 1,000

Capital in excess of par 104,000

Negative retained earnings .... 10,000)

TOTAL SHAREHOLDERS' EQUITY ....$ 95,000

SECOND YEAR

ASSETS

Cash .... $ 75,000

Accounts receivable 50,000

Inventory 100,000

Nevada real estate 200,000

Equipment 75,000

TOTAL ASSETS $500,000

LIABILITIES

Accounts payable .... $ 95,000

Note payable to Bank X 105,000

Note payable to Bank Y 100,000

TOTAL LIABILITIES $300,000

SHAREHOLDERS' EQUITY

1,000 shares of $1 par value
common stock ....$ 1,000

Capital in excess of par 149,000

Retained earnings 50,000

TOTAL SHAREHOLDERS' EQUITY $200,000

(You may assume that Fox Corp. is solvent and none of the transactions described **below** would impair Fox's ability to operate.)

24. Which of the following numbers represents the net worth of Fox Corp. at the end of the second year?

   A. $50,000.

   B. $100,000.

C. $200,000.

D. $350,000.

25. The book value of one share of stock in Fox Corp. at the end of the second year is:

    A. $100.

    B. $200.

    C. $500.

    D. $1,000.

26. For purposes of this question only, assume that, after the second year, Fox Corp. purchased Jr. Fox's 250 shares in exchange for a five-year, $100,000 promissory note made by Fox Corp. in favor of Jr. Fox. Would Jones's voting rights be *adversely* affected as a result of this transaction?

    A. Yes.

    B. No.

    C. Cannot tell without knowing the number of directors at Fox Corp.

    D. Cannot tell without knowing whether Fox Corp. has cumulative voting.

27. In a retained earnings jurisdiction, on the first day after the first year, Fox Corp. may:

    A. Pay each shareholder a dividend not exceeding $35,000.

    B. Pay each shareholder a dividend not exceeding $2,500.

    C. Pay each shareholder a dividend not exceeding $37,500.

    D. Not pay any of its shareholders a dividend.

28. For purposes of this question only, assume that Fox Corp. sold its Nevada real estate on the first business day after the first year to Mr. and Mrs. Fox for $175,000. Would this transaction dilute the present fair market value of Jones's shares?

    A. Yes.

    B. No.

    C. Cannot tell without additional facts pertaining to the Nevada real estate.

    D. Cannot tell without additional facts pertaining to whether Fox has straight or cumulative voting.

29. For purposes of this question only, assume that Fox Corp. has a board of five directors who are elected each year. Would Fox Corp.'s payment of a 10 percent common stock dividend **adversely** affect Jones's voting rights?

   A. Yes, regardless of whether Fox Corp. has straight or cumulative voting.

   B. No.

   C. Yes, but only if Fox Corp. has cumulative voting.

   D. Yes, but only if Fox Corp. has straight voting.

30. If Fox Corp. is incorporated in a typical nimble dividend state, immediately after the first year it may:

   A. Issue no dividends.

   B. Issue dividends in an amount not exceeding $250 per shareholder.

   C. Issue dividends in an amount not exceeding $2,500 per shareholder.

   D. Issue dividends in an amount not exceeding $140,000 per shareholder.

31. If Fox Corp. is incorporated in a state that permits dividends to be paid only from retained earnings or earned surplus, could Fox Corp., on the first business day immediately after the second year, repurchase Jr. Fox's shares in exchange for its $100,000, five-year promissory note?

   A. Yes.

   B. No, because the purchase price exceeds $50,000.

   C. No, because Fox Corp. would become insolvent as a result of this transaction.

   D. Cannot tell without additional facts.

32. If Fox Corp. is incorporated in a state that permits distributions to be paid out of retained earnings or earned surplus, on the first business day after the second year, it could:

   A. Pay a dividend of $10,000 to each shareholder.

   B. Pay a dividend of $13,000 to each shareholder.

   C. Pay a dividend of $37,500 to each shareholder.

   D. Pay a dividend of $50,000 to each shareholder.

33. Bob Barbell is the principal shareholder and president of CG Corporation. The corporation incurred a large unsecured obligation to Barbell as a result of consultation and management services he

rendered to CG. (You may assume that these transactions were **not** fraudulent in nature and that CG's board approved them. You may also assume that the transactions were **not** ultra vires.) As a result of partial payments to Barbell and several high-risk transactions undertaken by him on behalf of CG, CG became insolvent and filed for bankruptcy. The other unsecured creditors of CG want Barbell's claim disallowed entirely or at least subordinated to their claims.

Based on the foregoing, which of the following statements is most likely correct?

A. The indebtedness of CG to Barbell will be unenforceable because a corporation cannot validly transact business with its officers.

B. The indebtedness of CG to Barbell may be subordinated to the claims of other unsecured creditors under the *Deep Rock* doctrine; *Taylor v. Standard Gas & Electric Company*, 306 U.S. 307 (1939).

C. The indebtedness of CG to Barbell will be subordinated to the claims of CG's other unsecured creditors because Barbell is a share-holder of CG.

D. Barbell will be able to enforce his claim against CG on par with all of CG's other unsecured creditors.

34. At the liquidation of a corporation, which of the following best describes the priority of claims as between shareholders and creditors of a corporation?

A. Secured creditors are paid first to the extent of their security. The remainder, if any, is split between the shareholders and unsecured creditors.

B. First, preferred shareholders are paid any dividend arrearages. Next, the creditors are paid their debts. The remainder, if any, is distributed to the shareholders according to their rights and preferences.

C. First, secured creditors are paid to the extent of their security. They then become unsecured creditors for any remaining deficiency. Next, the unsecured creditors are paid. Finally, the remainder, if any, is distributed to the shareholders according to their rights and preferences.

D. First, creditors are paid in full. The remainder, if any, is distributed to the shareholders according to their respective rights and preferences.

Questions 35-36 are based on the following fact pattern:

On January 2, XYZ Corporation entered into a contract with Paula to purchase her bowling alley. XYZ's articles of incorporation expressly state that it is empowered only to operate a restaurant. The purchase price of the bowling alley is $200,000, which is to be paid at the change of possession of the premises. The date established for this to occur is April 4.

35. Assume that XYZ repudiates the contract on April 2. In a suit brought by Paula for breach of contract, XYZ asserts the ultra vires doctrine as a defense. Assuming this is a common law jurisdiction, which of the following statements best describes the most likely result?

   A. XYZ will prevail because the ultra vires defense is available to it under these circumstances.

   B. XYZ will prevail *if* Paula had not reviewed its articles of incorporation prior to entering into the contract.

   C. Paula will prevail because only XYZ's shareholders can assert the ultra vires defense under these circumstances.

   D. Paula will prevail *if* XYZ's shareholders had ratified the transaction prior to the board's attempted repudiation of the contract.

36. For purposes of this question, assume that the contract required a prepayment of $25,000 by XYZ to Paula on February 1 and that this payment was made. On February 20, XYZ entered into a two-year contract with Oliver to operate the bowling alley. If Paula tenders the $25,000 back to XYZ and repudiates the contract on March 30, which of the following is the most likely result in a common law jurisdiction?

   A. Paula will prevail because the contract constitutes an ultra vires transaction.

   B. Paula will prevail because she gave notice of repudiation and returned the down payment prior to the April 4 closing date.

   C. XYZ will prevail because it had made the prepayment and relied on consummation of the agreement to a substantial degree.

   D. XYZ will prevail, **unless** its shareholders had approved the transaction prior to Paula's repudiation.

37. Simone, the treasurer of Fruitco, Inc., was given authority by a properly passed resolution to purchase fruits and vegetables from local growers. After Simone performed this function for one year, another resolution was validly passed, limiting the dollar amount of the transactions into which she could enter. During the next year, Simone entered into agreements on behalf of Fruitco with several growers who had not sold

to Fruitco in the past. However, these transactions exceeded Simone's monetary limitation. Fruitco recently learned of these contracts and seeks to repudiate them. (You may assume the agreements are **not** ultra vires transactions.)

Based on the foregoing, which of the following statements is most likely correct?

A. Fruitco can rescind the transactions because they exceeded the express monetary limitation set forth in the applicable resolution.

B. Fruitco can rescind the transactions because the growers are deemed to be on constructive notice of all Fruitco resolutions.

C. Fruitco cannot rescind the transactions because Simone had apparent authority to enter into these agreements.

D. Fruitco cannot rescind the transactions because Simone had the inherent authority of her office to enter into these agreements.

38. Matt is the secretary of ABC Corporation, a corporation formed for the purpose of manufacturing and selling bedroom furniture. Matt enters into a contract with Elmer to purchase the land on which ABC's factory is to be built. Subsequently, Matt enters into a contract with Joanne to acquire the steel needed to produce the bed frames. When ABC's board learns of these transactions, it seeks to rescind the one with Joanne (but **not** the one with Elmer).

Based on the foregoing, which of the following statements is most likely correct?

A. ABC cannot rescind the transaction with Joanne because Matt had the inherent authority of office to enter into it.

B. ABC cannot rescind the transaction with Joanne because Matt had apparent (or ostensible) authority to enter into it, based on his agreement on behalf of ABC with Elmer.

C. ABC can rescind the transaction with Joanne because Matt lacked authority to enter into such an agreement.

D. ABC can rescind the transaction with Joanne **if** it also repudiates the agreement with Elmer.

39. Charles, the secretary of XYZ Corporation, signed a contract to lease commercial premises at which XYZ's products would be sold. (You may assume that the contract did **not** pertain to an ultra vires matter.) When the board was apprised of the lease at its next meeting, it neither ratified nor rejected the contract. It did, however, approve a resolution instructing XYZ's president to obtain at least three bids for remodeling

the premises. A short time later, however, the board determined that it would be unwise to market XYZ's products through retail premises and passed a resolution that expressly rejected the lease.

Based on the foregoing, which of the following statements is most likely to be correct?

A. The corporation can rescind the lease because Charles lacked authority to enter into the transaction.

B. The corporation can rescind the lease because it was expressly rejected by the board.

C. The corporation cannot rescind the lease because it was within Charles's apparent authority.

D. The corporation cannot rescind the lease because, although Charles lacked authority to enter into the transaction, the contract was implicitly ratified by the board.

40. Joan, the president of Bilko Corporation, entered into an agreement to merge Bilko into Apex Corporation. In return for conveying all of Bilko's assets to Apex, Bilko shareholders would receive Apex stock with a fair market value that was slightly higher than that of their Bilko shares. The boards of Apex and Bilko, at properly called meetings, approved the transaction.

Based on the foregoing, which of the following statements is most likely correct?

A. The transaction is invalid because it involves the sale of all of Bilko's assets.

B. The transaction is invalid because Joan is not a proper officer to sign the applicable documents for Bilko.

C. The transaction is valid because it was approved by the Apex and Bilko boards.

D. The transaction is valid because Joan had authority to enter into it, regardless of whether the board approved it.

41. The articles of incorporation of Buildco require that the corporation have five directors and that resolutions be passed by a "majority vote" of the directors at a properly called meeting. Buildco Corporation was formed to "acquire land for the purpose of subdividing it and constructing tract homes for sale to the public." For this purpose, the corporation validly acquired a large parcel of farmland.

However, when the permits necessary to develop the land were delayed as a result of lawsuits initiated by environmental groups, a board meeting was properly called to decide whether farming operations should be commenced on the land until the development permits could be obtained. Only three of the five directors attended this meeting, and two of them voted to undertake farming operations until the land could be subdivided. When the two nonattending directors were told of this resolution by the dissenting director, they indicated that, had they been at the meeting, they would have voted *against* the resolution.

Based on the foregoing, which of the following statements is most likely correct?

A. The resolution is invalid because it authorizes an ultra vires activity.

B. The resolution is invalid because less than a majority of the entire board voted for it.

C. The resolution is invalid because a majority of the entire board actually disapproved of it.

D. The resolution is valid because the activity authorized is reasonably necessary for the accomplishment of Buildco's express purposes.

42. The bylaws of Ajax Corporation state that, on the first Monday of each month (or the next business day thereafter, if that Monday is a legal holiday), the board of directors shall meet. Soon after Carson was elected to be a director on Ajax's five-member board, she missed a Monday meeting. At that gathering, the board approved, by a 3-to-1 vote, a management contract with Paul. Carson now contends that the resolution approving this contract was invalid because she failed to receive written notice of the meeting. (You may assume the agreement would otherwise be valid.)

Based on the foregoing, which of the following statements is most likely correct?

A. The resolution is invalid because Carson failed to receive written notice of the meeting.

B. The resolution is invalid *if* the board had failed to inform Carson that its meeting was held each month.

C. The resolution is valid because it would have passed even if Carson had received proper notice.

D. The resolution is valid because the meeting was properly held.

43. Oilco Corporation was interested in purchasing an extensive oil field from Nancy. (You may assume Oilco is empowered by its articles of

incorporation to enter into all legal transactions.) At a special meeting of the board, six of the nine directors were present. The purchase was approved by a vote of 5 to 1. The other three directors failed to receive the written notice required by the bylaws for a special meeting, nor did they execute written waivers of notice.

Sally, the secretary of Oilco, when requested by Nancy, showed her the resolution approving the transaction. Upon presentation of this resolution, Nancy executed the purchase and sale documents. They were executed on behalf of Oilco by Arthur, its president.

Based on the foregoing, which of the following statements is most likely correct?

A. Oilco can rescind the transaction because the meeting at which the resolution was approved was not properly noticed.

B. Oilco can rescind the transaction because a corporate president lacks actual or apparent authority to enter into a transaction of this magnitude.

C. Oilco cannot rescind the transaction because Nancy had a right to rely on the resolution presented to her by Sally.

D. Oilco cannot rescind the transaction because the resolution would have passed even if the three absent directors had attended the special meeting.

44. Ajax Corporation recently acquired Greenacre from Mary Nelson for $300,000. Greenacre consisted of land with a pen-manufacturing facility on it. (You may assume that this transaction was *not* ultra vires.) However, the board of directors of Ajax, after consideration at a properly noticed board meeting, voted to decline to acquire fire insurance for the building. This 4-to-3 decision was made because Ajax had not declared a dividend in over two years and a majority of the directors, fearing shareholder backlash against them, wanted to have funds available for this purpose. Subsequently, a fire occurred, causing damage to the premises in the amount of $100,000.

Based on the foregoing, which of the following statements is most likely correct?

A. The directors have no liability under the business judgment rule.

B. The directors who failed to approve the insurance are jointly and severally liable for the $100,000 loss, plus any consequential damages (e.g., lost business profits).

C. The directors who failed to approve the insurance are liable only for their proportionate share of the $100,000 loss, plus any consequential damages (e.g., lost business profits).

D. The directors who voted in favor of purchasing fire insurance are liable to the same extent as those voting against the insurance.

45. At a properly called meeting, the directors of Beta Corporation approved a resolution to purchase, for cash, many of the assets of Alpha, Inc., another corporation, including a leasehold Alpha possessed. This leasehold had almost three more years to run prior to its expiration. Because the lease payments required of Alpha were less than the present market value, acquisition of the lease was an important aspect of the transaction.

An officer of Alpha informed Beta's directors that there was an outstanding dispute in the amount of approximately $10,000, resulting from the landlord's claim that Alpha was responsible for certain improvements that had been made to the premises by the lessor. Alpha agreed that funds in this amount should be left in an escrow account, which Beta could access if the matter was not successfully resolved by Alpha.

Soon after the transaction was consummated, the lessor informed Beta that Alpha was in arrears in rental payments in the amount of $50,000 and that eviction proceedings would commence immediately if Beta (as assignee of the leasehold) did not pay the full amount of this delinquency.

Based on the foregoing, which of the following statements is most likely correct?

A. The directors who approved the transaction have no liability to the corporation because they relied on the statements of Alpha's officer.

B. The directors who approved the transaction have no liability to Beta under the business judgment rule.

C. The directors who approved the transaction are liable to Beta because they failed to obtain shareholder approval prior to entering into the agreement with Alpha.

D. The directors who approved the transaction are liable to Beta because they should have ascertained Beta's complete liability to the lessor.

46. The articles of incorporation and bylaws of Acme, Inc., provide for three directors and state that a director can be removed without cause

by majority vote of its shareholders. The bylaws also provide that directors shall serve for three-year terms. At the annual shareholders' meeting, a proposal was put forth to remove Mitchell, one of the directors, two years prior to expiration of his term, because of his anti-abortion stance. The resolution was approved by the shareholders, 600 to 400 (there are 1,000 shares of Acme stock issued and outstanding).

[handwritten: only needed 334 to be elected]

Based on the foregoing, which of the following statements is most likely correct?

A. Mitchell cannot be removed because the shareholders lack the authority to do so.

B. Mitchell cannot be removed because no gross abuse of his corporate position has been alleged.

C. Mitchell can be removed by the shareholders because the articles and bylaws of Acme permit such action to be undertaken.

D. Additional facts are necessary to determine whether Mitchell may be removed under these circumstances.

47. At the annual shareholders' meeting of Apex, Inc., the shareholders undertook the following actions:

[handwritten: SH elect D's, appointment is irrelavant]

(1) Elected Joan as a director in place of Paul, who had resigned during the previous year, even though the board had appointed Edward to fill this position only six weeks prior to the shareholders' meeting.

(2) Elected Adolpho president. *[handwritten: → action by BOD]*

[handwritten: Not enough disinterested SHs]

(3) Ratified a contract to acquire Blackacre, which is jointly owned by three of Apex's five directors.

(4) Elected Tina as a director in place of Allen, who had been properly removed for cause as a director during the prior year.

Based on the foregoing, which of the following statements is most likely correct?

A. All of the actions undertaken by the shareholders are valid.

B. Actions (1), (2), and (4) are valid, but not (3).

C. Actions (1), (3), and (4) are valid, but not (2).

D. Actions (1), (2), and (3) are valid, but not (4).

48. The three directors of XYZ Corporation are elected each year. The annual meeting at which the new board is to be elected is usually held on January 15. However, because this date was inconvenient for most of the seven shareholders, the annual shareholders' meeting was rescheduled for March 1. On January 11, the board entered into a two-

year employment agreement with Kent, whereby Kent was to make all corporate decisions with regard to the selection and termination of officers, the determination of their salaries, and all expenditures to be incurred by XYZ. The agreement with Kent provided that he could be dismissed for incompetence and failure to satisfy specifically described performance standards.

Based on the foregoing, which of the following statements is most likely correct?

A. The contract with Kent is invalid because it exceeds one year (the term of each directorship).

B. The contract with Kent is invalid because it encroaches upon the management decisions of the corporation.

C. The contract with Kent is invalid because the directors had no authority to bind the corporation after January 15, when a new board was to be elected by the shareholders.

D. The contract with Kent is valid.

Fundamental management decisions often cannot be delegated by the board

49. The directors of ABC Corporation learned that one of their employees had embezzled corporate funds in the amount of approximately $12,000. At the next board meeting, which was properly noticed and conducted, the board decided, by a vote of 5 to 4, to decline to seek recovery of the embezzled funds from the employee. This decision was premised on the directors' good-faith belief that (1) the corporation would be adversely affected by the publicity that litigation would cause, and (2) any judgment that might be obtained would be difficult to collect.

Shawn, a director and shareholder who believed that an action against the employee was warranted, wants to commence a derivative action against the directors who voted *against* commencing the lawsuit. However, an independent attorney, appointed by the entire board, advised against commencing a derivative action.

Based on the foregoing, which of the following statements is most likely correct?

A. A derivative action can be commenced because directors cannot condone criminal conduct.

B. A derivative action can be commenced *if* a majority of ABC shareholders vote to pursue it.

C. A derivative action cannot be commenced by Shawn because the board has considered the matter after receiving disinterested expert advice.

D. A derivative action cannot be commenced by Shawn because she was present and voted at the board meeting that declined to seek recovery from the employee.

50. Alice is a shareholder of ABC Corporation. She seeks to bring a derivative lawsuit in *federal* court (based on diversity jurisdiction) against two of the directors, Ted and Michael, claiming that they had usurped a corporate opportunity, resulting in lost income to ABC of $500,000. ABC has three directors.

Based on the foregoing, which of the following statements is most likely *incorrect*?

A. Alice cannot commence a personal action directly against Ted and Michael.

B. Alice is probably excused from making a demand on the directors.

C. Alice need not (1) make a demand on the directors or (2) show adequate reason for failing to make a demand (assuming she is not required to do so by applicable state law).

D. Alice must post a bond if required to do so under applicable state law.

51. Mike, a shareholder of ABC Corporation, alleges that certain directors engaged in the following actions:

(1) Deliberately sold off corporate assets at less than fair market value to induce Mike to sell his shares for a sum below their actual worth.

(2) Refused to permit him to vote at a recent shareholders' meeting, on the pretext that he had previously given another person a proxy for his shares.

(3) Issued additional shares without honoring Mike's preemptive rights.

(4) Negligently entered into various contracts that resulted in financial loss to ABC.

Which of the foregoing assertions would most likely be the subject of a derivative action?

A. (1), (2), and (3).

B. (1), (2), and (4).

C. (1) and (4).

D. (4) only.

52. Alex, a shareholder of XYZ Corporation, asserts that the directors have breached their duty of loyalty by entering into a certain contract with an entity in which they had a personal interest. The contract occurred one year prior to the time Alex inherited her XYZ shares from her deceased father. Alex also contends that, following her acquisition of the stock, the directors acted negligently by allowing XYZ to enter into particular transactions that resulted in significant financial loss to the corporation.

    Based on the foregoing, which of the following statements is most likely correct?

    A. Alex can bring a derivative suit *only for* the breach of loyalty.

    B. Alex can bring a derivative suit *only for* the negligence.

    C. Alex can bring a derivative suit for both breach of loyalty and negligence.

    D. Additional facts are needed to determine which of the three preceding answers is correct.

53. Moe, a shareholder of XYZ Corporation, commences a derivative action in federal court against three of the five directors, alleging that the three directors are liable to the corporation under SEC Rule 16(b). The alleged transactions occurred five weeks prior to the time that Moe purchased his shares in XYZ.

    Based on the foregoing, which of the following statements is most likely correct?

    A. The action is barred because Moe was not a shareholder when the alleged wrongs occurred.

    B. The action is barred, unless Moe makes a demand on the three directors to reimburse XYZ for the profits they made from the transactions in question.

    C. State law requiring a bond or other security is superseded in this instance.

    D. Any recovery by Moe will be distributed, on a pro rata basis, to XYZ's shareholders.

54. Chris, a shareholder of Boynton Corporation, alleges that the directors unanimously approved a dividend distribution that was contrary to the applicable state law (because the dividend was not made from

Boynton's retained earnings). If Chris commences a derivative action in federal court, based on diversity jurisdiction, asserting that an illegal distribution was made, which of the following statements is most likely correct?

A. Chris can dispense with the requirement, if any exists in this jurisdiction, of obtaining shareholder approval.

B. Chris must make demand upon the directors prior to commencing a derivative action against Boynton.

C. Any bond or security requirements are inapplicable because the action was commenced in federal court.

D. Chris is barred from commencing a derivative action because, as a shareholder, she accepted and benefited from the distribution.

55. Alpha Corporation has seven directors, four of whom are members of a single family (a father and three adult children). The corporation decides to purchase land owned by the father. At a properly noticed meeting, the father-director discloses his interest prior to the vote on the purchase. The purchase is then approved by a vote of 5 to 1 (the father-owner and his children voting in favor of the sale). At the annual shareholders' meeting held soon afterward, the purchase is ratified by a 42-to-18 vote of Alpha's disinterested stockholders.

Based on the foregoing, which of the following statements is most likely correct?

A. The transaction is invalid because it was not approved by a majority of the disinterested directors.

B. The transaction is invalid because shareholders cannot become involved in the management of a corporation by ratifying the board's action.

C. The transaction is valid because it was approved by a majority of the disinterested directors.

D. The transaction may be challenged in a derivative lawsuit by a disinterested shareholder who did *not* vote for the purchase, if the transaction is patently unfair to Alpha.

56. Charles is one of the five directors of Tilden Corporation. He is also a general partner of Unger Enterprises, a fact that is not known to the other four Tilden directors. Knowing that Tilden is considering the acquisition of another plant, Charles persuades Unger Enterprises to purchase a nearby plant suitable for Tilden's market needs. Unger buys the plant for $300,000. Charles then recommends to the Tilden board

that the plant be acquired by the corporation, but he does not reveal his interest in Unger.

One month after Unger buys the plant, the Tilden board, by a vote of 4 to 0, approves the purchase of the facility for $450,000. Charles does not attend the meeting at which the purchase is approved; he advises the board that he is too ill to attend. An agreement to purchase the facility is then entered into between Tilden and Unger. Prior to the closing of title of escrow, the other board members discover Charles's interest in Unger.

Based on the foregoing, which of the following statements is most likely correct?

A. Tilden cannot rescind the purchase because Charles did not vote on the matter.

B. Tilden cannot rescind the purchase if the board, in good faith, concludes that the transaction was fair to the corporation.

C. Tilden cannot rescind the purchase because it would be unfair to the other general partners of Unger.

D. Tilden may either rescind the transaction or recover $150,000 from Charles.

Questions 57-58 are based on the following facts:

Prior to becoming president of Drugco, Inc., Green entered into an employment agreement that, among other things, contained the following provision:

> Drugco, Inc., agrees to indemnify Green against all liabilities, costs, and expenses, _including_ attorneys' fees and any amounts paid in settlement of threatened or pending claims or lawsuits, incurred by Green _in connection with her duties as president of this corporation._

Two years later, while Green is president of Drugco, a chemist employed by the company advises Green that he has just discovered a cure for the common cold. Before anyone else knows about the discovery, Green purchases 10,000 shares of the company's stock at $5 per share, the closing price of Drugco shares on the New York Stock Exchange on the day the stock is purchased.

Green is sued in **state** court. The action seeks rescission of the stock purchase by Green.

57. If the complaint alleges a cause of action against Green under SEC Rule 10b-5, will a motion by Green to dismiss the action be granted?

A. Yes.

B. No, assuming it is alleged that no instrumentality of interstate commerce was used in Green's purchase.

C. No, assuming a state law claim was also made in the pleading.

D. Additional facts are necessary to determine whether Green's motion will be successful.

58. Assume that Green settles the action against her for $15,000, without any admission of liability, after expending $10,000 on legal fees and court costs.

Based on the foregoing, which of the following statements is most likely correct?

A. Drugco should indemnify Green for the entire $25,000.

B. Drugco should indemnify Green for only $10,000.

C. Drugco should indemnify Green for only $15,000.

D. Drugco should refuse to indemnify Green for any amount.

59. Hannah, a shareholder of Island Corporation, properly commenced a derivative action against Joe and Todd, directors, alleging that they failed to exercise adequate diligence in selecting an officer who subsequently embezzled a substantial sum of money from the corporation. The case proceeded to trial. Judgment was rendered, resulting in findings that (1) Joe was not liable, but (2) Todd was negligent and thereby liable to the corporation for its losses due to the embezzlement. (You may assume that there was no specific finding that Joe and Todd were "fairly and reasonably" entitled to reimbursement for their expenses.)

Based on the foregoing, which of the following statements is most likely correct?

A. Both Joe and Todd may validly be indemnified for their litigation expenses and attorneys' fees from Island.

B. Neither Joe nor Todd may validly be indemnified by Island for his litigation expenses and attorneys' fees.

C. Joe (but not Todd) may validly be indemnified by Island for his attorneys' fees and litigation expenses.

D. Todd may validly be indemnified by Island for his attorneys' fees and litigation expenses, but not for the amount of the judgment rendered against him.

60. Karl is the president of Acro Corporation. Jill, a vice president of Acro, commenced an action against Karl, personally, contending that, because of sexual harassment by Karl, it had become necessary for her to cease employment with the corporation. In his answer, Karl denied Jill's assertions and contended that she failed to perform her functions

in a competent manner, requiring criticism of her performance, which, in turn, brought about Jill's decision to leave Acro.

Subsequently, the action was settled for $10,000 (20 percent of the amount demanded in Jill's complaint), part of which was paid by Karl. The board approved a resolution stating that Karl had acted in good faith and for purposes that he reasonably believed to be in the best interests of the corporation. (You may assume that Karl is not a director and that he did not influence the board's determination with regard to his conduct.)

Based on the foregoing, which of the following statements is most likely correct?

A. Karl cannot be validly indemnified by Acro because he was named personally in Jill's action.

B. Karl may be validly indemnified by Acro for his attorneys' fees, litigation expenses, and the $10,000 settlement.

C. Karl cannot be validly indemnified by Acro because he was not successful "on the merits."

D. Karl may be validly indemnified by Acro for the sum of money paid to Jill in settlement of her action, but *not* for his attorneys' fees and litigation expenses.

61. The board of directors of Beta Corporation approved a resolution to make a $50,000 payment to the Ministry of Ashwan. (You may assume that Ashwan is a foreign country with which many U.S. corporations have previously had business dealings.) The board was advised by its agent in Ashwan that a payment of this type was a necessary prerequisite to consummation of all transactions with that government.

Subsequently, the U.S. Justice Department charged Beta Corporation, its directors, and the agent with violation of a federal criminal statute that prohibits bribing foreign officials. After being advised by counsel that a successful criminal prosecution was a "realistic possibility," Beta's board settled the proceeding by authorizing payment of a $150,000 fine.

Based on the foregoing, which of the following statements is most likely correct?

A. The board members cannot validly be indemnified for their attorneys' fees and litigation costs because they were charged with a criminal offense.

B. The board members cannot validly be indemnified for their attorneys' fees and litigation costs because they did not prevail on the merits.

C. The board members can validly be indemnified for their attorneys' fees and legal costs, provided a majority of the disinterested shareholders approves a resolution finding that the board acted in good faith and reasonably believed their actions were in Beta's best interests.

D. The board members can validly be indemnified for their attorneys' fees and legal costs, if a majority of disinterested shareholders determines that the board acted in good faith, reasonably believed their actions were in Beta's best interests, **and** had no reason to believe that their actions were unlawful.

62. The articles of incorporation of Tool Corporation authorized the issuance of 1,000 shares of common stock. All of the shares were purchased by Underhill (300 shares), Barnes (400 shares), and Whitson (300 shares). Subsequently, Tool properly amends its articles of incorporation so that the authorized number of shares is increased by 1,500 shares. The board undertakes this action, in part, so that it can acquire a unique patent from Smith in exchange for 500 of the newly authorized shares. The board believes this patent will revolutionize its industry. The rest of the shares are to be sold for cash. (You may assume that no state law or provision in the articles of incorporation or bylaws addresses the assertion of preemptive rights.)

Based on the foregoing, which of the following statements is most likely correct?

A. Underhill may assert preemptive rights for up to 300 of the newly authorized shares.

B. Underhill may assert preemptive rights for up to 450 of the newly issued shares.

C. Underhill may not assert preemptive rights in the newly issued shares because they had not been authorized at the time she acquired her original stock in Tool.

D. Underhill may not assert preemptive rights to any of the newly issued shares because some of this stock is being exchanged for property rights.

63. Ajax Corporation originally authorized the issuance of 1,000 shares of $100 par value common stock. It sold these shares at $100 per share. Arthur purchased 50 of these shares. Subsequently, Ajax repurchased 500 shares (none of which belonged to Arthur), which it held as treasury stock. Ajax now wishes to sell 1,000 common shares of $100 par value stock for $150 per share (the stock's present fair market value).

[handwritten note in left margin: Preemptive rights apply ~~only~~ to the original 1000 shares]

It has properly amended its articles of incorporation to authorize issuance of 500 more shares. (You may assume that no state law or provision in the articles of incorporation or bylaws addresses the assertion of preemptive rights.)

Based on the foregoing, which of the following statements is most likely correct?

A. Arthur may exercise preemptive rights to purchase 25 of the newly authorized shares at $150 per share.

B. Arthur may exercise preemptive rights to purchase 50 of the newly issued shares at $100 per share.

C. Arthur may exercise preemptive rights to purchase 50 of the newly issued shares at $150 per share.

D. Arthur may exercise preemptive rights to purchase 50 shares at $100 per share, and another 50 shares at $150 per share.

64. Vernon Corporation originally authorized and sold 1,000 shares of its common stock for $100 per share. Williams purchased 400 of these shares. After a management dispute arose between Williams and the other two stockholders who owned the balance of Vernon's outstanding shares, the articles of incorporation were properly amended to authorize issuance of another 1,000 shares. The other two shareholders each purchased 500 of these shares for $200 per share (the stock's fair market value), without offering Williams an opportunity to acquire any of the newly authorized stock.

There is **no** indication that the additional capital raised by the sale of the newly authorized stock was necessary for any of Vernon's business purposes. (You may assume that no state law or provision in the articles of incorporation or bylaws addresses the assertion of preemptive rights.)

[handwritten note in left margin: to enhance other SH power so may be able to rescind]

Based on the foregoing, which of the following statements is most likely correct?

A. Williams has no preemptive rights because the additional 1,000 shares had not been authorized when she originally purchased her stock.

B. Williams has preemptive rights, but her exclusive remedy is to purchase 40 percent of the newly authorized shares at $200 per share.

C. Williams has no preemptive rights because, at common law, such rights did not exist unless specifically provided for in the articles of incorporation.

D. Williams has preemptive rights and may be able to obtain a court order rescinding the issuance of the newly authorized shares.

65. Joan and Mervin are two stockholders of Delta Corporation. Mervin gave Joan a proxy to vote his shares at the upcoming annual shareholders' meeting. He did this because he planned to be on vacation when this meeting was scheduled to occur. However, Mervin had to cancel his vacation due to an illness in his immediate family, and he was present at the meeting. → *mere revocation is not enough to revoke proxy*

    Based on the foregoing, which of the following statements is most likely correct?

    A. Joan cannot vote Mervin's shares *if* Mervin attends the meeting.

    B. Joan cannot vote Mervin's shares because the purpose for which the proxy was given has ceased to be applicable.

    C. Joan can vote Mervin's shares, unless Mervin objects to this action by Joan.

    D. Joan can vote Mervin's shares, provided the articles of incorporation expressly authorize voting by proxy.

66. Mindy sold her shares of Zebco stock to Sally. Because the annual shareholders' meeting was to occur in two weeks and the record date for voting at that event had passed one week prior to the transaction, Mindy delivered a written proxy to Sally relating to the purchased shares. The proxy states that it is irrevocable. *sally has a coupled interest in voting since she now owns the shares*

    Based on the foregoing, which of the following statements is most likely correct?

    A. If Mindy attends the shareholders' meeting and expressly revokes her proxy, Sally cannot vote the shares.

    B. Sally cannot vote the shares because, despite the proxy, Mindy is the stockholder of record for that meeting.

    C. Sally can vote the shares, even if Mindy personally appears at the shareholders' meeting and insists upon voting the shares herself.

    D. Because there was an outright sale of shares to Sally, the corporation must allow Sally to vote her shares, regardless of whether she obtained a written proxy from Mindy.

67. Elmer is a shareholder of Fairway Corporation. (You may assume this corporation is subject to Section 14 of the Securities Exchange Act of 1934.) He owns approximately 2 percent of the corporation's outstanding common stock.

Elmer has learned that the management of Fairway intends to send out proxy solicitations to its shareholders for the purpose of obtaining their votes to reelect the present board of directors. Elmer makes a written demand on the board to include the following proposals in their solicitation materials: (1) that Jones be appointed chief financial officer (basically, the equivalent of treasurer) and (2) that a coffee room for employees be installed in Fairway's manufacturing facility.

Based on the foregoing, which of the following statements is most likely correct?

A. Management is *not* required to include either proposal in its solicitation materials.

B. Management must include the first proposal (pertaining to Jones), but not the second one (pertaining to the coffee room), in its solicitation materials.

C. Management must include both proposals in its solicitation materials if Elmer has owned his shares for at least one year.

D. Management must include the second proposal in its solicitation materials, but not the first one.

68. Emma is a shareholder of Belton Corporation. (You may assume this corporation is subject to Section 14 of the Securities Exchange Act of 1934.) She owns stock in the corporation that has a value of $6,000, and she has been a shareholder for 14 months.

Emma wants to submit an advisory proposal to the stockholders of Belton, urging the corporation to expand its operations into the nuclear energy field via the purchase of a defunct reactor in a nearby town. Belton was formed for the purpose of developing energy sources, but has not previously been involved in nuclear power. (You may assume that this proposal does *not* relate to Belton's ordinary business operations and that the directors intend to make a proxy solicitation.)

Based on the foregoing, which of the following statements is most likely correct?

A. Management must include Emma's proposal in its proxy solicitation materials, because of its significance, regardless of its length.

B. Management must include Emma's proposal in its proxy solicitation materials *if* it does not exceed 500 words.

C. Management must include Emma's statement in its proxy solicitation materials, but may charge Emma for the reasonable costs associated with mailing her proposal to Belton's shareholders.

D. Management is *not* required to include Emma's proposal in its solicitation materials, but must provide her with a mailing list of Belton's shareholders, or else independently mail her proposal to the shareholders at the corporation's expense.

69. Ralph is a director of Zeta Corporation. (You may assume this corporation is subject to Section 14 of the Securities Exchange Act of 1934.) The board of Zeta solicited proxies for their reelection. Although other members of the board had, from time to time, heard rumors of Ralph's criminal background, no conclusive proof of this background had ever been brought to their attention. However, a reasonably thorough investigation would have disclosed that, before his first election to the board, Ralph had been convicted of several crimes involving breach of trust.

The proxy solicitation failed to make mention of Ralph's prior contacts with the criminal justice system, and Ralph was elected. Following the election, Mary, a shareholder with *less* than 1 percent of Zeta's stock who did not want Ralph to sit on Zeta's board, commenced an action to rescind the proxy votes obtained by Ralph immediately before the election. (You may assume Mary gave her proxy to reelect the board and that Ralph would *not* have been elected but for the proxies obtained via the solicitation.)

Based on the foregoing, which of the following statements is most likely correct?

A. Mary should be successful and will probably be awarded her reasonable attorneys' fees and litigation expenses.

B. Mary's suit will not be successful because she lacks standing (i.e., she owned less than 1 percent of Zeta's stock).

C. Mary is not likely to be successful because she did not commence her action until *after* Ralph's election.

D. The omission of Ralph's past criminal background was probably not material because his convictions did not involve his conduct as a director of Zeta.

70. Jim and Phillip together own 65 percent of the outstanding stock of Acorn Corporation, but they are not directors or officers of the company. After meeting Cindy at a class reunion, Jim and Phillip signed an agreement with her, whereby it was agreed that she would serve for one year as secretary of Acorn. The previous secretary of Acorn had recently resigned.

When Jim and Phillip advised the three Acorn directors by telephone of the contract with Cindy, two of the directors signed a typewritten resolution that appointed Cindy the secretary of Acorn. The third director refused to sign the resolution, asserting that he wanted to do more research into Cindy's qualifications for this office.

Based on the foregoing, which of the following statements is most likely correct?

A. Cindy is the secretary, based on her written agreement with Jim and Phillip.

B. Cindy is the secretary, based on the resolution signed by a majority of the directors.

C. Cindy is *not* the secretary because she has not been properly appointed by the directors.

D. Cindy is *not* the secretary because shareholder appointment of officers must be unanimously ratified by the board to be valid.

71. Paula is a shareholder of Weldon Corporation. She is unhappy with management because, although the corporation was profitable last year, it lagged behind the growth of similar companies. Paula advises management that, during regular business hours, she intends to review the corporate books of account and all agreements entered into by Weldon throughout the most recent fiscal year for the purpose of determining why its profits have been relatively low.

Based on the foregoing, which of the following statements is most likely correct?

A. Paula may view the books of account, but not the contracts entered into by Weldon.

B. Paula may view the books of account and the contracts entered into by Weldon.

C. Paula may *not* view the items she seeks because the corporation has been profitable and no wrongdoing by management is evident.

D. Paula may *not* view the items she seeks because she has an absolute right only to inspect basic corporate documents, such as the articles of incorporation, bylaws, and resolutions.

72. John, a shareholder of Boolon Corporation, heard rumors that the corporation had entered into a number of "sweetheart deals" with firms owned by friends of the directors. As a consequence, John advises the board that, during regular business hours, he wants to review the corporate books of account and shareholder lists. The shareholder lists

are sought for the purpose of obtaining proxies to elect John as a director at the upcoming annual shareholders' meeting.

An applicable state statute provides that shareholders may inspect corporate **books of account** only after they have owned the company's stock for no less than 12 consecutive months. John has owned his shares for only seven months.

Based on the foregoing, which of the following statements is most likely correct?

A. John may inspect the shareholders list, but not the corporate books of account.

B. John may inspect the shareholders list and the corporate books of account.

C. John may **not** inspect either set of documents because an intent to unseat management in the absence of evidence of wrongdoing is an improper purpose for the solicitation of proxies.

D. John may **not** inspect either set of documents because the inspection of corporate documents is limited to books of account and John has not been a shareholder for the required period of time.

73. The directors of Bota Corporation unanimously passed a resolution that required compensation for the president (Josephine) of the corporation in the sum of about $2 million. James, a shareholder of Bota, immediately complained to the directors that Josephine's compensation was excessive. Nevertheless, the Bota directors unanimously approved an employment contract with Josephine that included compensation close to that described in the resolution. The disinterested shareholders of Bota ratified the contract, although by an extremely close vote (252 for approval of the resolution, 238 against ratification).

Assuming James can show that Josephine's compensation is clearly excessive in view of salaries received by presidents of similarly situated corporations, which of the following statements is most likely correct?

A. James's derivative suit will probably be allowed, but he will **not** be permitted to recover his attorneys' fees and court costs (even if successful).

B. James's derivative suit will probably be allowed because shareholders cannot ordinarily ratify corporate waste.

C. James's derivative suit will probably **not** be allowed because the shareholders have ratified the directors' action.

D. Under ordinary common law principles, James's derivative suit will probably **not** be allowed, **unless** he makes a formal demand on the directors to rescind the agreement.

74. Belton Corporation enters into an agreement to sell substantially all of its assets to Carlton Corporation. The consideration is 40 percent cash and an adequately secured promissory note for the balance. The transaction is properly approved by the directors of both corporations, as well as the necessary proportion of Belton's shareholders. However, the board of Carlton does not attempt to obtain approval of Carlton shareholders. Johnson, a shareholder of Carlton, contends that she is entitled to exercise appraisal rights with regard to her shares. (You may assume that the applicable jurisdiction empowers shareholders with appraisal rights.)

Based on the foregoing, which of the following statements is most likely correct?

A. Johnson is entitled to assert appraisal rights with regard to her shares in Carlton Corporation.

B. Johnson has no right to assert appraisal rights, but can probably obtain a court order enjoining the transaction (at least until the requisite proportion of Carlton shareholders authorizes the purchase).

C. The transaction is invalid and can, therefore, be enjoined because legislation in most states requires that a purchase of all (or substantially all) of a corporation's assets must be approved by the purchaser's shareholders.

D. Johnson is **not** entitled either to assert appraisal rights or to enjoin the transaction.

75. The directors of Ablon Corporation properly noticed a special meeting of the shareholders to approve the statutory merger of Ablon into Didon Corporation for stock of Didon. Amy, a shareholder of Ablon, wrote the boards of Ablon and Didon, advising both bodies that it was "unclear" to her whether or how the transaction would be beneficial to either corporation. Amy decided not to attend the shareholders' meeting pertaining to this transaction as a sign of her protest against the proposed merger.

At the meeting, the requisite proportion of Ablon's shareholders approved the transaction. The next day, Amy gave written notice to the board of Ablon that she intended to exercise her appraisal rights. (You may assume that the applicable jurisdiction empowers shareholders with typical appraisal rights.) Within six days after the shareholders' meeting, the boards of both Ablon and Didon properly approved the merger, as did the secretary of state.

Based on the foregoing, which of the following statements is most likely correct?

A. Amy may exercise her appraisal rights because she communicated her disapproval to the board in a prompt manner.

B. Amy may exercise her appraisal rights *if* she tenders her shares to Ablon within a reasonable period of time.

C. Amy may *not* exercise appraisal rights because she is a shareholder of the corporation whose assets are being sold.

D. Amy may *not* exercise appraisal rights because she failed to vote against the sale.

76. The board of directors of Gibble Corporation passes a resolution whereby its assets will be conveyed to Helton Corporation concurrently with Helton's transfer of shares of its stock to Gibble shareholders. Pursuant to the terms of this *statutory* merger, Gibble will dissolve after the transaction is authorized by the secretary of state. The board of Helton passes a resolution that approves the transfer of its stock in exchange for Gibble's assets. The requisite shareholder approvals are obtained, and the secretary of state approves the transaction.

Bo, one of *Helton's* shareholders, notified the board of his opposition to the transaction and voted against undertaking this transaction. (You may assume that the typical appraisal rights are recognized in the applicable jurisdiction.)

Based on the foregoing, which of the following statements is most likely correct?

A. It was not necessary for Helton's board or shareholders to approve this transaction.

B. Bo, being a shareholder of the acquiring corporation, is *not* entitled to assert appraisal rights in this situation.

C. Creditors of Gibble can pursue Helton for any obligations owed to them by Gibble, whether or not Helton expressly assumed Gibble's debts.

D. Assuming Bo is entitled to assert appraisal rights, he would receive the fair market value of Helton shares as of one month subsequent to completion of the merger.

77. Melton Corporation agrees to sell all of its assets to Nolton Corporation. The consideration for this sale will be Nolton stock. Because all of Nolton's originally authorized stock has been sold, its articles of incorporation must be amended to allow the issuance of additional shares. As part of the transaction, the Melton board has promised to distribute the Nolton stock it receives to its shareholders and then cause Melton's dissolution. (You may assume that the de facto merger doctrine is recognized in the applicable jurisdiction.)

Based on the foregoing, and assuming the transaction is consummated, which of the following statements is most likely correct?

A. Nolton will *not* be liable for Melton's debts.

B. The stockholders of Nolton need not approve the authorization of additional shares.

C. Shareholders of both corporations may assert appraisal rights.

D. Assuming there is nothing in the articles of incorporation or bylaws to the contrary, Nolton's shareholders may assert preemptive rights with respect to the newly authorized shares.

78. Megon Corporation, which is listed on the New York Stock Exchange, has entered into an agreement to merge into Polton Corporation, which is also listed on the New York Stock Exchange. This statutory merger is subject to approval by the shareholders of both corporations. The board of Megon solicits proxies from its shareholders and obtains a positive vote regarding the merger.

Elwood, a Megon shareholder, believes that the proxy solicitation contained fraudulent, materially misleading information. (You may assume this contention could be proved successfully at trial and that the applicable jurisdiction recognizes the typical appraisal rights.)

Based on the foregoing, which of the following statements is most likely correct?

A. Elwood can obtain rescission of the merger under SEC Rule 10b-5 *if* he bought (rather than inherited) his shares.

B. Elwood can exercise his appraisal rights *regardless* of whether he votes at the shareholders' meeting.

C. Assuming Elwood has an action under SEC Rule 10b-5 or Section 14 of the Securities Exchange Act, it can be commenced in either federal or state court.

D. Elwood could probably commence an action under state law to rescind the merger or exercise his appraisal rights.

79. Felton Corporation and Carlton Corporation agree to effectuate a **statutory** merger, pursuant to which Felton will exchange 10 percent of its outstanding shares (which previously were held as treasury stock) for Carlton's assets. The transaction is approved by the appropriate state authority. (You may assume that there would be **no** change in Felton's articles of incorporation as a consequence of this merger.)

Based on the foregoing, which of the following statements is most likely correct?

A. The shareholders of both Carlton and Felton must approve the transaction.

B. The shareholders of both Carlton and Felton have appraisal rights.

C. Felton would be liable for Carlton's outstanding obligations.

D. The transaction described above is sometimes referred to as a "short-form merger."

80. ABC Corporation authorized and has issued 1,000 shares of its common stock. The board of ABC has concluded that it would be beneficial to the corporation to raise additional capital by the issuance of a new class of preferred stock. These shares would be nonvoting, but would have priority with regard to the distribution of dividends. The ABC board passes a resolution approving the issuance of this new class of preferred stock.

Based on the foregoing, which of the following statements is most likely correct?

A. ABC's articles of incorporation probably require unanimous shareholder approval for the resolution to be effective.

B. Approval of an amendment to the articles of incorporation by the holders of ABC common stock is **not** required in this situation.

C. It is illegal to create a class of shares that have priority in the distribution of dividends, unless the issuance of these shares is authorized in the original articles of incorporation.

D. The holders of common stock must approve an amendment to the articles of incorporation before the preferred shares can be validly issued.

81. Ogden Corporation had a net profit of $30,000 last year. However, its books and records reveal a deficit to earned surplus of $21,000. Nevertheless, the board of directors of Ogden declares a dividend of $1 per share. There are 1,800 shares issued and outstanding. (You may assume this dividend would *not* cause Ogden to become insolvent and that there are no preferred shares that require priority in the payment of dividends.)

Based on the foregoing, which of the following statements is most likely correct?

A. The dividend is valid because it will be paid out of Ogden's net profits.

B. The dividend is invalid because dividend payments cannot be made while an earned surplus deficit exists.

C. The dividend is valid because it will not cause Ogden to become insolvent.

D. It is necessary to research applicable law to determine whether dividends may be paid under these circumstances.

82. Samuels, Tilden, and Underwood enter into a two-year voting trust that complies with all necessary requisites and under which Watson is appointed as their trustee to vote their shares with respect to certain specified matters, including the election of directors. Samuels and Tilden each own 20 percent of the corporation's shares, and Underwood owns 15 percent.

Watson decides to use the votes assigned to her under the trust to elect Martha as a director at the next shareholders' meeting. Watson believes Martha will do a good job as director of the corporation and that the interests of the beneficiaries will be served by her election. However, Samuels and Tilden do not like Martha and do not want her to be appointed. (You may assume that Martha is otherwise competent to handle this position.) Underwood is *not* opposed to Martha's election.

At the annual shareholders' meeting, Samuels and Tilden are present. They announce that they are repudiating the voting trust and attempt to vote their shares for a candidate other than Martha. Underwood makes no objection to Watson's voting his shares. (You may assume that the voting trust can be revoked by unanimous vote of the shareholder-beneficiaries.)

Based on the foregoing, which of the following statements is most likely correct?

A. Watson can vote the shares for Martha's election as a director because she believes her election would be beneficial to the members of the voting trust.

B. Watson can vote the shares for Martha because she is competent.

C. Watson *cannot* vote the shares for Martha because it would frustrate the purpose of the voting trust to ignore the wishes of two of the shareholder-beneficiaries.

D. Watson *cannot* vote the shares for Martha because her authority was revoked by Samuels and Tilden at the meeting and because of their express objection to voting Watson's shares for Martha's election.

83. Mary, Katey, and Mandy are shareholders of Guildco Corporation. Mary owns 32 percent of the corporation's shares, Katey 11 percent, and Mandy 18 percent. They enter into a pooling agreement, under which they each agree to vote their shares with regard to any matter as any two or more of them shall decide. The agreement is to be in effect for two years.

Prior to the next annual shareholders' meeting, Katey and Mandy decide to vote against a derivative action that another shareholder seeks to commence. Learning of their intention prior to the meeting, Mary declares that the pooling agreement is rescinded and advises Katey and Mandy that she (Mary) is not bound by their decision. (You may assume that the pooling agreement was *not* filed with Guildco for inspection and that there is nothing on the face of Mary's shares that makes reference to the pooling agreement.)

Based on the foregoing, which of the following statements is most likely correct?

A. Mary can vote her shares as she wishes because she holds a majority of the stock that is subject to the pooling agreement.

B. Mary can vote her shares as she wishes because the pooling agreement was not filed with the corporation.

C. Mary can vote her shares as she wishes because no reference to the pooling agreement appears on the face of Mary's shares.

D. Katey and Mandy can enforce the agreement by obtaining a decree of specific performance, if necessary.

84. Congolea Corporation is interested in acquiring control of Beldola Corporation. For cash, Congolea acquires an 82 percent interest in Beldola by purchasing the shares of Beldola's two largest stockholders, Bob and Beula Simpson. Congolea now is thinking about initiating a "short form" merger with Beldola.

Fred Farkel, a minority shareholder of Beldola, opposes this transaction. (You may assume that the purchase of Beldola shares was **unanimously** approved by Congolea's five-member board of directors. You may also assume that neither corporation is subject to federal securities laws.)

Based on the foregoing, which of the following statements is most likely correct?

A. Fred can invalidate Congolea's purchase because it was not approved by Congolea's shareholders.

B. Fred can invalidate Congolea's purchase because it was not approved by Beldola's board.

C. Fred cannot invalidate Congolea's purchase because it was **unanimously** approved by Congolea's board.

D. Fred will not be able to challenge Congolea's purchase.

85. Harrold owns a controlling interest (62 percent of the shares) in Ajax Corporation. Ajax is in the car wash business. Ianco Corporation is a competitor of Ajax, and it owns a car wash located a short distance from one operated by Ajax. Ajax shares have a fair market value of $30 per share. Ianco, after a properly approved resolution by its board of directors, offers to purchase Harrold's stock for $40 per share.

Frances, a minority shareholder of Ajax, objects to the control premium that Harrold will receive. Frances can show that, once the transaction is completed, Ianco is likely to (1) reduce the price of car washes at the Ajax facility to bring it in line with the price charged at Ianco's premises and (2) reduce advertising for the Ajax site so that more business will accrue to Ianco's facility. (You may assume that the applicable jurisdiction recognizes appraisal rights in both merger and de facto merger situations. You may also assume that this jurisdiction follows the holding and rationale of *Perlman v. Feldman*, 219 F.2d 173 (2d Cir. 1955).)

Based on the foregoing, which of the following statements is most likely correct?

A. Frances has **no** right to receive a pro rata portion of Harrold's premium because there is no proof that Ianco intends to loot Ajax.

B. Frances has **no** right to receive a pro rata portion of Harrold's premium because she has appraisal rights.

C. Frances can invalidate the sale because it has not been approved by Ajax's board.

    D. Frances *cannot* invalidate the transaction, but can probably obtain a pro rata portion of Harrold's premium.

86. Biltmore Corporation wishes to acquire a controlling interest in Park Place (PP) Corporation. To achieve this objective, Biltmore purchases all of the shares of PP owned by Joe Randolph. This purchase represents 58 percent of PP's outstanding shares. Randolph receives a $15 per share control premium for selling his interest to Biltmore.

    As part of the transaction whereby the purchase of Randolph's PP stock is to occur, Randolph promises to cause the seriatim resignation of PP's directors and the appointment of new directors, so that Biltmore would effectively have control of PP's board.

    There is *no* reason to believe that (1) Biltmore's management intends to loot or otherwise undertake acts detrimental to PP, or (2) Biltmore's control of PP will result in any lessened profitability to PP.

    Based on the foregoing, which of the following statements is most likely correct?

    A. The minority shareholders of PP are entitled to a pro rata distribution of Randolph's premium.

    B. The minority shareholders are *not* entitled to receive a pro rata distribution of Randolph's premium, but the directors' resignation and the appointment of new directors is invalid.

    C. The minority shareholders of PP are *not* entitled to receive a pro rata distribution of Randolph's premium, and the seriatim resignation and appointment of new directors is valid.

    D. The seriatim resignation of the present board and appointment of new directors is invalid.

87. Carla and John decide to incorporate for the purpose of operating an airport shuttle service. Each pays $10,000 to the corporation and receives 1,000 shares of stock. In addition, John lends $5,000 to the corporation, which is evidenced by a promissory note. The $5,000 is used for the down payment on a van the corporation purchases.

    One week after the shuttle service begins, the van is involved in an accident, resulting in two wrongful death judgments against the corporation. These judgments exceed the corporation's liability insurance (which was $250,000) by $500,000. The corporation then files a voluntary bankruptcy petition.

    Based on the foregoing, which of the following statements is most likely to be correct?

(1) Carla and John are personally liable for the corporation's debts.

(2) Assuming strict adherence to the necessary formalities for incorporation and the conduct of corporate business, Carla and John have no personal liability.

(3) John's promissory note may be subordinated by a court to the claims of the corporation's other creditors.

A. (2) only.

B. (1) only.

C. (1) and (3).

D. (2) and (3).

88. There are seven directors of XYZ Corporation. Prior to the annual directors' meeting, Art, Sam, and Kelly (three of the directors) agreed to vote in favor of retaining Oscar as president, even though XYZ had just experienced a very mediocre fiscal year. (The president of XYZ is chosen by a majority of the directors.) Later, but still prior to the meeting, Art became ill and gave Sam a proxy to cast his (Art's) vote for Oscar.

At the meeting, Carla (another director) argued so forcefully against retaining Oscar, that Kelly decided to vote for Elmer to be president. Elmer was the candidate proposed by Carla. Elmer received the four votes necessary to become president. The other three directors voted for Oscar (Sam cast his own vote and voted Art's proxy for Oscar).

Based on the foregoing, which of the following statements is most likely correct?

A. Art and Sam can successfully maintain an action against Kelly for breach of their agreement.

B. Sam was entitled to cast Art's vote for the election of Oscar.

C. The agreement among Art, Sam, and Kelly was unenforceable, and the proxy was invalid.

D. Oscar is entitled to have Elmer's election rescinded under third-party beneficiary principles.

89. The articles of incorporation of XYZ Corporation provide that shareholders must, prior to any sale or conveyance of their shares, offer them for sale to the other shareholders for their fair market value (as determined by an independent appraiser). The shares issued by XYZ contain the following legend, noted conspicuously: "These shares are subject to a restriction contained in the articles of incorporation."

Joe, one of XYZ's shareholders, agrees to sell his shares to Bertha for an amount per share that exceeds their fair market value. Bertha agrees to purchase these shares without actually seeing the certificates. On the date of the sale, Bertha tenders payment to Joe, and he hands Bertha a certificate reflecting his shares, along with a power of attorney. When Bertha delivers the share certificate to XYZ's secretary, he refuses to transfer the shares to her name.

Based on the foregoing, which of the following statements is most likely correct?

A. Bertha can obtain an order compelling XYZ to transfer the shares to her name because she was unaware of the restriction when she entered into the agreement with Joe.

B. Bertha can obtain an order compelling XYZ to transfer the shares to her name because the notation on the share certificate did not recite the specific restriction contained in the articles of incorporation.

C. Bertha can obtain an order compelling XYZ to transfer the shares to her name because, regardless of her constructive knowledge of the restriction, the provision pertaining to transferability is invalid.

D. Bertha cannot compel XYZ to transfer the shares to her name because the restriction is noted on the share certificate.

90. Under the laws of State X, which otherwise generally follows the Model Business Corporations Act (MBCA), any attorney who acts as incorporator in the articles of incorporation must attach an affidavit affirming his or her authority to practice law. John Avocat was one of three incorporators who signed the articles of incorporation for ABC Corporation. The other two were A and B. John knew that his license was **not** in force because he failed to file the annual certificate evidencing malpractice insurance coverage as required by the state bar authorities or to pay his required annual fees and, therefore, did not attach the affidavit.

The articles were filed with the secretary of state, and a certificate was issued by the state to that effect. Subsequently, shares were issued to A and B, directors were elected, and officers were appointed. Shortly thereafter, a customer of ABC sued A and B personally in contract, claiming that he had been delivered a defective product.

Based on the foregoing, which of the following statements is most likely correct?

A. ABC is a corporation.

B. The only way for A and B to avoid personal liability is to establish that ABC is a de facto corporation.

C. The only way for A and B to avoid personal liability is to assert the corporation-by-estoppel doctrine against the customer.

D. ABC would probably be viewed as a partnership for purposes of any recovery by the customer.

91. Gerber, Hall, and Jackson are the *original* shareholders, directors, and officers of Island Corporation. Included in the bylaws of Island is a provision requiring that, in the event any of the three ceases to be employed by Island, his or her shares must be offered to the other two at fair market value (as determined by an independent appraiser), before the stock may be sold to anyone else. The bylaws also provide that, once this value is determined, it may be paid by the purchasing shareholder(s) over a three-year period, with interest at 5 percent per annum.

    Hall decides to leave Island, but wants to sell her shares to Natalie. Hall honestly believes that Natalie would greatly complement the managerial skills of Gerber and Jackson.

    Based on the foregoing, which of the following statements is most likely correct?

    A. Hall does not have to offer her shares to the other shareholders because the bylaw provisions are unreasonable.

    B. Hall does not have to offer her shares to the other shareholders because she is acting in good faith.

    C. Hall must offer her shares to the other shareholders because the bylaw provisions are reasonable.

    D. Hall does not have to offer her shares to the other shareholders because the agreement restricting transferability is not shown on the stock certificates.

92. Anticipating the production needs of the new company, Alex, a promoter for Bennett Corporation, entered into a preincorporation contract with Castleton Industries for the purchase of grain. Alex did not expressly tell Castleton that he would not be personally liable on the contract if the Bennett board failed to approve it. After Bennett was validly incorporated, Castleton delivered the grain to Bennett's premises. Believing that the grain was delivered pursuant to a valid agreement between Castleton and the president of Bennett, Bennett's employees used 15 percent of the grain in the week following delivery.

When Bennett's board learned that the grain was delivered under the contract with Alex, it refused to approve the contract and returned the unused grain to Castleton.

Based on the foregoing, which of the following statements is most likely correct?

- **A.** Alex has no liability to Castleton because Bennett used some of the grain.
- **B.** Alex can recover in *quasi* contract from Castleton for the grain that was used by Bennett.
- **C.** Bennett is liable to Castleton for the grain it consumed.
- **D.** By using some of the grain, Bennett became liable to Castleton for the entire contract price.

93. Able, a promoter of Benson Corporation (a corporation that had not yet been formed), purchased a parcel of land in her own name for $50,000. Able purchased the parcel because she believed Benson would probably require the site for the retail toy store business it intended to operate. Able transferred the parcel to a partnership called Belbow Brothers, which she controlled. Subsequently, Benson was validly formed.

Shortly afterward, Belbow and Benson entered into an agreement, under which Benson was to purchase the realty for $75,000. The partnership was *not* represented by Able, but by another partner. One week after the land purchase agreement was made, the directors of Benson learned of Able's interest in Belbow Brothers.

Based on the foregoing, which of the following statements is most likely correct?

- **A.** Able has no liability to Benson because she was not a director or officer of the corporation when the purchase agreement occurred.
- **B.** Able is not liable to Benson because the transaction was negotiated by a partner of Belbow other than Able.
- **C.** Able is liable to Benson for her profit because she failed to disclose her interest in the property.
- **D.** Able is not liable to Benson for her profit *if* she can prove that the fair market value of the land was $75,000 at the time the directors of Benson entered into the transaction with Belbow Brothers.

94. Minefield Incorporated is a corporation that is empowered by its articles to acquire, operate, and sell the minerals extracted from the earth. The bylaws of Minefield provide that the treasurer has the authority

to receive funds, provide receipts therefore, and make deposits into the corporate bank account.

A little over one year ago, Jack, the treasurer of Minefield, entered into a one-year agreement with a boarding house for employees of Minefield. The contract authorized the purchase of food by the boarding house for the account of Minefield. The food was to be used to feed Minefield employees. When Minefield's board became aware of this agreement, it instructed Jack to make *no* contracts for the corporation in the future.

However, with the knowledge of the president of Minefield, Jack entered into a one-year renewal of the contract with the owner of the boarding house. The renewal was performed by both parties over several months. When the contract was brought to the attention of the board of directors by a disgruntled employee, the board passed a resolution repudiating the contract. The owner has sued Minefield to compel the corporation to honor the contract.

Based on the foregoing, which of the following statements is most likely correct?

A. The agreement is enforceable because it was within Jack's implied authority.

B. The agreement is enforceable because it was within Jack's apparent authority.

C. The agreement is enforceable because it was ratified by the board of directors of Minefield.

D. The agreement is unenforceable under the ultra vires doctrine.

95. Joanne was a C.P.A. with Wilkes & Wilkes. Belmont Incorporated was a client of the accounting firm. One day, while Joanne was at Belmont's premises performing work on behalf of Wilkes & Wilkes, she reviewed a company file disclosing an offer by Ajax Corporation to acquire all of the outstanding shares of Belmont. Without disclosing this nonpublic information to anyone, Joanne purchased 1,000 shares of Belmont stock. After the purchase, Joanne owned 3 percent of Belmont's outstanding stock. About two months later, Ajax publicly offered to acquire all of Belmont's outstanding shares, resulting in a $2 per share increase in Belmont stock.

Based on the foregoing, which of the following statements is most likely correct?

A. Joanne has no liability because she was not a corporate insider.

B. Joanne has no liability because she made no material misrepresentations with respect to her acquisition of Belmont stock.

C. Joanne is liable under SEC Rule 10b-5 because she failed to disclose the information to the seller of her stock.

D. Joanne is liable to the sellers of the shares under the special-facts doctrine.

96. X, a vice president of ABC Corporation, overheard the president advise the secretary in the company corridors that the corporation had just been awarded a valuable government contract. This fact would definitely make ABC stock more valuable. X immediately purchased 300 shares of ABC stock from Y. After news of the government contract became public two weeks later, ABC stock increased in value by $5 per share. ABC Corporation sued X to recover the profit he made as a consequence of his purchase of ABC shares from Y.

Based on the foregoing, which of the following statements is most likely correct?

A. The corporation should be successful under SEC Rule 10b-5 *if* an instrumentality of interstate commerce was used in the X-Y transaction.

B. The corporation should be successful under SEC Rule 10b-5 *only if* ABC shares are sold on a national stock exchange.

C. The corporation should be successful in its action against X under SEC Rule 10b-5, regardless of whether an instrumentality of interstate commerce was used or ABC stock is sold on a national stock exchange.

D. The corporation might be successful in its action against X under the special-facts doctrine.

97. Barnes is the president of Acme Corporation. On June 1, Acme purchased 1,000 shares of Caswell Incorporated common stock. Caswell stock is *not* traded on a national stock exchange. At the September 1 shareholders' meeting following Acme's acquisition of Caswell stock, Barnes was elected to Caswell's board of directors. Unknown to Acme or Barnes, Caswell had just patented an important medical device.

On November 11, Barnes acquired knowledge of this patent as a consequence of being a director of Caswell. On November 15, news of the patent became public, and Caswell stock increased by $5 per share. On November 22, Acme sold its Caswell stock, making a profit of $5 per share. (You may assume that Caswell has assets in excess of $11 million and 512 holders of Class A common stock. You may also assume that Caswell is engaged in interstate commerce.)

Based on the foregoing, which of the following statements is most likely correct?

A. Acme has no liability to Caswell because it is neither an officer, director, or 10 percent shareholder of Caswell stock.

B. Acme has no liability to Caswell because the corporation is *not* traded on a national stock exchange.

C. Acme is liable to Caswell for the profit it made from the sale of its Caswell shares.

D. Acme is liable to Caswell for the profit it made from the sale of Caswell shares *if* it became at least a 10 percent shareholder as a consequence of its purchase of Caswell stock.

98. Abby and Brandon entered into an agreement with Carlson, the president of Davis Corporation, under which Abby and Brandon each agreed to purchase 50 shares of Davis stock at $30 per share. The par value of Davis stock as set forth in the articles of incorporation is $25 per share. The subscription agreement was executed by Carlson on behalf of Davis Corporation pursuant to a board resolution authorizing him to enter into the agreement. Abby and Brandon agreed to complete the purchase "within three months." Two months after the agreement, Abby and Brandon sent the board of Davis a letter repudiating their obligations under the subscription agreement.

Davis Corporation is authorized to issue 10,000 shares of common stock. It had issued 8,000 prior to the date of the subscription agreement with Abby and Brandon.

Based on the foregoing, which of the following statements is most likely correct?

A. Because there are no other subscribers, Abby and Brandon can revoke the subscription agreement at any time until the shares are actually issued.

B. Abby and Brandon may repudiate the subscription agreement because it requires them to pay an amount in excess of the par value of the shares as set forth in the articles of incorporation of Davis.

C. Abby and Brandon must purchase the shares because their agreement with Davis is enforceable.

D. The subscription agreement is enforceable against Abby and Brandon only *if* they owned Davis stock at the time the subscription agreement was made.

99. Victor is the vice president of Quickie Finance, Inc., a company that makes cash quickly available to strapped borrowers – but at the price of a very high interest rate. He finds himself in desperate need of a very large amount of cash. He explains his situation to the board, making full disclosure of his financial situation. The members of the board are quite sympathetic and agree that Quickie Finance will loan Victor the money he needs, even though the amount of the loan is larger than usual for Quickie Finance. Because the members of the board believe that Victor is a good credit risk, notwithstanding his current troubles, they agree to a slightly lower interest rate than is usually charged.

Based on the foregoing, which of the following statements is most likely to be correct?

A. The board has acted properly because Quickie Finance, Inc. is in the business of making loans to people in Victor's situation.

B. The members of the board are in breach of their duty of care.

C. Victor is in breach of his duty of loyalty.

D. Whether or not the board has acted properly depends on whether Quickie Finance, Inc. has registered under the Securities Exchange Act of 1934.

100. Audrey, Benjie, and Caitlin form Zedcorp. Its articles of incorporation provide that it is to have three classes of shares: Class A, Class B, and Class C. One hundred shares of Class A are issued to Audrey, one hundred shares of Class B are issued to Benjie, and one hundred shares of Class C are issued to Caitlin. Each class of stock is entitled to elect one member of the three-member board of directors but otherwise is identical. Each of the shareholders votes his or her shares to elect him- or herself. There is nothing in Zedcorp's articles of incorporation with respect to the method of their amendment.

Based on the foregoing, which of the following is most likely correct?

A. Zedcorp's articles of incorporation cannot be amended; therefore, the right of each shareholder to elect a director is fully protected.

B. Zedcorp's articles of incorporation can be amended by the recommendation of the board and the vote of less than all of the shareholders; nonetheless, the right of each of the shareholders to elect a director is fully protected.

C. Zedcorp's articles of incorporation can be amended upon the recommendation of the board of directors and the approval of a majority of the shareholders; therefore, the right of each shareholder to elect a director is not fully protected.

D. The vote of all of the shareholders would be required to amend Zedcorp's articles of incorporation with respect to the election of directors; therefore, the right of each shareholder to elect a director is fully protected.

101. Alphacorp was formed in a state the statutes of which permit a corporation's articles of incorporation to control on the matter of cumulative voting. There is nothing in the state's constitution that would contradict this. Alphacorp's articles of incorporation do provide that its shareholders will have the right to cumulate their votes for Alphacorp's three directors. Xerxes, Yves, and Zelda are Alphacorp's only shareholders, each owning 40 of the corporation's 120 outstanding shares of common stock. There is nothing in Alphacorp's articles of incorporation with respect to the method of their amendment or with respect to the existence of preemptive rights.

Based on the foregoing, which of the following statements is most likely correct?

A. Zelda can elect herself director, even if opposed by Xerxes and Yves; her ability to do so is fully protected because the articles of incorporation cannot be amended without her consent.

B. Zelda can elect herself director, even if opposed by Xerxes and Yves; her ability to do so is not fully protected, however, because the articles of incorporation can be amended by a majority vote of the shareholders.

C. Zelda can elect herself director, even if opposed by Xerxes and Yves; her ability to do so is fully protected because, if additional shares are issued by the corporation, she would have the preemptive right to acquire a proportional share of them.

D. Zelda cannot elect herself director without the cooperation of either Xerxes or Yves.

Questions 102- 105 are based on the following facts:

Darius is a very wealthy television celebrity who has invested in and serves on the board of We-Build, Inc., a publicly held corporation that manufactures modular homes. Darius also serves on the board of Bankorp, Ltd., one of the many banks that We-Build regularly taps for credit. Darius has no business background and finds business matters quite boring; he long ago ceased attending the meetings of either board (although a series of creative excuses thus far has kept him from being dropped from the boards). He thus is absent on the day that We-Build's board unanimously votes to approve the borrowing of a very substantial amount of money from Bankorp. The loan is to bear a floating interest rate with no cap. Although very significant to We-Build, the amount of the loan is below the limit set by Bankorp's board (at a meeting Darius did not attend) as requiring its specific approval; Bankorp's loan officers simply batch it with other, similar floating-rate loans and regularly report to the board on the status of the entire loan class, along with the other classes of loan in Bankorp's portfolio. As it turns out, economic conditions quickly push floating interest rates sky-high; the debt service on the loan from Bankorp turns out to be the straw that breaks the camel's back for the financially struggling We-Build. It goes into default on the Bankorp loan. As is often the case, the default also is a breach of covenants in agreements with other lenders. It is clear that none of the lenders will get back more than pennies on the dollars they loaned We-Build. We-Build's shares will have no value whatsoever.

102. Paloma is a long-time holder of We-Build shares and is very unhappy about what has happened. She is looking for someone with a lot of money to sue on behalf of We-Build, and Darius has attracted her attention.

Based on the foregoing, which of the following statements is most like to be correct?

A. Darius has violated the duty of care that he owes to We-Build, Inc.; he appears to lack the requisite skill to serve and thus probably will be liable for damages.

B. Darius has violated the duty of care that he owes to We-Build, Inc.; he missed the meeting at which the floating interest rate loan from Bankorp was approved, thus failing to act with the requisite diligence. He thus probably will be liable for damages.

C. Darius has violated the duty of care that he owes to We-Build, Inc., because the floating interest rate loan from Bankorp was so imprudent; Darius thus probably will be liable for damages.

D. Darius may have violated the duty of care that he owes to We-Build, Inc., but he is unlikely to be liable for damages.

103. Paloma is aware of additional theories she would like to explore with respect to Darius's possible liability.

Based on the foregoing, which of the following statements is most likely to be correct?

A. Darius's service on the board on Bankorp constituted a conflict of interest; he therefore has violated the duty of loyalty that he owes to We-Build, Inc.

B. The floating rate interest loan made by Bankorp constitutes self-dealing by Darius; he therefore has violated the duty of loyalty that he owes to We-Build, Inc.

C. Darius's total failure to pay attention to We-Build's affairs exhibits a lack of good faith; he therefore has violated the duty of loyalty that he owes to We-Build, Inc.

D. There does not seem to be any serious argument that Darius has violated the duty of loyalty that he owes to We-Build, Inc.

104. Peyton is a long-time holder of Bankorp, Ltd. shares. When the loan to We-Build tanked, so did a lot of other Bankorp loans. As a result, Bankorp has had to write off a number of loans and its own share price has suffered. Peyton is looking for someone to sue on behalf of Bankorp and Darius has attracted his attention.

Based on the foregoing, which of the following statements is most likely to be correct?

A. Darius did nothing to disclose to Bankorp, Ltd. the imprudence of making the floating interest rate loan to We-Build. This was a violation of Darius's duty of care.

B. Darius did nothing to disclose to Bankorp, Ltd. the imprudence of making the floating interest rate loan to We-Build. This was a violation of Darius's duty of loyalty.

C. Darius did not attend Bankorp, Ltd. board meetings, including the one at which the board set the limit for loans requiring specific board approval. This was a violation of Darius's duty of care.

D. It does not appear that Darius has violated any fiduciary duty owed to Bankorp, Ltd.

105. Darius is not the only person on Peyton's radar screen.

Based on the foregoing, which of the following statements is most likely to be correct?

A. If it can be shown that the board of Bankorp, Ltd. made no effort to monitor the practices of its loan officers the members of the board may be liable in damages for a breach of the duty of loyalty.

B. If it can be shown that the board of Bankorp, Ltd. made no effort to monitor the practices of its loan officers the members of the board may be liable in damages for a breach of the duty of care.

C. If it can be shown that no other bank would have loaned money to We-Build at the time of the floating interest rate loan from Bankorp,Ltd., a breach of the duty of care by Bankorps' board would be adequately proven.

D. If it can be shown that the limit placed on loans not requiring the specific approval of Bankorp, Ltd.'s board was significantly higher than the limit imposed by any other bank of similar size, a breach of the duty of loyalty by Bankorp's board would be adequately proven.

Questions 106-120 call on your knowledge about the distinctions between different types of business entities and the factors that might be relevant in choosing among them.

106. The availability of limited liability for investors is usually a very important factor in choosing among business entities.

Based on the foregoing, which of the following statements is most likely to be correct?

A. Limited liability is most likely to be important to the sole shareholder of a closely held corporation who also is the corporation's sole employee.

B. Limited liability is most likely to be important to the passive investors in a business enterprise.

C. Limited liability is of equal importance to all participants in any business enterprise.

D. The best way to attain limited liability is to form a corporation.

107. Limited liability partnerships are a fairly recent innovation. They bear similarities to other business entities, but also have differences.

Based on the foregoing, which of the following statements is most likely to be correct?

A. Insofar as management structure and profit-sharing are concerned, limited liability partnerships are more like general partnerships than they are like limited partnerships.

B. Insofar as management structure and profit-sharing are concerned, limited liability partnerships are more like limited partnerships than they are like general partnerships.

C. Insofar as management structure and profit-sharing are concerned, limited liability partnerships are unlike either general partnerships or limited partnerships.

D. Insofar as management structure and profit-sharing are concerned, limited liability partnerships are more like limited liability limited partnerships than they are like any other type of entity.

108. Limited liability companies are a fairly recent innovation. They bear similarities to other business entities, but also have differences.

Based on the foregoing, which of the following statements is most likely to be correct?

A. Insofar as management structure and profit-sharing are concerned, limited liability companies may be functionally identical to general partnerships.

B. Insofar as management structure is concerned, the default rule for limited liability companies is to centralized management.

C. Insofar as management structure and profit-sharing are concerned, limited liability companies are unlike either general partnerships or limited liability partnerships.

D. Insofar as management structure and profit-sharing are concerned, limited liability companies are more like limited liability limited partnerships than they are like any other type of entity.

109. ABC, LLC and XYZ, LLP are planning to form and invest in a brand new business. They have certain goals, including pass-through taxation, that they would like to achieve.

Based on the foregoing, which of the following statements is most likely to be correct?

A. The most logical choice of entity would be a joint venture.

B. The new business could not be formed as a limited liability partnership.

C. The new business could not be formed as a limited liability company.

D. The new business could not qualify for the Subchapter S election.

110. There are many doctrines applicable to corporations and their shareholders that may or may not be equally applicable to other forms of entity.

Based on the foregoing, which of the following statements is most likely to be correct?

A. Preemptive rights should apply to partners in a limited liability partnership just as they do to corporate shareholders.

B. Equitable subordination should apply to members in a limited liability company just as it does to corporate shareholders.

C. Piercing the veil of limited liability is a concern with respect to limited liability companies but not with respect to limited liability partnerships.

D. Fiduciary duties owed to one another by the members of a limited liability partnership are identical to the fiduciary duties owed to one another by the shareholders of a closely-held corporation.

111. Jackson, a famous and wealthy singer, has patented a portable recording device, which he wants to manufacture and sell. If Jackson chooses to do business under a sole proprietorship structure, which of the following statements best describes Jackson's personal liability to contract creditors of the proprietorship?

A. Jackson has no personal liability to the proprietorship's contract creditors.

B. Jackson is personally liable to the proprietorship's contract creditors.

C. Jackson is liable to the proprietorship's contract creditors *if* he had personally guaranteed their obligations.

D. None of the above.

112. Cook formed a general partnership with two other individuals. Which of the following best describes Cook's liability to the partnership's creditors?

A. Cook is personally liable to the partnership's creditors, but only up to the amount of her contribution to the partnership.

B. Cook is personally liable to tort, but *not* contract, creditors of the partnership.

C. Cook is personally liable to contract, but *not* tort, creditors of the partnership.

D. None of the above.

113. Jack and Jill are partners in a general partnership to conduct a mobile, on-call manicure business for a period of one year. They agree that Jill will contribute the initial required capital to get the business started, as well as perform all management functions. They further agree that Jack will perform the manicures and will drive his own car to clients' offices and homes. They will split the profits equally. Pursuant to their agreement, Jill contributes $10,000. Of that amount, $5,000 is used to buy state-of-the-art equipment and supplies. The remainder is spent on advertising. During the second week of business, all of the new equipment and supplies are stolen from Jack's car. In frustration,

Jack and Jill agree to terminate the partnership. While in operation, it earned $1,000.

Based on the foregoing, which of the following statements is most likely correct?

A. Jack and Jill are each entitled to receive a $500 distribution; the partners' financial obligations to one another then will be at an end.

B. Jack is owed the value of his services, and Jill is owed the return of her capital.

C. Jill is owed the return of her capital, and Jack is owed nothing for his services.

D. Jill is entitled to receive $1,000 from the partnership as a return of her capital; the partners' financial obligations to one another will then be at an end.

114. Pansy and Begonia are partners in Flower Girls, a general partnership that carries on a landscaping business. Pansy advises Greens, a local nursery, that she is not happy with the quality of Greens' plants and will not be responsible for any more bedding stock ordered from Greens by Begonia. Pansy mentions this to Begonia, who protests that Greens is the only nursery that regularly stocks her favorite flowers. Pansy is unmoved. Begonia goes right ahead and orders $5,000 worth of bedding stock from Greens on behalf of Flower Girls. The stock is delivered to Flower Girls' place of business, where it is, as customary, left outside. Unfortunately, it is totally destroyed by an unforeseeable cold snap.

Based on the foregoing, which of the following statements is most likely correct?

A. Only Begonia is liable to Greens.

B. Only Flower Girls is liable to Greens.

C. Flower Girls is liable to Greens; in the event Flower Girls does not pay Greens, only Begonia will be liable.

D. Flower Girls is liable to Greens; in the event Flower Girls does not pay Greens, both Pansy and Begonia will be liable.

115. Several years ago, X formed X Corp., of which X is the sole shareholder, officer, and director. The only function of X Corp. is to act as the sole general partner of X Limited Partnership, a venture capital

firm formed, as the name indicates, as a limited partnership. X and nine other individuals own limited partnership interests in X Limited Partnership. X Corp. was formed and is run with all appropriate formalities; in addition, there is no question that its capitalization is adequate for its purpose.

Based on the foregoing, which of the following statements is most likely correct?

A. There is no apparent risk to X of personal liability for the debts of X Limited Partnership.

B. X is at risk for personal liability for the torts of X Limited Partnership.

C. X is at risk for personal liability for the contracts of X Limited Partnership.

D. X is at risk for personal liability for all of the debts of X Limited Partnership.

116. Peter and Paul have, for many years, been the only two partners in Peter Paul Pastries (Pastries), a general partnership formed for the purpose of manufacturing and selling various baked goods. Although Pastries has never been sued, Peter and Paul are aware that a number of their competitors have been and have wound up making hefty payments to people who have chipped teeth on nutshells, been shocked by the discovery of foreign items in their pies, and so forth. They realize that they have been lucky thus far and it is just a matter of time before Pastries discovers itself liable for an amount greatly in excess of its assets (which have been kept relatively low, in light of the partners' practice of withdrawing all profits on an annual basis). Peter and Paul have maintained a significant amount of liability insurance for Pastries, but are becoming concerned about its expense. They have heard about limited liability partnerships and are intrigued. They contact Lois, a lawyer, and tell her that they would like to convert Pastries from a general partnership to a limited liability partnership so they will no longer need to carry liability insurance.

Based on the foregoing, which of the following is the best advice for Lois to give them, assuming that their jurisdiction is one that provides for limited liability partnerships?

A. Forming a limited liability partnership will provide them with the protection that they are looking for, but at a price of significant changes in Pastries' management structure.

B. Forming a limited liability partnership will provide them with the protection that they are looking for and should have no effect on Pastries' management structure.

C. Forming a limited liability partnership almost certainly is advisable, but failure to carry liability insurance could subject Peter and Paul to personal liability for at least some of Pastries' debts.

D. Forming a limited liability partnership always is inferior to forming a limited liability company.

117. Alice (A) and Becca (B) both are hair stylists. Each has owned her own business for several years, and each has built up a stable of devoted clients. They also are similar in that they are the mothers of small children and work only part time. When A and B meet at a party, they start to discuss how expensive it is to maintain a beauty salon. A suggests that they consider sharing A's current salon space pursuant to an arrangement in which A will work on Mondays, Wednesdays, and Fridays, and B will work on Tuesdays, Thursdays, and Saturdays. The two women will share all the expenses equally, but each will keep the money paid by her own clients. The salon is, and will continue to be, called "Hair." B agrees to the plan. She knows, though, that she is going to have to borrow money to see her through the transition. She contacts her wealthy sister, Susan (S), and asks for a loan. S says she is happy to lend B whatever she wants, but she doesn't want B to worry about having to make interest payments if she isn't making money. They agree that the only interest S will receive is 2 percent of B's annual profits and that B can pay back the principal whenever she sees fit.

Based on the foregoing, which of the following statements is most likely correct?

A. A and B will be partners.

B. B and S will be partners.

C. There is not enough information available to know whether A and B will be partners.

D. There is not enough information available to know whether B and S will be partners.

118. Angus and Babs are equal partners in a general partnership (Ogee) formed to carry on an oil and gas drilling business. Their business plan calls for the acquisition and exploitation of drilling rights throughout the State of Y. One day, Angus receives a call from Oscar. Oscar has

options on the drilling rights on substantial oil and gas properties in State Z. Oscar comments admiringly on the job that Ogee has done in the State of Y and asks if Angus and Babs would like to "partner up" with him and expand their work to State Z. Angus and Babs have not been getting along, so Angus says, "I'd be happy to, but I won't work with Babs again." Oscar is satisfied with this response; he and Angus form a State Z general partnership (Geo) for purposes of exercising and exploiting Oscar's options. Oscar assigns the options to Geo, and Angus contributes a substantial amount of cash to permit their exercise. (You may assume that there is no statute that purports to define the fiduciary duties of general partners.)

Based on the foregoing, which of the following is most likely correct?

A. Babs will be entitled to 50 percent of any profit earned by Angus from Geo; she will not, however, be liable for any of Geo's obligations.

B. Babs will be entitled to 50 percent of any profit earned by Angus from Geo; she will not, however, be liable for any of Geo's obligations, unless the money contributed to Geo by Angus came out of Ogee's partnership funds.

C. Babs will be entitled to 50 percent of any profit earned by Angus from Geo and will be liable as a partner for Geo's obligations.

D. Babs will not be entitled to any profit earned by Angus from Geo and will not be liable for any of Geo's obligations.

119. Gladys (G) and Harold (H) agree to carry on a catering business. G will invest $100,000, and H will carry on the day-to-day business. H bargains for and receives G's agreement that H will receive a salary of $3,000 per month. G and H further agree that the profits remaining after the payment of expenses, including H's salary, will be split 60 percent/40 percent, with G receiving the larger share. G seeks the advice of Amanda, an attorney, as to the choice of business entity. G tells Amanda that H is a great cook, well organized, and generally a fine worker, but is not very strong in business judgment. Thus, G is anxious to have a veto power over any contracts entered into by H.

Based on the foregoing, which of the following would be correct advice, assuming that the entity will be formed under the laws of a jurisdiction that does not permit the formation of limited liability partnerships and specifies that every limited liability company (LLC) must have at least two members?

A. Formation of a general partnership is advisable because, in that form, management power is shared equally; thus, H would be unable to subject G to contractual liability without G's consent.

B. G should carry on business as a sole proprietorship and hire H as an employee; thus, H would be unable to subject G to contractual liability without G's consent.

C. If G and H form a two-member LLC, the formation documents may specify that H has no authority to enter into contracts without G's consent; thus, G could not be held personally liable for any of H's acts, and any contracts made by H would not be binding on the LLC.

D. If G and H form a two-member LLC, the formation documents may specify that H has no authority to enter into contracts without G's consent; thus, G could not be held personally liable for any of H's acts, although contracts made by H might, under some circumstances, be binding on the LLC.

120. A provision in the state constitution of State Q directs that licenses to distribute liquor can be issued to sole proprietorships and general partnerships, but cannot be issued to corporations. This provision was adopted shortly after the repeal of federal prohibition and has not since been amended. State Q has, in the last 20 years, adopted statutory provisions permitting the formation of both limited liability companies and limited liability partnerships. Ethel and Fred are in the process of setting up a business to engage in the distribution of liquor.

Based on the foregoing, which of the following statements is most likely correct?

A. Ethel and Fred probably can conduct their liquor distribution business as a limited liability partnership.

B. Ethel and Fred probably can conduct their liquor distribution business as a limited liability company.

C. Ethel and Fred probably cannot conduct their liquor distribution business as either a limited liability company or a limited liability partnership.

D. Ethel and Fred probably can conduct their liquor distribution business as either a limited liability partnership or a limited liability company.

Multiple-Choice
Answers

1. **A** In a (dwindling) number of states, where shares are *not* issued for money paid, labor done, or property actually transferred to the corporation, the transaction is voidable by the corporation. Because the majority view in these jurisdictions is that an unsecured promissory note does not constitute "money paid," the transaction is voidable (not void) by ABC. Thus, the corporation can rescind its sale of the shares. In some jurisdictions, ABC alternatively could require Bill to make the payments due under the note. Choice **B** is incorrect because judgment creditors of ABC would not be permitted to enforce the note unless ABC was in bankruptcy (which it is not). Choice **C** is incorrect because ABC's shareholders cannot enforce the note. Rescission or demand for payment must be made by ABC through its officers and directors. In fact, in many jurisdictions, the corporation cannot obtain a *monetary judgment* for stock issued for inadequate value. It must either rescind or affirm the transaction. Finally, choice **D** is wrong because choice **A** is a correct answer.

2. **D** If stock is issued in good faith and with the reasonable belief that the stated par value is equal to the value of the property received in exchange, the shares are *not* watered. Although there may be some evidence that the property received was not exactly equal in value to the shares, this fact alone is insufficient to characterize the shares as being watered. The evidence of the expert as to the worth of the property goes to its *present* value. It is entirely possible that the property had a higher value one year ago, when it was received in exchange for the shares. Choices **A**, **B**, and **C** are incorrect because the shares, having been issued in good faith with the reasonable belief that their par value was equal to the value of the property, are *not* watered. We do not have to consider whether creditors and/or stockholders would have standing to recover from Jackie because the stock is not watered.

3. **A** The watered amount of shares can ordinarily be recovered by judgment creditors of the corporation. Under the trust fund theory, all judgment creditors of a corporation can usually recover the watered amount of shares measured at the time of issue. Under the misrepresentation theory, only persons who extended credit to ABC after the transaction with Jackie could recover the $2,000 difference. The fact that Jackie no longer owns the stock is irrelevant. Choices **B** and **C** are incorrect because the shareholders cannot personally recover the watered amount. Their remedy would be to commence a derivative action on behalf of ABC to rescind the transaction to the extent

the stock was watered. Choice **C** is incorrect also because the share-holders could only recover $2,000, not $5,000. Finally, choice **D** is incorrect because judgment creditors of ABC can recover the watered amount from Jackie.

4. **A** Under the common law, a subscriber can repudiate his or her obligation under a subscription agreement at any time prior to formation *and acceptance by* the corporation. Although X Corporation was formed, no resolution was passed affirming the subscription agreement prior to A's repudiation. Choice **B** is incorrect because the corporation must be formed *and* must accept the subscription agreement for it to be binding on the subscriber. Choice **C** is incorrect because B's failure to join A in revoking the subscription agreement is irrelevant (unless, of course, the subscription agreement specifically provided that B's promise was contingent on performance by A). Finally, choice **D** is incorrect because, once the corporation was formed, the board of X was the proper party for A to notify of her revocation, not the promoter.

5. **C** Once a subscription agreement is accepted by the corporation, the subscribers are ordinarily liable to pay for the shares they have promised to purchase. Although there is a minority view that a subscriber is relieved of liability if the corporation has become insolvent prior to delivery of the shares (i.e., there has been a material failure of consideration by reason of the corporation's insolvency), the majority view still holds the subscriber liable. Choice **A** is incorrect because A became liable under the subscription agreement when the contract was affirmed by the corporation. Choice **B** is incorrect because, in most jurisdictions, a subscriber remains liable even though the corporation becomes insolvent prior to delivery of the stock. Finally, choice **D** is incorrect because the subscriber is liable to judgment creditors of an insolvent corporation. The trustee-in-bankruptcy enforces the rights of all creditors of the corporation.

6. **A** When a promoter signs a contract on behalf of a corporation "to be formed," he or she is usually personally liable under that agreement. In the absence of proof of a contrary understanding, it is ordinarily assumed that the obligee expects the promoter to be bound by the contract because the corporation (1) may never be formed or (2) may fail to ratify the agreement. Thus, in the absence of a specific disclaimer to the contrary, Zeek is personally liable to Paula. Choice **B** is incorrect because, under the circumstances, Zeek is liable to Paula. Choice **C** is incorrect because Amco would be liable to Paula *only* if it

affirmed the agreement. Finally, choice **D** is wrong because choice **A** is a correct answer.

7. **C** Ordinarily, a promoter is **not** relieved of liability under a preincorporation contract simply by reason of ratification of that agreement by the corporation. Although Amco approved the agreement, Zeek is **not** automatically relieved of personal liability. The subsequent ratification by Amco is likely to be viewed as merely an implied assignment by the original obligor (Zeek) to Amco. Choice **A** is incorrect because, by approving the contract, Amco became liable under the agreement along with Zeek. Choice **B** is incorrect because Zeek is still liable under the contract. Finally, choice **D** is wrong because choice **C** is a correct answer.

8. **B** When a corporation knowingly accepts the benefits of a contract, it may have implicitly approved the agreement. In the alternative, the corporation may be liable under *quantum meruit* principles for the value of the benefit bestowed upon it. Because Alice worked at the corporation for five months, Exco would appear to have implicitly ratified the entire agreement. In the alternative, Alice should at least be able to recover the reasonable value of the benefit of her services under *quantum meruit* principles. Choice **A** is incorrect because John specifically exculpated himself from personal liability (i.e., " . . . but not for himself personally"). Choice **C** is incorrect because, although John is not liable, Exco may be liable for the entire agreement (if it implicitly ratified the contract) or at least for the reasonable value of the services Alice bestowed on it over five months. Finally, choice **D** is wrong because choice **B** is a correct answer.

9. **C** A de jure argument cannot be made successfully until the articles of incorporation have been filed. Thus, choice **A** is incorrect. Under the common law, a de facto corporation exists where there has been (1) a good-faith attempt to comply with the statutory filing requisites and (2) some significant use of the corporate form (e.g., directors elected, officers appointed, stock issued, business conducted). Because there has been virtually no use of the corporate form (the facts fail to indicate that any directors have been elected, officers appointed, or stock issued), a de facto corporation argument would probably be unsuccessful. While there was a reference to the corporate form in the transaction A had with Billie, A alluded only to the future formation of Exco. Moreover, the de facto corporation doctrine is deemed to be abolished by statute in some jurisdictions. Thus, choice **B** is incorrect. Finally, choice **D** is incorrect because the corporation-by-estoppel

doctrine is applicable only when a plaintiff believes, or has reason to believe, that he or she has transacted business with a corporation. Chuck had no such belief prior to the accident with B. Therefore, choice **C** must be correct.

10. C Under the corporation-by-estoppel doctrine, if a person reasonably believes he or she is dealing with a corporation, a corporate structure is deemed to exist *for purposes of that transaction.* Because Billie presumably believed she was dealing with a corporate entity (A signed the agreement, "A, future president of Exco Corporation"), the corporation-by-estoppel doctrine would arguably apply. Although A's use of the word "future" makes the corporation-by-estoppel argument more problematic, this contention nevertheless represented his best means of avoiding personal liability. Because the articles of incorporation were never approved by the secretary of state, a de jure corporation does not exist. Thus, choice **A** is incorrect. Under the common law, a de facto corporation exists when there has been (1) a good-faith attempt to comply with the statutory filing requisites and (2) some significant use of the corporate form (e.g., directors elected, officers appointed, stock issued, business conducted). As stated above in Question 9, a de facto corporation argument would probably be unsuccessful. Thus, choice **B** is incorrect. Finally, choice **D** is incorrect because (1) A will be entirely relieved of personal liability if the corporation-by-estoppel doctrine is applicable, and (2) there is no factual basis to assert that he is personally liable for one-third of Billie's claim.

11. B Although there are cases to the contrary, the traditional common law view is that, prior to the time a corporation is properly formed, the entity created by the proposed incorporators exists as a partnership. Each partner is ordinarily jointly and severally liable for the obligations of a partnership. Neither a de jure nor a de facto corporation existed at the time of the accident. Thus, A, B, and C were acting as a partnership. As such, A is jointly and severally liable for Chuck's damages. In some jurisdictions, only those partners who have assumed a management role are personally liable. However, even under that view, A would be jointly and severally liable to Chuck, because he entered into a contract on behalf of Exco. The corporation-by-estoppel doctrine is *not* applicable because Chuck could not be aware that a corporation might be involved. While A is liable for the full amount of Chuck's injuries, as a partner, he can seek reimbursement from B and C for their proportionate (i.e., one-third each) shares of liability. Choice **A** is incorrect because A is liable to Chuck as B's partner, even though B was the driver of the vehicle involved in the accident. Finally, choices **C** and **D** are incorrect because each partner is jointly and severally liable to the tort victim for the full amount of his injuries.

12. **C** Under SEC Rule 10b-5, a corporate insider who fails to disclose nonpublic, material facts in connection with a purchase or sale of securities is liable to the seller or purchaser, as the case may be. An insider is generally a person who is advised of material, nonpublic information as a consequence of (1) his or her position with the corporation or (2) being retained by the corporation to perform a confidential function. X may or may not be an insider. He merely overheard a conversation between the geologist and the president of ABC; he was not advised of the facts by anyone. As an agent of the company, he nonetheless owes a duty of confidentiality and quite arguably misappropriated the information in violation of this duty, thus violating SEC Rule 10b-5. Because the duty of confidentiality was owed to ABC, not to the persons from whom he purchased the shares, however, he probably is **not** liable to the sellers of ABC stock under SEC Rule 10b-5. Therefore, choice **C** is correct, and choice **B** is incorrect. Choice **A**, which relies on SEC Rule 16(b) liability, is incorrect because the facts indicate that X was a mailperson (not an officer or director) who was not already a 10 percent shareholder at both the purchase and the sale of the stock. Choice **D** is incorrect because choice **C** is correct.

13. **A** A director, officer, or 10 percent shareholder of a corporation that (1) is traded on a national exchange or (2) has a net worth of at least $10 million and at least 500 shareholders is strictly liable **to that corporation** for any profits derived from (1) a sale and purchase or (2) a purchase and sale of the corporation's securities within any period of less than six months. X, as an officer of ABC, is liable to the corporation for profits she derived from the purchase and sale of its stock, even though X may have lacked scienter. SEC Rule 16(b) is a **strict liability** measure. Choice **B** is incorrect because (1) X lacked scienter (i.e., she did **not** act on nonpublic information known to her as a consequence of her corporate position), and (2) the facts **do not** indicate that ABC was directly involved in these transactions. Choice **C** is incorrect because X lacked scienter. Finally, choice **D** is incorrect because, there being no misuse of insider information, X has no liability to ABC under the special-facts doctrine.

14. D Under the special-facts doctrine, when, as a consequence of one's corporate position, one obtains material, nonpublic information about the stock, there is a fiduciary duty to disclose those facts **to existing shareholders** in connection with a sale or purchase of the corporation's shares. In some jurisdictions, the corporation can assert an action under this theory **if** the aggrieved buyer or seller fails to do so; *Diamond v. Oreamuno*, 248 N.E.2d 910 (N.Y. 1969). Assuming (1) Bob does **not** assert an action against X and (2) this jurisdiction permits a corporation to seek recovery if the aggrieved buyer or seller fails to commence an action, X may be liable to ABC for the profit obtained in her transaction with Bob. Choice **A** is incorrect because, although X is the vice president, the facts fail to indicate that she has sold the stock she purchased from Bob. Choice **B** is incorrect because, under SEC Rule 10b-5, only the aggrieved buyer or seller may commence an action. Finally, choice **C** is incorrect because no instrumentality of interstate commerce was used during the transaction between X and Bob. Thus, this is the rare case in which a jurisdictional requirement for application of SEC Rule 10b-5 is absent.

15. C A director, officer, or 10 percent shareholder of a corporation that (1) is traded on a national exchange or (2) has a net worth of at least $10 million and at least 500 shareholders is strictly liable to that corporation for any profits derived from (1) a sale and purchase or (2) a purchase and sale of the securities of that corporation within any period of less than six months. Under SEC Rule 16(b), all transactions within any six-month period are analyzed for purposes of determining whether a profit was made. Because Ossie was a director when he sold 100 shares for $50 per share and purchased 100 shares only one month later for $10 per share, for purposes of SEC Rule 16(b), he has achieved a profit of $40 per share. Thus, he would be liable to ABC for $4,000. Choice **A** is incorrect because Ossie, as a director of ABC, has liability under SEC Rule 16(b), even though he actually lost money in his overall transactions involving ABC stock. Choice **B** is incorrect because the correct calculations are those involving the sale of ABC stock for $50 per share and the subsequent repurchase of those shares for $10 per share. No liability would result to Ossie from the relationship between the transaction occurring on January 4 and the sale of the stock three months later for $50 per share. On these two transactions, Ossie derived no profit for SEC Rule 16(b) purposes. Finally, choice **D** is incorrect because, for SEC Rule 16(b) purposes, Ossie's profit is $4,000. The first and last purchases are *not* compared. Liability under SEC Rule 16(b) must be based on (1) purchase and sale or (2) sale and purchase.

16. **C** For purposes of liability under SEC Rule 16(b), one need be a director or officer only at the time of *either* the purchase or the sale of the securities. Because Ossie was a director at the time of the sale of the shares he had acquired within the six-month period, Ossie is liable to ABC under SEC Rule 16(b) for $3,000. Choice **A** is incorrect because, as discussed above, Ossie is liable to ABC under SEC Rule 16(b). Choice **B** is incorrect because the facts fail to provide any basis for concluding that Ossie used any nonpublic, material information during these transactions, even assuming that an instrumentality of interstate commerce was used. Finally, choice **D** is incorrect because the facts fail to state any basis for liability to the original seller of the shares.

17. **D** Under SEC Rule 10b-5, an aggrieved buyer or seller may recover the damages he or she has incurred in a transaction, provided the defendant intentionally (or at least recklessly) acted to deceive, manipulate, or defraud. Neither Smith & Smith nor ABC had any actual knowledge that negative data had been omitted, and there is no indication that they acted recklessly. Because scienter is lacking, neither party is liable to Joan under SEC Rule 10b-5. In fact, because ABC retained an established and prominent accounting firm, the negligence of the firm cannot be attributed to it. Choices **A**, **B**, and **C** are incorrect because they each assert that either Smith & Smith or ABC is liable to Joan under either SEC Rule 10b-5 or the special-facts doctrine, which usually only applies to purchases or sales made to or from existing shareholders. (It should be noted that Joan may have an action against Smith & Smith under common law negligence principles.)

18. **D** Under SEC Rule 10b-5, it is unlawful for any person to use any fraudulent or manipulative means *in connection with the sale or purchase* of securities by means of an instrumentality of interstate commerce. Because Amy kept her stock, she could not sue Paul under any of the doctrines described in choices **A**, **B**, or **C**. Choice **A** is incorrect because SEC Rule 10b-5 is applicable only where the aggrieved party has purchased or sold stock. Choice **B** is incorrect because SEC Rule 16(b) constitutes a basis for recovery *by the corporation* whose stock was traded by an officer, director, or 10 percent shareholder within a six-month period. Finally, choice **C** is incorrect because (1) there

is no indication that Paul is an insider, and (2) he did not purchase or sell ABC stock. The special-facts doctrine usually applies only to purchases or sales of stock between an existing shareholder and an insider who possesses material, nonpublic information.

19. A A director, officer, or 10 percent shareholder of a corporation that (1) is traded on a national exchange or (2) has a net worth of at least $10 million and at least 500 shareholders is strictly liable **to that corporation** for any profits derived from (1) a sale and purchase or (2) a purchase and sale of that corporation's securities within any period of less than six months. Because Arlo is a director, she would be liable to ABC if she had purchased her shares within six months and made a profit from their sale. Choice **B** is incorrect because, as an insider, Arlo would have an obligation to disclose negative financial information about ABC. Choice **C** is incorrect because Arlo would be liable under SEC Rule 10b-5 regardless of the price she paid for her shares. Her liability typically would be determined by the buyer's losses. Finally, choice **D** is incorrect because, as discussed above, Arlo would have liability under SEC Rule 16(b) **if** she had purchased the stock for less than $20 per share within the preceding six months.

20. D One is an insider for purposes of SEC Rule 10b-5 when one learns of material, nonpublic information as a consequence of (1) one's position with the corporation or (2) being retained by the corporation to perform a confidential function. In addition, one may have a duty of disclosure by reason of having established a relationship of trust with the plaintiff; *UTE Citizens of Utah v. United States*, 406 U.S. 128 (1972). Under these circumstances, Gale probably has no liability. Choice **A** is incorrect because there is no indication that SEC Rule 16(b) is applicable. Choice **B** is incorrect because Gale did not learn of the material, nonpublic information as a consequence of a position with the corporation. Thus, she is not an "insider" for purposes of SEC Rule 10b-5. In addition, Gale probably has no liability as a tippee. A tippee is liable only if the tipper would have been culpable. An insider is liable for "tipping" material, nonpublic information to someone who purchases or sells without disclosing the "tipped" facts **if** disclosure was made by the tipper to (1) acquire some type of personal gain or advantage or (2) bestow a gift upon the tippee. Because Arlo made only an absentminded comment, there is no evidence that she sought to acquire any type of personal gain from her statement or to benefit Gale. Finally, choice **C** is incorrect because Gale was **not** an officer, director, or key employee.

21. **B** For purposes of liability under SEC Rule 16(b), one must be at least a 10 percent shareholder at ***both*** the time of (1) the purchase and sale or (2) the sale and purchase. Choice **A** is incorrect because Mark was not at least a 10 percent shareholder when he bought the shares that he sold one month later—that is, he was not at least a 10 percent shareholder ***both*** prior to, and at the time of, the purchase and sale of his ABC stock. Choice **B** is correct because, even though Mark is ***not*** a tippee (for the same reasons Gale is not a tippee in Answer 20 above), he owes a duty of confidentiality to his employer and quite arguably misappropriated the information he learned from Arlo. Trading on misappropriated information gives rise to liability under SEC Rule 10b-5. Finally, choice **C** is incorrect because Mark did not learn of ABC's financial downturn by reason of his position with the corporation.

22. **D** M is liable to Zeta Corp. because she was a 10 percent stockholder prior to her first purchase and her last sale. The amount recoverable under SEC Rule 16(b) is computed in a manner that maximizes the profits recoverable (e.g., the lowest purchase and highest sale prices within the six-month period are matched, then the second lowest purchase and sale prices are matched). M is liable to Zeta Corporation for $800. This amount is computed as follows: Because the greatest disparity is between the 200 shares of stock purchased at $6 per share and the stock sold at $8 per share, this calculation is done first (200 shares times $2 per share equals $400). Next, the remaining 400 shares sold by M on May 5 are matched against those purchased at $7 per share, resulting in another $400 difference. Choice **A** is incorrect because M, as a holder of more than 10 percent of Zeta's common stock prior to the times of purchase and sale, is liable to that corporation under SEC Rule 16(b). Finally, choices **B** and **C** are incorrect because they fail to state the proper recovery by Zeta under SEC Rule 16(b).

23. **D** Majority or controlling shareholders of a corporation have a fiduciary duty to refrain from exercising their position in a manner that takes undue advantage of, or oppresses, minority shareholders. In addition, directors owe a duty of good faith to their corporation. This obligation requires directors to place the interests of shareholders before their personal interests. Because the minority shareholders did not purchase or sell any of their Aardvark stock, they ***cannot*** obtain recovery under SEC Rule 10b-5. Choices **A** through **C** are potentially successful causes of action. In engineering a negative

vote with respect to the sale to Ant Corporation, Martin arguably took undue advantage of the other shareholders, so that he could subsequently sell his shares to Zoo for a premium. Although a majority shareholder may ordinarily obtain a premium for selling a controlling interest, when a director rejects a bona fide offer made to all the shareholders in order to obtain greater personal profit, he may have violated the obligation of good faith. The individual shareholders may also have personal actions against Martin, because his rejection of Ant's offer arguably resulted in direct financial loss to them (measured by the difference between $35 and the present $30 per share value of Aardvark stock). Thus, choice **B** is a correct statement. Choices **A** and **C** are correct statements because a director must act in good faith with regard to his or her corporation and all shareholders. Martin should have disclosed his negotiations with Zoo and refrained from voting or influencing other directors with regard to this matter. Also, if Zoo's operation of Aardvark might result in Aardvark shares becoming less valuable, Aardvark has been harmed.

24. **C** A corporation's net worth is equal to its total assets minus its aggregate liabilities. Because Fox's assets are $500,000 and its liabilities are $300,000, its net worth after the second year is $200,000.

25. **B** The book value of outstanding shares is ordinarily determined by dividing the stated capital and any surplus by the total number of outstanding shares. The stated capital ($150,000) and retained earnings surplus ($50,000) are divided by the 1,000 outstanding shares of stock. This results in a book value of $200 per share.

26. **B** Under straight voting, each shareholder may vote his or her total number of shares for each candidate for a directorship. Under cumulative voting, a person's shares are multiplied by the number of directors being elected, but these shares can be cast only once. Because Jones would possess one-third (rather than one-fourth) of the corporation's outstanding shares as a consequence of this transaction, Jones's personal voting rights are *not* adversely affected. This would be the case whether the corporation had cumulative or straight voting, regardless of the number of directors chosen at the annual shareholders' meeting. Thus, choice **B** is the correct answer.

27. **D** In a "retained earnings" jurisdiction, dividends may only be paid out of earned surplus (also known as "retained earnings"). The balance sheet reveals that, after year 1, Fox Corp. had negative retained

earnings (a deficit of $10,000). As a consequence, *no* dividends may be paid to any of the shareholders. Thus, choices **A-C** are incorrect.

28. **C** The fair market value of shares takes into consideration the appreciation and depreciation of the corporation's assets, as well as the future prospects of the business activity involved. Although the Nevada real estate is reflected in Fox's balance sheet as being equal to $400,000, this is merely the price Fox Corp. *originally* paid for this asset. Its fair market value (i.e., the price at which a willing buyer and a willing seller, each being under no pressure to buy or sell, would conclude the transaction for this land) may have appreciated or depreciated significantly due to market conditions. Thus, it is impossible to determine whether the sale of the Nevada real estate for $175,000 after year 1 increased or decreased the fair market value of Fox Corp. shares. Thus, choice **C** is the correct answer. Choices **A** and **B** are incorrect because there is not enough information provided to give a definite answer either way. Choice **D** is incorrect because the effect of cumulative or straight voting was reflected in the fair market value of Jones's shares independently of the sale of the Nevada real estate.

29. **B** Under straight voting, each shareholder may vote his or her total number of shares for each candidate for a directorship. Under cumulative voting, each stockholder's shares are multiplied by the total number of directors, but may be voted only once. Jones's rights are not adversely affected regardless of whether Fox Corp. has straight or cumulative voting. Jones's rights are also *not* impacted in a positive manner, either. With each shareholder holding 250 shares, Jones can elect *no* directors under a straight voting scheme. Even if each shareholder held 275 shares, Jones could still not elect any directors under a straight voting approach. Under cumulative voting, Jones could elect only one director regardless of whether she has 250 or 275 shares. The other three choices are wrong because they are all premised on an adverse effect on Jones's voting rights.

30. **A** In nimble dividend states, a corporation may issue dividends from the current year's profits (or, in some states, the current and prior year's profits, taken as a whole), even though an overall deficit (i.e., negative retained earnings) remains after the dividends are paid. After its first year of operation, Fox Corp. has *no* net profits. In fact, it has a deficit (i.e., negative retained earnings) of $10,000. Some jurisdictions permit dividends as long as the corporation's total

assets exceed its total liabilities, but these are not known as nimble dividends. Because choice **A** is correct, choices **B-D** are incorrect.

31. **D** The board of directors may repurchase outstanding shares of the corporation's stock, if (1) a legitimate corporate purpose is served by this action, and (2) the repurchase will not cause the corporation to become insolvent or impair its ability to operate. Because Fox Corp. has a net worth of $200,000, the purchase of Jr. Fox's stock will **not** cause the corporation to become insolvent. In addition, the facts stipulate that none of the transactions would impair Fox Corp.'s ability to operate. However, because other factors must be considered, it **cannot** be stated unequivocally that Fox Corp. could repurchase Jr. Fox's shares for $100,000, so choice **A** is incorrect. More facts are needed to resolve this inquiry, such as (1) whether this is an excessive price for Jr. Fox's shares (we know the aggregate book value of Jr. Fox's shares is $50,000, but we do not know the stock's fair market value) and (2) what corporate purpose will be achieved by purchasing Jr. Fox's shares (the mere fact that Jr. Fox would like to sell his stock is no reason for Fox Corp. to incur a $100,000 obligation). Choice **B** is incorrect because the fact that the purchase price exceeds $50,000 is not, per se, a reason to conclude that the purchase is improper. Finally, choice **C** is incorrect because Fox Corp. would **not** become insolvent as a result of this transaction. (Note that, although nondividend distributions to shareholders, including repurchases, often are subject to the same restrictions as payment of dividends, a rule to this effect is not indicated by the question. This is yet another reason to select choice **D**.)

32. **A** Profits earned by the corporation since its inception are retained earnings or earned surplus. Dividends can always be paid from this sum (assuming the payments will not cause the corporation to become insolvent or impair its ability to operate). Remember that the introductory paragraph preceding this series of questions (preceding Question 24) stated that none of the transactions would impair Fox Corp.'s ability to operate. Because Fox Corp. has retained earnings or earned surplus of $50,000, it can issue dividends in the amount of $10,000 to each shareholder. Actually, it could issue dividends in an amount up to $12,500 to each shareholder, if it chose to do so. Choices **B**, **C**, and **D** are all incorrect because the dividend payments described in those answers would exceed Fox Corp.'s retained earnings of $50,000.

33. B Under the *Deep Rock* doctrine, when a corporation has become insolvent, its obligations to a shareholder may be subordinated to the claims of other creditors, if it would be inequitable (e.g., the shareholder-creditor was, in some manner, responsible for the corporation's inability to satisfy its debts) for the shareholder-creditor to participate equally with the corporation's other creditors. Because Barbell caused CG to (1) incur substantial obligations to him and (2) enter into several high-risk transactions—situations that resulted in CG's bankruptcy—Barbell's debt will probably be subordinated to the claims of other creditors. Choice **A** is incorrect because there is no per se rule invalidating a corporation's obligations to its corporate officers. Choice **C** is similarly incorrect because there is no per se rule subordinating debts owed to shareholders. Finally, choice **D** is incorrect because, in view of the fact that Barbell's actions were in large part the cause of CG's insolvency, Barbell will probably not be allowed to enforce his claim on par with CG's other creditors.

34. C At the dissolution of a corporation, its assets are distributed in the following priority. First, secured creditors are paid to the extent their obligations are collateralized by specific property of the corporation. Next, unsecured creditors are paid. (If a secured creditor's collateral is insufficient to satisfy the obligation owed, he or she becomes an unsecured creditor for the balance.) Next, preferred shareholders are paid in accordance with their rights and preferences. Finally, the other shareholders receive whatever remains. Choice **C** most closely coincides with the order of priority set forth above. Choice **A** is incorrect because unsecured creditors are paid before shareholders. Choice **B** is incorrect because secured and unsecured creditors are paid before preferred shareholders. Finally, choice **D** is incorrect because it fails to point out that (1) secured creditors take prior to unsecured creditors and (2) preferred shareholders are ordinarily satisfied prior to common shareholders.

35. A At common law, either the corporation or the other party to the contract could disaffirm an ultra vires contract that was fully executory. The contract is ultra vires because XYZ is authorized only to operate a restaurant. Thus, XYZ can assert the defense of ultra vires before either side commences performance of the agreement. Choice **B** is incorrect because, even if Paula had read the articles of incorporation prior to entering into the transaction with XYZ, XYZ could still assert the ultra vires doctrine. If this had occurred, Paula would have been on notice that XYZ could repudiate the transaction. Choice **C**

is incorrect because, at common law, a corporation can assert the ultra vires doctrine. (The shareholders can assert this theory only if the corporation fails to do so.) Finally, choice **D** is incorrect because, even if the shareholders had ratified the transaction, Paula would **not** prevail. Shareholders are incapable of approving an ultra vires act. It should be pointed out that some courts take the view that shareholder ratification, if accomplished by a vote of the shareholders sufficient to change the articles of incorporation, constitutes an implied amendment of that document. In such a jurisdiction, the transaction would not be ultra vires, and Paula would prevail.

36. **C** At common law, when there was part performance of, or reliance upon, a transaction by either party, the other party was ordinarily estopped from asserting the ultra vires doctrine. The $25,000 payment made to Paula constitutes part performance of the agreement. In addition, the two-year contract with Oliver probably constitutes substantial reliance on the transaction by XYZ. As a result, XYZ may enforce the agreement. Choice **A** is incorrect because, although the contract is ultra vires, there has been part performance and reliance by XYZ. Choice **B** is incorrect because mere return of the consideration Paula had received is not a basis for allowing her to avoid the contract. Finally, choice **D** is incorrect because XYZ can prevail with or without stockholder approval.

37. **A** When a corporation should recognize that, based on his or her **prior** dealings with the corporation, a third party will be likely to view an officer or agent as possessing authority to enter into the agreement in question, the corporation **cannot** avoid that transaction. However, even though Simone had undertaken similar transactions in the past, the growers with whom she contracted after the resolution was passed were **not the ones with whom she had previously dealt.** Thus, any "apparent authority" argument **would not** prevail in this instance. Although there is no indication that the growers were aware of the resolution limiting the monetary amount of contracts into which Simone could enter, a corporate treasurer is ordinarily **not** empowered to bind the corporation contractually. Choice **B** is incorrect because the growers would **not** be deemed to be on constructive notice of the resolution setting Simone's contractual limits. Choice **C** is incorrect because there is no basis in the hypothetical to assume that the growers in question knew of the transactions Simone had previously entered into on behalf of Fruitco. Finally, choice **D** is incorrect because the "inherent authority of office" doctrine would

allow the growers only to assume that Simone had the normal powers of a corporate treasurer. As already noted, a treasurer does *not* ordinarily have the authority to bind the corporation to a contract.

38. C Each corporate officer has the authority to enter into transactions that are reasonably related to the performance of the normal duties of his or her office. A corporate secretary ordinarily certifies the records of the corporation, including the board's resolutions. He or she does not enter into contracts to buy land or inventory. ABC can probably rescind the transaction to acquire the steel because the vendor should have recognized that a corporate secretary lacks the authority to bind the corporation contractually. Choice **A** is incorrect because a secretary lacks the implied authority of office to bind the corporation to land or inventory contracts. Choice **B** is incorrect because the facts fail to indicate that the steel vendor was aware of the transaction with Elmer or that she believed that the corporation had approved of it. Finally, choice **D** is incorrect because ABC's right to avoid the second transaction is not contingent upon repudiation of the initial one. The vendor of the land could raise Matt's lack of authority, if he chose to do so.

39. D Acts of a corporate officer or agent that are beyond his or her authority may be implicitly ratified by the board by its action or inaction. By approving a resolution to obtain bids for remodeling the premises subsequent to acquiring knowledge of the lease and by taking no action to repudiate the lease, the XYZ board probably implicitly ratified the contract. Thus, even though the secretary of a corporation ordinarily lacks authority to bind the company contractually, XYZ implicitly ratified the lease by passing a resolution that approved steps in furtherance of the lease. Choice **A** is incorrect because, while Charles lacked authority to enter into the lease, the board implicitly approved the transaction by instructing XYZ's president to obtain bids for remodeling the premises. Choice **B** is incorrect because, once having approved the lease, the board could no longer repudiate that contract. Finally, choice **C** is incorrect because there is nothing to indicate that the lessor had reason to believe Charles had authority to enter into the lease.

40. A When a corporation sells all, or substantially all, of its assets, by merger or otherwise, the transaction must be approved by the board and a majority (in some jurisdictions even a greater proportion) of its shareholders. Because the transaction involves the sale of *all* of Bilko's assets, it must be approved by the shareholders of Bilko. (In some states, the shareholders of Apex must also approve the transaction.) The facts do not indicate that the Bilko shareholders knew of the transaction or approved it. Choice **B** is incorrect because Joan is the proper officer to enter into this type of transaction for Bilko (subject to shareholder and director approval). Choice **C** is incorrect because approval by the Apex and Bilko boards is not enough; the transaction must be approved by Bilko's shareholders. Finally, choice **D** is incorrect because **both** Bilko's board and its shareholders must approve the transaction.

41. **D** Resolutions ordinarily need be passed only by a majority vote of directors present at a properly called meeting at which a quorum exists. The facts indicate that that's what happened here. A corporation ordinarily has the implied power to perform acts that are reasonably necessary to accomplish its express or authorized purposes (and that are not otherwise prohibited or unlawful). Undertaking farming operations until the necessary permits could be obtained would arguably, under these circumstances, be viewed as reasonably necessary to Buildco's main purpose of subdividing land for the purpose of constructing tract homes. Otherwise, the land would be totally unproductive during the period before the permits could be obtained. The fact that the nonattending directors would have voted against the resolution does **not** undermine its validity, so long as the meeting was properly called and a quorum was present. The directors had the power to call another meeting to overturn the resolution. Choice **A** is incorrect because undertaking farming operations while awaiting the necessary permits would appear to be reasonably necessary to preserve Buildco's express purposes and, therefore, **not** ultra vires. Choice **B** is incorrect because only a majority vote of a duly constituted quorum is usually necessary to pass a resolution. Finally, choice **C** is incorrect because the resolution was properly passed at a meeting at which a quorum was present.

42. **D** If the time of regular meetings is stipulated in the articles of incorporation or bylaws, no additional notice is required. Directors are ordinarily deemed to be on constructive notice of their corporation's articles of incorporation and bylaws. Because corporate bylaws ordinarily require only that a majority of directors be present for a proper quorum, the meeting was properly held. Because a majority of those attending voted in favor of the resolution, it is valid. Choice **A** is incorrect because Carson is on constructive notice of Ajax's bylaws. Choice **B** is incorrect because the board was under no obligation to

give additional notice to Carson of a regularly scheduled meeting. Finally, choice **C** is incorrect because there was no obligation to give specific notice to Carson. Thus, it is wrong to state that she failed to receive **proper** notice.

43. C A corporation cannot use as a defense against parties with whom it has contracted and who acted in good faith that it failed to give adequate notice to its directors for a meeting at which the transaction was approved. Those parties ordinarily have a right to assume that facially valid resolutions were properly undertaken. Although the resolution was not properly passed because three of the directors failed to receive the written notice required for a special meeting, Nancy had the right to rely on the resolution presented to her by the secretary. Choice **A** is incorrect because Nancy had a right to rely on a facially valid resolution. Choice **B** is incorrect because liability is **not** based on the president's actual or apparent authority to enter into the agreement with Nancy. Rather, it is based on an express resolution by the board approving the transaction. Finally, choice **D** is incorrect because Oilco would have been able to rescind the transaction but for the fact that Nancy was presented with a resolution that appeared to be valid. If a meeting is improperly noticed, any action undertaken by the board at the meeting is invalid (even if it appears that votes of the absentee directors would have had no impact upon the resolution). It is possible that if the nonnoticed directors had attended, they would have been able to persuade the other directors to vote in a different manner.

44. B Under the director's duty of due care, directors must exercise the same degree of care and skill with respect to corporate matters as a reasonably prudent person would with respect to his or her own affairs (or, in a number of jurisdictions, the care of a reasonably prudent person in like position). A director's reasonable business judgment that proves, in retrospect, to have been erroneous, is **not** actionable, because of the protection afforded by the business judgment rule. However, on these facts, the directors who failed to approve the resolution requiring the purchase of insurance are probably jointly and severally liable for the losses resulting from their decision. It is ordinarily unreasonable to neglect to carry insurance on a substantial corporate asset. This error is compounded by the fact that funds that could have been used to purchase the insurance were retained for a nonbusiness purpose (the payment of dividends). Choice **A** is incorrect because, although wide latitude is given to the business judgment of directors, the failure to obtain fire insurance under these circumstances is probably actionable, particularly in light of the stated, self-interested motive of a majority of the directors to maintain their positions. Choice **C** is incorrect because the directors who voted against the acquisition of fire insurance would be jointly and severally liable (not proportionately) for the losses resulting from their action. Finally, choice **D** is incorrect because directors who voted in favor of purchasing the insurance would be absolved from liability.

45. D Under the director's duty of due care, directors must exercise the same degree of care and skill with respect to corporate matters as would a reasonably prudent person with respect to his or her own affairs (or, in some jurisdictions, the care of a reasonably prudent person in like position). Directors must make a reasonable effort to inform themselves of the facts necessary to make a proper decision. Prior to acquiring a lease, a reasonably prudent businessperson would verify whether there were any delinquencies or outstanding liabilities by the transferor-lessee. This is especially true when, as here, the directors know that the landlord has alleged a breach by the tenant. Thus, the directors who approved the transaction are probably liable for the losses that may be sustained by Beta. Choice **A** is incorrect because the fact that officers of Alpha may have misrepresented their liability to the lessor does not relieve Beta's directors of their obligation to make a reasonable inquiry with regard to all breaches under the lease. Choice **B** is incorrect because the business judgment rule would probably *not* protect the directors in this instance. Finally, choice **C** is incorrect because the directors of a corporation that is acquiring the assets of another entity for cash are ordinarily *not* required to seek approval by their shareholders.

46. D Under cumulative voting, each stockholder's shares are multiplied by the total number of directors to be chosen; the resulting number of votes may be cast for no more candidates than there are seats to be filled, but can be cast for fewer than all such seats. In most states, if cumulative voting for directors is required, a director may *not* be removed *without good cause* if the votes *against* removal are sufficient (if voted cumulatively) to have elected that director. If cumulative voting is applicable in Acme's state, Mitchell *cannot* be removed. Because only 334 votes are necessary to elect Mitchell, the votes against his removal are sufficient to preclude this action. Choices **A** and **B** are incorrect because the articles of incorporation specifically allow shareholders to remove directors without cause. Finally, choice **C** is incorrect because, even if cumulative voting is applicable, there were a sufficient number of votes cast against Mitchell's removal to prevent this action. (Editor's note: the student may wonder why, if we are hypothesizing a state in which cumulative voting is required, the articles and bylaws would contain a provision inconsistent with that hypothesis—that is, that a director can be removed without cause. The assumptions that should be made in such circumstances are something the student should specifically ascertain from the instructor before entering the final exam.)

47. C Ordinarily, the directors of a corporation appoint its officers. Because shareholders cannot ordinarily appoint officers, their election of Adolpho to be president was improper. Actions (1) and (4) are proper because the shareholders do elect directors. The fact that the directors had made an interim appointment of Edward is irrelevant; their action is superseded by the shareholder action. The action described in (3) is proper because, although shareholders cannot make management decisions pertaining to the operation of their corporation, they may ordinarily ratify transactions when a disinterested quorum of directors does *not* exist. Thus, choices **A**, **B**, and **D** all list an incorrect combination of selections.

48. B Fundamental management decisions and the appointment of corporate officers ordinarily *cannot* be delegated by the board of directors. Because the contract with Kent authorizes him to select officers and determine corporate expenditures, the employment agreement is probably invalid. The fact that he can be dismissed for incompetence or the failure to satisfy specific performance standards does not detract from the breadth of his initial authority. Choice **A** is incorrect because the agreement's invalidity is *not* predicated on the fact that it exceeds one year. Today, most jurisdictions permit a board to approve contracts that exceed the terms of the existing directors. Choice **C** is incorrect because a board can certainly approve a transaction that will bind the corporation beyond the date of the next board election; a contrary rule would inhibit a corporation unreasonably. Finally, choice **D** is incorrect because the contract with Kent is invalid for the reasons described above.

49. C When an independent litigation committee or consultant advises against a derivative action, the board is usually justified in deciding not to bring suit. Because an independent, disinterested attorney-consultant appointed by ABC's board of directors has advised against a derivative action, a lawsuit by Shawn (or any shareholder) should be barred. Choice **A** is incorrect because there is no requirement that a derivative action be commenced to compel recovery when an employee has committed a crime. Choice **B** is incorrect because the shareholders cannot override the directors in these circumstances. Finally, choice **D** is incorrect because her presence during the vote to refrain from commencing an action against the employee would *not*, in itself, preclude Shawn from pursuing a derivative action.

50. **C** Choice **C** is the correct answer because it is the only choice that is incorrect on the facts. When a derivative action is commenced in federal court on account of diversity, the complaint must allege the plaintiff's efforts to obtain action from the directors or explain his or her reasons for not making the efforts. Because Alice commenced the action in federal court, she is required to allege the efforts she made to obtain action by the directors (i.e., demanding that the directors sue Ted and Michael) or explain why she failed to make the efforts. Choice **A** is a correct statement because only a derivative action can be commenced against Ted and Michael. Alice cannot sue them on her own behalf, because the losses resulting from their allegedly improper actions were incurred primarily by ABC, not by individual shareholders. Choice **B** is a correct statement because Alice probably is excused on these facts from making a demand on the directors. Because two of the three directors are involved in the alleged wrongdoing, no disinterested majority exists upon whom such a demand can be made. Finally, choice **D** is a correct statement. Because Alice's derivative action is premised on diversity jurisdiction (rather than on a federal claim), she must post a bond if required to do so under applicable state law.

51. **C** A derivative action is appropriate when the harm complained about was done *primarily* to the corporation, rather than to the plaintiff-shareholder. The actions of the directors described in (1) and (4) resulted primarily in financial loss to ABC. Although the action described in (1) was allegedly premised on an intention to obtain Mike's shares at a discounted value, the complaint alleges the sale of corporate assets at less than market value, and the harm that resulted was incurred primarily by the corporation. On the other hand, the refusal to let Mike vote his shares and the dilution of his ownership interest in ABC were actions that impacted primarily on Mike, personally. The actions described in (2) and (3) did not *primarily* affect ABC and may not be made the subject of a derivative action.

52. **D** To maintain a derivative action, the plaintiff must ordinarily have been a shareholder at the time the harm to the corporation occurred. However, the date of acquisition for a plaintiff who acquires her shares through operation of law (e.g., inheritance, intestacy) is the date upon which her decedent acquired the shares. Although the facts tell us that Alex inherited her stock from her father, they do **not** disclose whether her father was a shareholder at the time the directors breached their duty of loyalty. If Alex's father acquired his shares **after** that time, Alex could not commence a derivative action for that breach. Although Alex could bring a derivative action based on the directors' negligence with regard to her second assertion, because she was a shareholder at the time of the negligence, it still would be necessary to ascertain when her father acquired the XYZ shares to determine whether a derivative action alleging a breach of the duty of loyalty (for the first assertion) can also be maintained. (Note, moreover, that, with respect to the negligence claim, it would be necessary to determine whether the statutes of the state provided for, and the articles of incorporation took advantage of, the ability to limit directorial liability for negligence.)

53. **C** When a derivative action is based on SEC Rule 16(b), it is **not** necessary for the plaintiff to have been a shareholder at the time of the alleged wrong. Also, when a derivative action in federal court is based on a **federal claim**, state laws requiring a bond or other security are superseded. Because Moe's claim is based on SEC Rule 16(b), any otherwise applicable state law requiring a bond or other security is superseded. Choice **A** is incorrect because, under federal law, one does not have to have been a shareholder at the time of an alleged wrong to maintain an SEC Rule 16(b) action. Choice **B** is incorrect because, in view of the fact that all three directors were the alleged wrongdoers, it would be futile to demand that they take action against themselves. Finally, choice **D** is incorrect because, if Moe's derivative action is successful, the entire recovery will be paid to the corporation. (Moe could, however, recover his reasonable attorneys' fees and court costs.)

54. **A** In some states, the plaintiff must request that a majority of the **disinterested** shareholders ratify a derivative action. However, when the derivative action is premised on acts that are prohibited by statute, shareholder approval is usually unnecessary. In most states, the circumstances under which dividends may be paid are statutorily mandated. In these states, the shareholders cannot approve or ratify

an improper or illegal dividend distribution. Choice **B** is incorrect because all of the directors participated in the allegedly improper conduct. Chris must, however, describe in her pleadings the reason why a demand would be futile. Choice **C** is incorrect because state bond or security requirements are applicable when a derivative action in federal court is predicated upon ***diversity*** jurisdiction. Finally, choice **D** is incorrect because, under these circumstances, Chris had no choice but to accept any dividend payment that was tendered to her. Her acceptance of the dividend cannot be used to justify improper distribution by the board.

55. **D** When a director or officer has a direct financial interest in a transaction, he or she is ordinarily obliged to disclose that interest and refrain from voting on the matter. If, after his or her disclosure, the transaction is approved by a majority of the disinterested directors or a majority of the disinterested shareholders, it will be valid unless shown to be unfair. However, because the transaction described was patently unfair to Alpha (i.e., would constitute a waste of corporate assets), it cannot be validly ratified even by the disinterested shareholders. Choice **A** is incorrect because, although the resolution was not approved by a majority of disinterested directors, a majority of disinterested shareholders can nevertheless ratify a transaction that is not prohibited or patently unfair to the corporation. Choice **B** is incorrect because the shareholders may ratify a transaction even if approval by the board was defective because it was voted on by interested directors. Because (1) the owner-director and his family should have refrained from voting, and (2) the disinterested directors split 1 to 1 on the transaction in question, shareholder ratification was appropriate (subject to the caveats above). Finally, choice **C** is factually incorrect because the vote of the ***disinterested*** directors was 1 to 1.

56. **D** A director or officer cannot exploit for personal gain information acquired or made available to him or her as a consequence of his or her corporate position, ***unless*** the corporation (1) declines to pursue the same opportunity after full disclosure or (2) is, and would continue to be (despite any reasonable efforts), unable to take advantage of the opportunity. If the officer breaches this rule, the corporation can obtain either equitable relief or damages equal to the profit derived by the wrongdoer. Because Charles has appropriated a corporate opportunity by purchasing the manufacturing plant through his partnership, Tilden can either rescind the purchase or recover

the $150,000 profit made by Unger. Charles also breached his duty of loyalty by failing to inform the Tilden board of his personal interest in the transaction. Choice **A** is incorrect because Charles's failure to vote on the matter does *not* absolve him of culpability. Choice **B** is incorrect because the board can rescind the transaction to prevent unjust profit to Charles even if it finds that the purchase price of the facility was fair. Finally, choice **C** is incorrect because, even if the other general partners of Unger were unaware of Charles's personal interest, his misdeed would probably be attributed to the partnership, of which he was an agent; further, the equities would still favor Tilden.

57. **A** Actions based on SEC Rule 10b-5 or SEC Rule 16(b) *must* be commenced in federal court. Because the SEC Rule 10b-5 action was commenced in *state* court, a motion by Green to dismiss the case will be successful. Choices **B** and **C** are incorrect because a state court action does not lie even if a valid state claim is asserted or an allegation is made that interstate commerce was not involved. Finally, choice **D** is incorrect because *no* additional facts are necessary to conclude that Green's motion will be successful.

58. **D** When an action against a director or officer based on an act or omission in connection with his or her duties is settled prior to judgment, the corporation may indemnify the defendant for his or her attorneys' fees and litigation expenses (provided a majority of disinterested directors or shareholders determines that the defendant was acting in good faith). Notwithstanding this general rule, because the basis of the action in this case is not a lawsuit, act, or omission *connected with* Green's duties as president of Drugco, Drugco should refuse to indemnify her for any amount whatsoever. Thus, choices **A**, **B**, and **C** are all incorrect.

59. **C** When a director or officer in a derivative suit is adjudged to have breached a duty owed to the corporation, indemnification is ordinarily not permitted. Because Joe was exonerated of negligence in selecting the employee who embezzled money from Island, he is entitled to be indemnified for his attorneys' fees and litigation expenses. Choice **A** is incorrect because Todd may *not* be indemnified for his litigation expenses and attorneys' fees. Choice **B** is incorrect because Joe may be indemnified for his litigation expenses and attorneys' fees by Island. Finally, choice **D** is incorrect because Todd, who was found to have breached his duty to Island, is *not* entitled to indemnification. In a few jurisdictions, a director who is found

liable may nevertheless be reimbursed for his or her attorneys' fees and litigation expenses *if* he or she is adjudged to be "fairly and reasonably" entitled to indemnification. However, in this instance, the facts tell us that no such finding was made.

60. B If a lawsuit against a director or officer does *not* allege a knowing breach of duties, and the suit is settled prior to trial, the officer or director may be indemnified by the corporation *if* a majority of disinterested directors determines that the defendant acted in good faith and for a purpose reasonably believed to be in the best interests of the corporation. Because the board approved a resolution stating that Karl had acted in good faith and for purposes that he reasonably believed to be in Acro's best interests, all of his expenses (including the settlement amount to the extent paid by Karl) may be reimbursed by the corporation. Choice **A** is incorrect because the fact that Karl was named personally in the action does *not* preclude reimbursement. Choice **C** is incorrect because, in the vast majority of states, it is not necessary for Karl to have been successful on the merits to obtain reimbursement from Acro; in the interest of avoiding litigation, a reasonable settlement is always encouraged. Finally, choice **D** is incorrect because Karl may, under these circumstances, be indemnified for his attorneys' fees and litigation expenses.

61. D Civil lawsuits against a director or officer that do *not* allege a knowing breach of duties and that are settled prior to trial may ordinarily be reimbursed by the corporation if a majority of the disinterested shareholders determines that the defendant acted in good faith and for a purpose reasonably believed to be in the best interests of the corporation. However, where a criminal action is involved, the director or officer must satisfy a third requirement—he or she must show that he or she had no reason to believe that his or her action was unlawful. If a majority of the disinterested shareholders determines that this tripartite test in a criminal action is satisfied, reimbursement may occur. Choice **A** is incorrect because a mere charge that a criminal offense has been committed does not preclude indemnification. Choice **B** is incorrect because indemnification under these circumstances is *not* contingent upon prevailing on the merits. Finally, choice **C** is incorrect because it does not satisfy the third part of the tripartite test—the shareholders must also conclude that the directors had no reason to believe that their actions were unlawful.

62. A At common law, when a *new* issue of shares occurred, an existing shareholder had the right to acquire the number of shares necessary to maintain his or her proportionate interest in the corporation. Underhill may assert preemptive rights in up to 30 percent of the newly issued shares (excluding the 500 that will be tendered to Smith). Thus, Underhill may purchase an additional 300 shares. Choice **B** is incorrect because Underhill may not assert preemptive rights with respect to the 500 shares that will be delivered to Smith. At common law, preemptive rights did **not** extend to newly issued shares that were to be exchanged for property other than cash. Choice **C** is incorrect because preemptive rights extend **only** to shares **not** previously authorized at the time the shareholder acquires his or her stock. Finally, choice **D** is incorrect because, although Underhill may not assert preemptive rights in the 500 shares to be given to Smith, she does retain those rights with regard to the remaining 1,000 shares of newly issued stock.

63. **A** In most states, preemptive rights ordinarily do **not** extend to the resale of treasury stock. Because Arthur purchased 5 percent of the originally issued shares, he is entitled to exercise preemptive rights in up to 5 percent of the **newly** authorized 500 shares of stock. But he has **no** preemptive rights with regard to the treasury shares that were previously repurchased by Ajax and that are now being sold by Ajax. Choice **B** is incorrect because Arthur (1) is only entitled to 25 shares and (2) would be obliged to pay the offering price of $150 per share. Choice **C** is incorrect because Arthur has preemptive rights only with regard to the 500 newly issued shares, not the 500 treasury shares. Finally, choice **D** is incorrect because, as described above, Arthur is entitled to purchase only 25 shares of the newly authorized stock at $150 per share.

64. **D** At common law, if there was an issue of new shares, an existing shareholder had preemptive rights—that is, the right to acquire the number of shares necessary to maintain his or her proportionate interest in the corporation. Williams has preemptive rights with respect to the newly issued shares. In addition, because the shares were not necessary for a valid business purpose, but were apparently issued only to enhance the ownership interest of the other two stockholders, Williams may be able to obtain a court order rescinding the issue of the newly authorized stock. She might seek such an order if purchasing 40 percent of the newly authorized stock would pose a financial hardship for her. Choice **A** is incorrect because preemptive rights extend **only to shares that were not authorized** at the time the plaintiff originally acquired her stock. Choice **B** is incorrect

because it would be essentially unfair to require Williams to expend the money necessary to buy her rightful share of the stock when there was no valid business purpose for the issue. Finally, choice **C** is incorrect because, at common law, preemptive rights existed whether or not they were specified in the corporate charter.

65. C A proxy is ordinarily revocable by the proxy giver who attends a shareholders' meeting, provided that he or she either (1) expressly revokes the proxy or (2) votes the shares subject to the proxy him- or herself. Mere attendance is not enough to accomplish revocation. Mervin's attendance at the shareholders' meeting would not prevent Joan from voting the shares that were subject to the proxy. However, if Mervin indicates in any manner that he no longer intends the proxy to be operative, the proxy is revoked. Choice **A** is incorrect because Joan can vote the shares unless Mervin expressly or implicitly revokes the proxy, notwithstanding his attendance at the meeting. Choice **B** is incorrect because a proxy is *not* inoperative merely because the original reason for its issuance has ceased to exist. Finally, choice **D** is incorrect because, even if the articles of incorporation expressly authorize proxy voting, Mervin can still revoke the proxy given to Joan.

66. C The purchaser of shares has a sufficient interest in the corporation to support an irrevocable proxy. Only stockholders on the record date (or those who have received proxies from these stockholders) may vote at a shareholders' meeting. Because Mindy's proxy to Sally was irrevocable, Sally may vote the shares. If Mindy attempts to revoke the proxy at the shareholders' meeting, she will be unable to do so. Choice **A** is incorrect because Mindy cannot repudiate the proxy she gave to Sally. Choice **B** is incorrect because, although Sally was not the shareholder of record for purposes of the meeting, she received an irrevocable proxy from Mindy at the time of sale. The proxy was valid because it was issued by the record owner. Finally, choice **D** is incorrect because, without the proxy from Mindy, Zebco could prevent Sally from voting the shares she purchased from Mindy, on the grounds that Sally was not a shareholder on the record date.

67. A Under SEC Rule 14a-8, shareholders who (1) own at least 1 percent or $2,000 in present value of the corporation's securities and (2) have held their shares for at least one year may submit a single proposal for inclusion in management's proxy materials to be voted on at the upcoming shareholders' meeting. The shareholder's proposal and supporting statement may not exceed 500 words. The proposal that

Jones be appointed chief financial officer may be rejected because it is *not a proper subject for shareholder action* (corporate officers are usually appointed by the directors). The second proposal—to install a coffee room for employees—can also probably be excluded because it relates to the company's ordinary business operations and is too routine a management matter to constitute a proper subject for stockholder action. Choice **B** is incorrect because major corporate officers are ordinarily chosen by the board of directors. Choice **C** is incorrect because, even if Elmer has owned his shares for a year, management is not required to include these kinds of proposals in its solicitation materials. Finally, choice **D** is incorrect because the second proposal relates to Fairway's ordinary business operations and is too routine a management matter to permit shareholder intervention.

68. **B** Under SEC Rule 14a-8, shareholders who (1) own at least 1 percent or $2,000 in present value of the corporation's securities and (2) have held the shares for at least one year may submit a single proposal for inclusion in management's proxy materials to be voted on at the upcoming shareholders' meeting. The shareholder's proposal and supporting statement may not exceed 500 words. Because Emma's proposal seems to be an appropriate one for consideration by the shareholders, management must include it in its solicitation materials, if the statement and its supporting materials do not exceed 500 words. The facts stipulate that Emma has been a shareholder for more than one year and that the value of her stock exceeds $2,000. Choice **A** is incorrect because the proposal and its supporting statement may *not* exceed 500 words, regardless of its content or significance. Choice **C** is incorrect because, under these circumstances, Belton *cannot* charge Emma for any costs associated with including her proposal in its proxy solicitation to the corporation's shareholders. Finally, choice **D** is incorrect because the board is *not* required to mail Emma's proposal at Belton's expense to the shareholders, except as a part of its own solicitation.

69. **A** When a proxy solicitation contains a material misstatement or omission, the court may rescind any corporate action that was undertaken on the basis of those proxies. A successful plaintiff can ordinarily recover his or her attorneys' fees and litigation expenses. On these facts, the solicitation of proxies for the reelection of Ralph without describing his past contacts with the criminal justice system would probably involve a material omission. Thus, Mary could

have Ralph's election set aside and recover the attorneys' fees and expenses incurred in her action. Choice **B** is incorrect because any shareholder may complain when proxies have been solicited on the strength of material omissions or misstatements, regardless of the amount of stock he or she owns. In a few jurisdictions, the shareholder will not have standing unless he or she has actually given his or her proxy in response to the solicitation. This is not an issue here, because Mary did give her proxy. Choice **C** is incorrect because the fact that Mary did not commence her action until after Ralph's election is not significant (unless she delays an unreasonably long period of time). Finally, choice **D** is incorrect because Ralph's contacts with the criminal system involved breach of trust and, thus, are probably material, even though his conduct as a Zebco director did not give rise to the convictions.

70. **C** Corporate action must ordinarily be undertaken pursuant to validly authorized resolutions validly adopted. The appointment of corporate officers must ordinarily be undertaken by resolution of the directors. The fact that a majority of directors have signed a typewritten resolution appointing Cindy as secretary is not controlling. Although recent legislation in many jurisdictions permits directors to act without a formal meeting, these statutes still ordinarily require that the action be taken in writing and be approved unanimously. In this instance, the resolution was not signed by *all* of the directors. Choice **A** is incorrect because shareholders ordinarily *cannot* appoint a corporate officer by agreement with the officer directly. Choice **B** is incorrect because there was no properly held meeting of the board to consider Cindy as secretary. Finally, choice **D** is incorrect for two reasons—officers must be appointed by the board rather than the shareholders, and the board does not need unanimous agreement to appoint an officer. A majority of directors is sufficient, provided all formal requirements for notice and/or waiver are met.

71. **B** Under the common law, shareholders may inspect corporate books and records, including board minutes, minutes of shareholders' meetings, bylaws, books of account, contracts, and other similar documents pertaining to the company's affairs. The inspection must be done in good faith, at a reasonable time, and for the purpose of advancing the interests of the corporation or its shareholders. Because Paula is asking to inspect Weldon's books of account and contracts for a proper purpose (to determine why the corporation has not been more profitable when others have), she should be permitted to examine these items. Choice **A** is incorrect because, her

purpose being a proper one, there is no basis for precluding preclude Paula from viewing the contracts entered into by Weldon. Choice **C** is incorrect because no assertion of wrongdoing by management is necessary before a shareholder is permitted to view corporate books and records. Finally, choice **D** is incorrect because, her purpose being a proper one, Paula may view both Weldon's books of account and its contracts.

72. **A** When a statute restricting the inspection of corporate books and records exists, it is usually construed narrowly to avoid encroaching on common law rights—in this case, the common law right to inspect all relevant books and records. Because the statute in this case is limited to inspections of corporate ***books of account,*** it will probably be construed as applying only to that category of records. Therefore, John can still assert his common law right to review the corporation's books, records, and documents ***other than*** its books of account, even though he has been a stockholder for only seven months. Because John's purpose in soliciting the shareholder lists is a proper one (i.e., to become a director for the purpose of determining whether fraud by members of the board has occurred), he should be able to view this data. Choice **B** is incorrect because he has owned Boolon stock for only seven months (not the one-year period of time required by the statute to inspect the books of account). Thus, John cannot inspect the books of account. Choice **C** is incorrect because John can properly inspect the shareholder lists, and the solicitation of proxies in an effort to unseat existing management is not an improper purpose. Finally, choice **D** is incorrect because John's common law rights of inspection would probably still extend to corporate documents ***other than*** the books of account.

73. **B** A derivative action to overturn an act of the board that is either unlawful or constitutes a waste of corporate assets cannot be prevented by stockholder ratification of the director's act—not even by a majority of disinterested stockholders. James's derivative suit should be allowed if Josephine's compensation is so excessive as to constitute waste of corporate assets. Because, on these facts, both the board and a majority of disinterested shareholders have approved the contract with Josephine, James will probably have the burden of showing that the contract was unfair. He may succeed in doing this if he can show that her contract was much more costly than the contracts of officers with comparable authority and duties in the same industry. Choice **A** is incorrect because, if James's suit is successful, he should be permitted to recover his attorneys' fees and court costs.

Choice **C** is incorrect because even disinterested shareholders cannot ratify corporate waste. Finally, choice **D** is incorrect because, in view of the fact that the directors had voted unanimously in favor of Josephine's compensation, a demand on the board would presumably be futile. This is not the case under some statutes.

74. **D** The sale of all, or substantially all, the assets of one corporation to another for cash or for cash and secured debt is usually followed by the liquidation of the seller and the distribution of its assets to its shareholders. The stockholders of the two corporations involved are not treated equally. The stockholders of the selling corporation must approve the sale. The shareholders of the purchasing corporation do not ordinarily have to approve the sale. Because the outstanding stock of the purchasing corporation is not affected by the purchase, appraisal rights do not apply. Therefore, Johnson does not have appraisal rights, and she cannot complain that the shareholders of Carlton have not been asked to approve the transaction. Choice **A** is incorrect because Johnson is not entitled to appraisal rights. Choice **B** is incorrect because consent by the Carlton stockholders is not required. Choice **C** is incorrect because most states do not ordinarily require approval by the stockholders of the purchaser.

75. **D** To exercise his or her appraisal rights, a shareholder must do the following: (1) give notice to the corporation *prior to the shareholder vote* that he or she is demanding payment of the fair value of his or her stock interest, (2) vote against the transaction or refrain from voting in its favor, and (3) as soon as possible (some states require that this be done before the vote), deposit his or her shares with the corporation. Because Amy failed to vote against the sale, she will probably *not* be permitted to exercise her appraisal rights. Choice **A** is incorrect because communication of disapproval is not enough; Amy failed to vote against the transaction. Choice **B** is incorrect because, having failed to appear at the shareholders' meeting, Amy forfeited her right to exercise her appraisal rights. Choice **C** is incorrect because appraisal rights were designed to protect the interests of shareholders in the selling corporation and Amy would be entitled to these rights, except for her failure to follow the required steps.

76. **C** When a statutory merger occurs (i.e., the transaction is effectuated pursuant to the applicable statutory requirements), the surviving corporation (Helton) automatically assumes the obligations of the target company (Gibble). Because a statutory merger has occurred, the creditors of Gibble can enforce collection against Helton for any

obligations owed to them by Gibble. This principle applies regardless of whether (1) Helton expressly assumed Gibble's debts, or (2) the obligations were known or unknown by Helton. Choice **A** is incorrect because a statutory merger requires approval by the boards of both the target and the survivor. Choice **B** is incorrect because, when a *statutory* merger occurs, the shareholders of *both* corporations may assert appraisal rights. In some states, the appraisal rights of the shareholders of the acquiring corporation will be unavailable if the resulting increase in outstanding stock is less than 20 percent. Finally, choice **D** is incorrect because, although Bo has appraisal rights as a stockholder in the target company, his recovery is the value of the stock as of the date immediately *preceding* the merger.

77. **C** When, as consideration for a sale of all (or substantially all) of its assets, the transferor corporation receives stock of the transferee and is required to dissolve soon afterward, many courts treat the transaction as a de facto merger. In these situations, the principles applicable to statutory mergers (e.g., approval of the directors and shareholders, appraisal rights, assumption by the survivor of the target corporation's debts) are applicable. Because we know that the de facto merger doctrine is operative in this jurisdiction, the shareholders of both corporations possess appraisal rights (except that the appraisal rights of shareholders in the acquiring corporation may not be as broad as those of the transferring shareholders). Choice **A** is incorrect because, assuming the transaction is viewed as a de facto merger, Nolton is liable for Melton's debts (regardless of whether Nolton has expressly agreed to assume these obligations). Choice **B** is incorrect because stockholders of the acquiring corporation would be obliged to approve the issuance of additional shares. Ordinarily, an increase in the amount of authorized stock is viewed as an "organic" change in the corporation and requires an amendment to the articles of incorporation. Finally, choice **D** is incorrect because preemptive rights are ordinarily *not* applicable to situations where stock is exchanged for specific property other than cash.

78. **D** Instead of resorting to the federal courts, a shareholder whose proxy has been fraudulently solicited may ordinarily commence an action for rescission against the culpable party in a state court, under applicable state law. Or, instead of his or her other remedies, an aggrieved shareholder in a merger or de facto merger may assert his or her appraisal rights. However, the shareholder can assert his or her appraisal rights only if he or she has *voted against the merger*. Choice

B is, therefore, incorrect. Choice **A** is incorrect because it does not matter whether Elwood purchased his shares or inherited them. He must, however, be a buyer or seller of securities *in the transaction under scrutiny* to assert SEC Rule 10b-5; the "forced seller" doctrine recognized in some circuits probably would suffice. Finally, choice **C** is incorrect because an action under SEC Rule 10b-5 or Section 14 of the Securities Exchange Act *must* be initiated in federal court.

79. **C** In a statutory merger, the general rule is that shareholders of both the target corporation and the surviving corporation must approve the transaction. However, in a whale-minnow merger, approval of the shareholders of the surviving corporation is not required. (See our discussion of appraisal rights of the Felton shareholders.) Choice **A** is, therefore, incorrect. Choice **B** is incorrect because both groups of shareholders do not have the same appraisal rights, either. If we view this as a whale-minnow merger (applicable here because Felton, the whale, is giving up only 10 pecent of its stock for all the assets of the minnow, Carlton), then this is an exception to the general rule requiring approval of the shareholders of the acquiring corporation. Under the MBCA the shareholders of the surviving corporation do not get appraisal rights if the increase in outstanding stock of the survivor is less than 20 percent. Choice **D** is incorrect because a short-form merger occurs when, prior to the transaction, the survivor owned a substantial proportion (e.g., often at least 90 percent) of the target's stock. There is *no* indication from the facts that this is the case. The correct answer is **C**. In a statutory merger, the surviving corporation is responsible for the debts of the target corporation.

80. **D** Unless the class is provided for in the original articles of incorporation, the holders of outstanding common stock must approve an amendment to the articles of incorporation before the issuance of a new class of stock that has priority in the distribution of dividends. Because ABC seeks to create a class of preferred stock having priority in the distribution of dividends, the requisite percentage of holders of common stock—usually, a majority—must approve an amendment to the articles of incorporation. Choice **A** is incorrect because *unanimous* approval by shareholders to create a new class of preferred stock is not necessary unless the articles require it. Choice **B** is incorrect because an amendment to the articles of incorporation is necessary in this situation. Changes in the right of shareholders to receive dividends are ordinarily viewed as being "organic" or "basic" in nature. Finally, choice **C** is incorrect because, provided it

is accomplished with the necessary percentage of common shares, the articles of incorporation can be amended to create a new class of stock that has priority in the distribution of dividends.

81. **D** To determine whether Ogden can pay dividends under these facts, it is necessary to research the law pertaining to dividends in the applicable jurisdiction. While some states still require that dividends be paid only from positive earned surplus, jurisdictions that allow nimble dividends permit distributions to be made from recent net profits. Nimble dividends are dividends paid from the corporation's net profits for the fiscal year in which the dividend is declared and/or the preceding fiscal year. Nimble dividend jurisdictions require, however, that the dividend not result in corporate insolvency. Some jurisdictions have enacted statutes that permit dividends to be paid as long as a corporation's total assets exceed its total liabilities. No decision on payment of dividends can be made without knowledge of the local laws. Choice **A** is incorrect because only a small minority of jurisdictions recognizes the payment of nimble dividends. Choice **B** is incorrect because some jurisdictions do allow dividend payments to be paid out of current operating profits, despite a deficit in the earned surplus account. Finally, choice **C** is incorrect because dividends cannot automatically be paid simply because the corporation won't be insolvent after the distribution.

82. **A** A voting trust is ordinarily enforceable according to its terms. The trustee has a fiduciary duty to act in the best interests of the beneficiaries (i.e., the participating shareholders). The trustee need not adhere to the wishes of any of the beneficiaries. Watson can vote the shares for Martha's election, assuming she possesses a good-faith belief that this action is beneficial to the shareholders of the trust. Because the trust is to operate for two years, the opposition of Samuels and Tilden to Martha's appointment is inoperative. Choice **B** is incorrect because Martha's competence is not sufficient. Watson must believe that Martha's election to the board will be beneficial to the trust's beneficiaries. Choice **C** is incorrect because Watson's obligation is to vote the shares in a manner that promotes the interests of the shareholder-beneficiaries as she sees them. She cannot disregard her judgment because it conflicts with the preferences of some of the beneficiaries. Finally, choice **D** is incorrect because Samuels and Tilden cannot revoke the trust by appearing at the stockholders' meeting or by objecting to the election of Martha. The trust can be terminated only by *unanimous* vote of the trust beneficiaries, and Underwood does *not* oppose Martha's election.

83. D A valid pooling agreement—that is, an agreement among stockholders to vote their stock together as a unit on certain or all matters—can ordinarily be enforced by a decree of specific performance. Because Katey and Mandy intend to vote in favor of the resolution preventing the derivative action, Mary **must** vote her shares in the same way because their agreement provides that a 2-out-of-3 vote will control. If Mary does not do so, Katey and Mandy can probably obtain a decree of specific performance. Choice **A** is incorrect because the fact that Mary owns more shares than the combined total of Katey and Mandy is irrelevant; their agreement controls. Choice **B** is incorrect because it is not necessary that the corporation receive a copy of the agreement before the agreement can be enforced against the original parties. Failure to file the agreement with the corporation might affect the rights of a bona fide purchaser from one of the three parties, but not the original parties. Finally, choice **C** is incorrect because the omission of any reference to the pooling agreement on the stock certificates is irrelevant among the original parties to the agreement. This omission would be significant if one of these parties transferred her shares to a person who did **not** know of the agreement.

84. D The courts in some states have applied the de facto merger doctrine, although all of the requirements of a statutory merger are not met, if the transaction is enough like a merger to be treated as one. When the doctrine of de facto merger is applied, the stockholders of the target corporation get appraisal rights, and, in some cases, the stockholders of the selling corporation get the right to vote on the transaction. Because Congolea purchased a controlling interest in Beldola from shareholders of Beldola *for cash*, it is extremely unlikely that any court would apply the de facto merger doctrine to this transaction. Fred is in no worse position now than if another person, or several persons, had purchased a majority interest in Beldola. But Fred may be able to assert appraisal rights when and if the "short form" merger of Beldola into Congolea occurs. Choice **A** is incorrect because, barring application of the de facto merger doctrine, approval by Congolea's shareholders is unnecessary. Choice **B** is incorrect because the transaction involved a purchase of stock for cash directly from *shareholders* of the target; thus, approval of Beldola's board was unnecessary. Finally, choice **C** is incorrect because Fred's rights are not governed by the actions of the Congolea board. It doesn't matter whether the board approved the merger unanimously or by a simple majority.

85. D In a jurisdiction that applies the reasoning in the *Perlman* case, the courts will scrutinize any transaction in which a controlling stockholder sells all his or her stock to an acquiring corporation at a premium. This would be especially so when the two corporations are direct competitors, because the instinct of the acquiring corporation is likely to be to reduce the impact of the competition, thereby injuring the minority stockholders in the target corporation. When the seller knows, or has reason to know, that the transfer will impair the value of shares held by the other shareholders, he or she is obliged to share the control premium with those other stockholders. The correct answer is **D**. Choice **A** is incorrect because the right under *Perlman* to obtain a pro rata share of the premium is ***not*** contingent upon proof that the new controlling shareholder intends to loot the corporation. As long as the seller has violated his or her fiduciary duty by negating a corporate opportunity, pro rata distribution of the control premium should apply. Choice **B** is incorrect because there is no basis on which Frances could assert appraisal rights in this situation. Finally, choice **C** is incorrect because Harrold's sale of his shares does ***not*** require approval by Ajax's board.

86. C In most states, a shareholder who obtains a premium for selling a majority or controlling portion of the corporation's stock ordinarily does ***not*** have to account to minority shareholders for this premium. Also, as part of the acquisition of a controlling interest in a corporation, the seller and purchaser may arrange a seriatim change in the directors elected by the seller. Because there is no reason on these facts to believe that Biltmore's control of PP will be detrimental to PP, its minority shareholders are ***not*** entitled to receive a pro rata portion of the "control" premium received by Randolph. In addition, the seriatim resignation and appointment of new directors is valid under these circumstances. The courts will not interfere with the seriatim transfer of control even though majority control is being sold for a premium. Choice **A** is incorrect because there is no indication that Randolph has breached his fiduciary duty to the corporation or the minority shareholders. Choice **B** is incorrect because seriatim transfer of control through orderly resignations of existing directors will not be disturbed by the courts. Biltmore may arrange for the replacement of the directors with individuals of its choosing. Finally, choice **D** is incorrect because, concurrently with obtaining control of a corporation, the acquiring party can arrange for the seriatim resignation and replacement of existing directors.

87. A When a corporation is capitalized with assets that are grossly inadequate to meet reasonably foreseeable obligations, considering the nature and purpose of the business, the corporate veil may be "pierced" (i.e., the shareholders may be held personally liable for the corporation's debts). This is especially true with respect to claims by involuntary creditors, as opposed to creditors who chose to do business with the company. However, the majority of states will not pierce the corporate veil on the basis of undercapitalization alone; other factors, such as fraud or misleading or a gross failure to follow corporate formalities also are required. Because no additional factors seem to be present here, Carla and John should be able to avoid personal liability, especially because they did secure liability insurance. Statement (2) is, therefore, correct. If Statement (2) is correct, then Statement (1) is incorrect. Statement (3) is incorrect because, in the bankruptcy proceeding, although John's note runs at least some risk of being treated as insider capital and may, therefore, be subordinated to the claims of general creditors, this is not a foregone conclusion. The court will consider other factors, including many that would overlap those relevant to piercing the corporate veil. The correct choice is, therefore, **A**, which adopts only Statement (2).

88. C Ordinarily, board members may *not* give proxies to other directors for the purpose of voting on corporate matters. A director must exercise his or her own independent judgment on all corporate matters and may *not* transfer his or her right to vote as a director to anyone else, including another director. The original agreement among Art, Sam, and Kelly was unenforceable. The proxy given by Art to Sam was also invalid. Directors may not vote by proxy. Choice **A** is incorrect because the original agreement among Art, Sam, and Kelly was invalid and unenforceable by any party. Choice **B** is incorrect because directors may not give or receive, or vote by, proxy. Finally, choice **D** is incorrect because Kelly had an absolute right (and obligation) to vote as she thought best for the corporation.

89. D Generally, a shareholder may transfer his or her stock, subject to any reasonable restrictions as to its alienability. These restrictions may be found in the articles of incorporation or bylaws or in shareholder agreements. A restriction on transfer of a security is ineffective against any person without actual knowledge of it, unless the restriction is conspicuously noted on the security. On these facts, the notation on Joe's stock certificate would be sufficient to place Bertha on notice of the restriction, even though the notation makes reference to another document that sets forth the terms of the restriction. The restriction described here (a right of first refusal by current shareholders at the stock's fair market value) is ordinarily viewed as reasonable. Choice **A** is incorrect because Bertha was not bound to complete the purchase when she was tendered the certificate bearing the legend. Until that time, she had suffered no damage. Choice **B** is incorrect because Bertha is deemed to have knowledge of the limitations on the transferability of the stock contained in the articles of incorporation by virtue of the legend on the certificate. She had the duty to pursue the reference by reading the articles. Finally, choice **C** is incorrect because a restriction that gives existing shareholders a right of first refusal at the fair market value of shares is ordinarily considered to be reasonable and valid.

90. A Under the Model Business Corporations Act, which has been followed by many states, acceptance of articles of incorporation by the state conclusively establishes the corporation's existence against anyone but the state. Therefore, choice **A** is correct. Choice **B** is not correct, both because some jurisdictions have abolished the de facto corporation doctrine and because those that recognize it also would accept arguments based on the corporation-by-estoppel doctrine. Choices **C** and **D** are not correct because choice **A** is correct.

91. C Generally, a shareholder may transfer his or her stock freely, subject only to any reasonable restrictions. These restrictions may be found in the articles of incorporation or bylaws, as well as in shareholder agreements. A bylaw provision that requires a stockholder to give the other shareholders a right of first refusal when he or she leaves is probably valid (especially because the shareholder is entitled to receive the stock's fair market value). The provision requiring that payment be made over three years is not unreasonable, nor is the provision limiting interest to 5 percent per annum. Choice **A** is incorrect because the provision is almost certainly a reasonable one. Choice **B** is incorrect because the mere fact that Hall is acting in good faith does ***not*** exempt her from compliance with valid restrictions in the bylaws. Finally, choice **D** is incorrect. As one of the original shareholders/directors/officers, she is deemed to have actual knowledge of the bylaws adopted by the corporation.

92. C A corporation is ***not*** liable for contracts made on its behalf by promoters prior to incorporation, unless the contracts are expressly or implicitly ratified by it after formation. A corporation may, however, be liable under *quasi*-contract principles if it has derived a benefit from a contract that the board of directors subsequently rejects. Because Bennett consumed approximately 15 percent of the grain, it is liable to Castleton for the reasonable value of the benefit it derived from the grain. Choice **A** is incorrect because Alex remained liable to Castleton under the contract, despite the fact that Bennett began using the grain. He failed to disclaim personal liability in his negotiations with Castleton. Choice **B** is incorrect because Alex will not be able to recover in *quasi* contract until Castleton obtains a judgment against Alex for the contract price. At that point, Alex may be able to recover an amount equal to the benefit that Bennett derived from the grain. Finally, choice **D** is incorrect because Bennett used only 15 percent of the grain prior to the time it discovered Alex's agreement, and then without any knowledge by its employees that the contract was not negotiated by an officer after incorporation. This would probably **not** be sufficient to constitute implied ratification of the entire contract.

93. **C** A corporate promoter owes a fiduciary duty to the corporation in formation. This duty includes the obligation to refrain from exploiting a corporate opportunity. Because Able purchased the land in anticipation of reselling it to Benson and did not divulge her interest in the partnership, she is probably obliged to remit the $25,000 profit to the corporation. This is true even if she paid a fair market price and earned her profit only because of an increase in property values generally. Choice **A** is incorrect because promoters owe a fiduciary duty to their prospective corporations. The fact that Able was not a director or officer of Benson when the purchase agreement was made is irrelevant. Also, the fact the transaction was negotiated by a Belbow partner other than Able is irrelevant. The facts tell us that the partnership was controlled by Able. Finally, choice **D** is incorrect because Able is liable for the profit, even if Benson was contracting with Belbow to pay what was then a fair market price.

94. **B** A corporate treasurer is not ordinarily empowered to negotiate contracts for the purchase of commodities required in the operation of the business. His or her duties usually consist of the collection and deposit of funds and the preparation of financial reports and documents. Each officer of the corporation has certain duties implied by the nature of his or her office. The treasurer does not have the implied authority to enter into contracts of the kind involved here. Choice **A** is, therefore, incorrect. Choice **C** is factually incorrect because the board did **not** ratify the second agreement with the

boarding house owner. In fact, the directors repudiated that agreement as soon as they all became aware of it. Choice **D** is incorrect because it is reasonable to conclude that a corporation engaged in mining operations—often in a remote area—would probably have to provide food and housing for its employees. Thus, the contract itself is not ultra vires. The correct answer is **B**. If the board is aware that an officer has exercised authority beyond the normal scope and that third parties have come to rely on the appearance of authority, the corporation will be liable on the theory of apparent authority. Here, the board is aware that the third party knows that the original contract entered into by Jack was performed by the corporation, evidently without objection. Moreover, Jack renewed the contract with the approval of the president, who has the inherent authority to approve contracts in the ordinary course of business. Furthermore, the renewal was performed by Minefield over several months, and the board is probably charged with notice.

95. **C** A person is a temporary insider for purposes of SEC Rule 10b-5 when he or she learns of material, nonpublic information as a consequence of his or her performance of a confidential function on behalf of the corporation. Such an insider is liable to an aggrieved party when he or she fails to disclose nonpublic, material information in connection with the purchase or sale of stock. Although Joanne was not an officer or director of the corporation, she was a "temporary insider" for purposes of SEC Rule 10b-5, because her company had been retained by Belmont to perform a confidential function (i.e., Belmont's accounting work). Thus, Joanne was obliged to disclose nonpublic, material information to the persons from whom she purchased Belmont stock. Choice **A** is incorrect because Joanne was a "temporary insider" for purposes of SEC Rule 10b-5. Choice **B** is incorrect because the fact that Joanne made no material misrepresentations is irrelevant. Her liability arises from her failure to disclose to the seller the material, nonpublic information she had obtained. Finally, choice **D** is incorrect because the special-facts doctrine has traditionally been applied only to officers, directors, or key employees of a corporation. Joanne does not satisfy any of these designations.

96. **D** Because the other answers are clearly wrong, the best answer is **D**. It must be noted, however, that the corporate remedy described in **D** is permitted only in a limited number of states, including New York. Under the special-facts doctrine, when, as a consequence of his or

her corporate position, a person acquires material, nonpublic information affecting the stock's value, there is a fiduciary duty to disclose those facts to an existing shareholder in conjunction with a sale or purchase of that shareholder's stock. In the few jurisdictions that follow New York, the corporation can bring an action under this theory if the aggrieved buyer or seller fails to do so; *Diamond v. Oreamuno*, 248 N.E.2d 910 (N.Y. 1969). Assuming this jurisdiction adheres to this holding, ABC could recover X's profit under the special-facts doctrine. Choice **A** is incorrect because the remedy provided in SEC Rule 10b-5 is available only to the buyer or seller of stock. Because ABC was not directly involved in the transaction between X and Y, it cannot recover under this doctrine (even if an instrumentality of interstate commerce was used). Choice **B** is incorrect because SEC Rule 10b-5 does *not* require that the security involved be sold on a national stock exchange; moreover, as we have noted, the rule can be asserted only by buyers or sellers of the security. Finally, choice **C** is also incorrect for the same reason—ABC was not involved in the purchase or sale of the shares in question, and SEC Rule 10b-5 can be asserted only by buyers or sellers of the security.

97. **C** When a person (or entity) uses his or her (or its) shares to elect an individual to sit on the board—in effect, *deputizing* that individual—that person or entity is deemed to be the director for purposes of SEC Rule 16(b), a rule that controls short-swing sales made within six months of stock acquisition. Upon the election of Barnes to the board of Caswell, Acme became (in effect) a director of Caswell for purposes of Rule 16(b). Because Acme sold its Caswell shares while (in effect) a director within six months of its purchase, Caswell can recover Acme's profit under SEC Rule 16(b). Choice **A** is incorrect because the SEC rule deems Acme to be a director of Caswell. Rule 16(b) is applicable to a corporation that is *either* traded on a national exchange *or* has assets greater than $10 million and a class of stock held by at least 500 stockholders. Choice **B** is incorrect because, although Caswell is not traded on a national stock exchange, it has assets in excess of $10 million and more than 500 shareholders of at least one class of stock. It is also engaged in interstate commerce. Thus, the transactions are subject to SEC Rule 16(b). Finally, choice **D** is incorrect because Acme's liability is premised on its position as constructive director and not on its percentage of stock ownership. It's not necessary to apply the 10 percent rule under these facts.

98. C When subscribers enter into a contract to purchase the shares of an *existing* corporation, and the shares in question are issued and tendered under proper authorization, the agreement is enforceable. Because Abby and Brandon have agreed to purchase validly authorized shares from an existing corporation, the subscription agreement is enforceable against them. Choice **A** is incorrect because the shares involved would, at the time of issuance, be validly authorized and tendered by an existing corporation. There is no need to look to the question of whether other subscribers may have given consideration to support Abby and Brandon's obligation. Choice **B** is incorrect because a corporation may charge more for its shares than the par value specified in its articles of incorporation. The par value stated in the articles is ordinarily only the minimum price at which the shares may be sold. Finally, choice **D** is incorrect because the obligations of Abby and Brandon are *not* contingent upon their prior ownership of Davis stock. Their obligation to perform is not diminished because they are strangers to the corporation.

99. D Since the passage of the Sarbanes-Oxley Act of 2002, companies required to register securities under the Securities Exchange Act of 1934 ('34 Act) have been subject to a variety of rules impacting corporate governance. One of these is that no loans may be made to corporate executives unless they are made on the same terms as those made available to others; in other words, no special deals. If Quickie Finance is registered under the '34 Act, Victor's special deal would be in clear violation of this rule. Choice **A** is incorrect: Just because Quickie Finance makes emergency loans to individual does not establish that a special deal with someone who appears to be a corporate insider is appropriate. Specific inquiry into whether the board has breached a fiduciary duty would be required. Choice **B** is incorrect because, just as being the business of making loans does not prove that the board breached no duty, the fact that a special loan was granted to Victor does not establish such a breach. To establish breach of the duty of care, it would have to be shown that the board did not adequately consider the matter or that the terms of the loan were so unreasonable as to amount to waste, thus depriving the substantive decision of the protection of the business judgment rule. To establish breach of the duty of loyalty, it would have to be shown that the board did not act in good faith in the best interests of Quickie Finance and there are nowhere near enough facts to suggest that showing could be made. Choice **C** is incorrect because, although

Victor clearly has engaged in self-dealing, that is only a breach of loyalty if the terms are unfair to the corporation. Victor has made full disclosure, and the board of directors authorized the loan; assuming the directors are not interested in the transaction, their approval probably would shift the burden with respect to fairness to anyone who wanted to challenge the loan. Although the board is portrayed as "sympathetic" to Victor, this does seem to constitute either the type of financial or close personal involvement that ordinarily might be regarded as an "interest" in the transaction.

100. **B** The usual statutory method for amending a corporation's articles of incorporation calls for (1) a recommendation by the board of directors, (2) subsequent approval by the shareholders, and (3) acceptance for filing by the proper state official, usually the secretary of state. Unless the articles provide otherwise, only a majority of the directors and a majority of the shareholders must vote in favor of the amendment. Nonetheless, the typical statute goes on to provide that if a class of shares is peculiarly affected by an amendment, it has the right to a class vote on the matter (effectively, a veto power). Thus, for instance, if Audrey and Benjie sought to amend Zedcorp's articles of incorporation to eliminate the right of the Class C shares to elect a director, they could satisfy the requirements of majority votes by the directors and the shareholders. Caitlin would, however, be entitled to cast a class vote and presumably would vote against the amendment, preventing its adoption. Choice **B** is correct because the rights of shareholders to elect directors are protected, even though the articles could be amended by the vote of less than all the shareholders (if, for instance, Benjie and Caitlin voted together to eliminate the right of Class C shares to elect a director). Choice **A** is incorrect. Even though the articles do not say anything about their method of amendment, the statutory method described above would be applicable. Choice **C** is incorrect because it fails to recognize class voting rights. Choice **D** is incorrect because only a majority vote of the shareholders, plus a class vote by an affected class, would be required.

101. **B** Under cumulative voting, a shareholder is entitled to a number of votes equal to her number of shares multiplied by the number of openings for director. These votes can be cast for all or fewer than all the openings. Thus, if Zelda casts her 120 votes (40×3) for herself, it will be impossible for Xerxes's and Yves's 240 votes (80×3) to be cast for more than 2 people with 120 votes apiece, and Zelda

will be entitled to be seated. However, if the articles of incorporation are amended to eliminate cumulative voting, Xerxes's and Yves's combined (2/3) voting power would be sufficient to elect all members of the board. The usual statutory method for amending a corporation's articles of incorporation calls for (1) a recommendation by the board of directors, (2) subsequent approval by the shareholders, and (3) acceptance for filing by the proper state official, usually the secretary of state. Unless the articles provide otherwise, only a majority of the directors and a majority of the shareholders must vote in favor of the amendment. Accordingly, Xerxes and Yves, acting together, could bring about an amendment in this case. Because all the shares are of a single class and would be similarly affected, there would be no question of a class vote (or veto) on these facts. Choice **A** is incorrect because the articles can be amended without her consent. Choice **C** is incorrect because, even if she is entitled to preemptive rights with respect to any newly issued shares, the articles can be amended to strip her right to cumulate her votes. Given the proportion of ownership described, choice **D** is incorrect as long as the right to cumulative voting is preserved.

102. **D** Darius rather clearly is in breach of his duty of due care owing to his lack of diligence. This does not necessarily translate into monetary liability for at least two reasons. First, it would be very difficult to prove that Darius's lack of diligence caused an injury to We-Build. Presumably, the directors who did attend the meetings voted for the loan from Bankorp; only if it were shown that Darius's presence would have prevented the loan from going forward would he be likely to be held liable for any monetary amount. Second, the facts state that We-Build is publicly held. Most publicly held corporations have taken advantage of statutes permitting adoption of a provision in the articles of incorporation eliminating monetary liability for most breaches of the duty of good faith. Choice **A** is incorrect because even though Darius lacks a business background, it is not clear that renders him unfit for the job of director of a company that manufactures modular homes. If he could, with moderate effort, understand the nuances of the business, he might be a perfectly qualified director. Moreover, proof of a causal link between Darius's lack of skill and injury to We-Build would be problematic; even if Darius had been more skillful there would be no reason to think the loan would not have been

approved. Finally, the probable presence in We-Build's articles of a provision limiting liability for breach of the duty of care means being answerable in damages is quite unlikely. Choice **B** is incorrect on somewhat similar reasoning. First, failure to attend a single meeting does not establish breach of the duty of care; any director might miss a meeting or two for a variety of reasons. Second, even if Darius had attended the meeting, there is no reason to think the loan would not have been approved, particularly since the vote was unanimous. Although Delaware arguably has dispensed with the requirement of a causal showing in lack of diligence cases, most jurisdictions still require one. Finally, and once again, the probable presence in We-Build's articles of a provision limiting liability for breach of the duty of care means being answerable in damages is quite unlikely. Choice **C** is a bit more complicated but still incorrect. Any claim against a director based on the imprudence of a decision is quite likely to be bested by the business judgment rule. Although it is likely that Darius would lose protection of the rule because of his lack of diligence, it still would be very difficult to show to show causation. The final nail in the coffin, however, is the probable presence in the articles of a provision limiting liability for breach of the duty of care.

103. **C** Delaware has led the way in characterizing "total failure" to monitor as a lack of good faith effort to protect the corporation's best interests. [Note that because good faith is a component of the duty of loyalty, this characterization has the effect of removing such cases from the protection of the statutorily authorized provisions appearing in the articles of incorporation of most publicly held corporations that limit liability for breach of the duty of care.] Although failure to monitor thus far has only arisen in cases against entire boards, there does not seem to be any logical reason the same concept could not be applied in the case of individual directors. Proof of a causal link to a complained of injury might be an impediment to the collection of damages, but this question does not ask about that. Choice **A** is incorrect because service on "interlocking" boards is not uncommon and is not *necessarily* a breach of loyalty. Many argue that having interlocks can be beneficial because the interlocked directors will have an appreciation for the possible synergies of the corporations involved. There certainly might be instances in which a director serving on multiple boards would be called upon to abstain from a particular decision, but

that is not what the questions asks. Choice **B** is incorrect because even if the loan by Bankorp to We-Build did count as self-dealing because of Darius's presence on both boards, only *unfair* self-dealing constitutes a breach of the duty of loyalty. Although the loan turned out badly for We-Build, that does not necessarily mean it was unfair. Choice **D** is incorrect because choice **C** is correct.

104. C Directors owe a duty of care which demands the skill, diligence and prudence of a reasonable person in managing his or her own assets (or, in many jurisdictions, a reasonable person in similar circumstances). Total failure to attend meetings and then giving creative excuses about it does not seem to satisfy this standard. Proof of a causal link to a complained of injury might be an impediment to the collection of damages, but this question does not ask about that. [Note, too, that Delaware appears to have dispensed with proof of causation in lack of diligence cases.] Choice **A** is incorrect because, as a director of Bankorp, Darius would have no reason to know that a loan was being made to We-Build. Choice **B** is incorrect for the same reason. Although it might be argued, with respect to both **A** and **B**, that if Darius had been discharging his duties to We-Build he would have had knowledge that should have been disclosed to prevent harm to Bankorp, it is not clear that his duty to Bankorp requires him to pay attention to another company's business. In any event, choice **C** is much more clearly true. Choice **D** is incorrect because choice **C** is correct.

105. A Delaware has led the way in characterizing "total failure" to monitor as a lack of good faith effort to protect the corporation's best interests. Because good faith is a component of the duty of loyalty, this characterization has the effect of removing such cases from the protection of the statutorily authorized provisions appearing in the articles of incorporation of most publicly held corporations that limit liability for breach of the duty of care. The concept has been applied in circumstances arguably quite similar to those in the fact pattern. Choice **B** is incorrect because even if a failure to monitor also were characterized as a question of lack of diligence and thus a breach of the duty of care, Bankorp probably does have one of the articles provisions just described. Choice **C** is incorrect because it is well established that failure to follow the pack does not prove that a board's decision was so unreasonable as to deprive it from the protection of the business judgment rule. A company and its shareholders are entitled to the independent judgment of the board the shareholders elected, not the judgment of other boards. It may well be that Bankorp has a different business model than other banks with different loan terms, etc. Choice **D** is incorrect because the type of delegation suggested does not seem to amount to the "total failure" to monitor called for to establish a lack of good faith amounting to a breach of the duty of loyalty.

106. B Limited liability is regarded as important in inducing passive investors to hand over their money to someone else to employ. If they were not promised limited liability for the obligations of the resulting enterprise, they presumably would feel they would have to pay closer attention to the business than they might be equipped to do. They also might be reluctant to diversify their investments, feeling that they could not possibly monitor more than a very few at a time. Choice **A** is incorrect because the sole shareholder of a closely held corporation is likely to be called upon to guarantee, and thus be personally liable for, many of the entity's debts. If he or she is the corporation's only employee, the shareholder also will be liable for most, if not all, of the corporation's tort obligations. Liability to unsophisticated contract creditors may be avoided, but, in general, limited liability is not nearly as important to sole shareholders as one might think. Choice **C** is incorrect because, as described above, passive investors are likely to be quite concerned about their inability to protect themselves. Investors who are actively involved in management are better able to protect against bad judgments and already may have significant personal exposure. Choice **D** is incorrect because the limited liability available through other forms of business entity is the same as the limited liability available to corporate shareholders.

107. A Limited liability partnerships are identical to general partnerships *except* with respect to the liability of the partners for obligations of the partnership. Although the precise management structure and profit-sharing rules applicable to any particular limited liability partnership or general partnership are subject to agreement by the partners, the default rules are the same: equal rights to manage and equal profit shares. By contrast, the limited partnership form generally calls for management only by the general partner(s) and has a default rule of sharing profits in proportion to capital contributions. Choice **B** is incorrect because choice **A**, its exact opposite, is correct. Choice **C** is incorrect because, as explained above, the default management structure and profit sharing rules for limited liability partnerships are identical to those of general partnerships. Choice **D** is incorrect because of the similarity of limited liability partnerships and general partnerships. Limited liability limited partnerships have the management and profit-sharing rules of limited partnerships (described above) and thus are dissimilar to limited liability partnerships.

108. A In fact, many limited liability company enabling statutes are virtually identical to limited liability partnership statutes. Thus, the default rules as to management structure and profit-sharing are the same. Even where the statutes differ, it is typical to permit the members of a limited liability company to design their own rules for management and profit-sharing. This means an entity with the same management structure and profit-sharing rules as a typical limited liability partnership would be quite possible. Choice **B** is incorrect in at least some states. In a number of states, the default is to an equal-participation-in-management model, similar to the default rule for limited liability partnerships. Choice **C** is incorrect because the management structure and profit-sharing rules of limited liability companies may be identical to those for limited liability partnerships. This necessarily means they also will be identical to the rules for general partnerships (which you might think about as limited partnerships minus limited liability). Choice **D** is incorrect because limited liability limited partnerships have the management and profit-sharing rules of limited partnerships. These generally call for management only by the general partner(s) and profit sharing in proportion to capital contribution.

109. D To qualify for a Subchapter S election, a corporation (1) must (with some exceptions) have only shareholders who are natural persons, (2) must have no non-resident alien shareholders, (3) must have no more than 100 shareholders, (4) must have no more than one class of shareholders (although classes differing solely with respect to voting rights are permitted), and (5) must allocate profit and loss in accordance with interests in the business. The proposed new business fails at (1): ABC LLC and XYZ LLP are not natural persons. Choice **A** is incorrect because it seems to call for formation of an entity that would not confer limited liability on its owners. ("Joint venture" has traditionally been used to refer to a general partnership formed for a specific, short-term purpose.) Although ABC LLC and XYZ LLP themselves are limited liability entities, it can still be desirable to isolate the obligations associated with a new line of business. That is, after all, why corporations form subsidiaries. Choice **B** is incorrect. Artificial entities can be partners in limited liability partnerships and there does not seem to be any other reason a limited liability partnership would not work (assuming the form is available in the desired jurisdiction). Limited liability partnerships are permitted to "check the box" to claim either pass-through or two-tier taxation, as desired, unless they are publicly traded. For a variety of reasons, limited liability partnerships are never publicly traded. Choice **C** is incorrect. Artificial entities can be partners in limited liability companies and there does not seem to be any other reason a limited liability company would not work (and this form is available in all states). Limited liability companies are permitted to "check the box" to claim either pass-through or two-tier taxation, as desired, unless they are publicly traded. Although limited liability companies occasionally are publicly traded, there is no indication that this is in the plans of ABC LLC and XYZ LLP.

110. **B** Equitable subordination is an equitable (surprise!) doctrine calling for subordination (surprise!) of debt owed to persons who also are owners of an entity, thus giving preference to payment of debts owed to non-owners. The circumstances in which it has been invoked are quite similar to those giving rise to an occasion to pierce the corporate veil (undercapitalization, siphoning of funds, misleading conduct, etc.), but the result is different. In equitable subordination, the owners are not made liable for the obligations of the entity; instead (and less drastically), their own claims against the entity are repaid after the claims of third parties. There is no reason to think that this doctrine would not apply to the members of limited liability companies on the same terms it has been applied to corporate shareholders. Choice **A** is incorrect because preemptive rights, when applicable, require that new shares be offered to the existing shareholders on a pro rata basis. The partners in a limited liability partnership have (unless otherwise agreed in advance) the ability to complete prevent new partners from entering the partnership, and thus would not seem to require the protection of preemptive rights. Choice **C** is incorrect because the same factors that make it equitable to pierce corporate veils equally pertain to both limited liability companies and limited liability partnerships. Both of the latter forms, like corporations, can be abused by those who undercapitalize them, siphon their funds, etc. Choice **D** is incorrect because choice **B** is a correct answer.

111. **B** An individual doing business as a sole proprietorship is personally liable for all debts incurred. Because Jackson is doing business as a sole proprietorship, he is personally liable for any obligation incurred by that entity. In fact, a sole proprietorship is not really a separate, distinct entity from the individual operating that business. Choice **A** is incorrect because the individual is personally liable for contractual obligations created by his or her sole proprietorship. Choice **C** is incorrect because Jackson is personally liable for the proprietorship's contractual obligations, regardless of whether he guaranteed those debts. Finally, choice **D** is incorrect because choice **B** is a correct answer.

112. **D** Each partner of a general partnership is generally jointly and severally liable for the obligations of the partnership. Cook is probably jointly and severally liable for ***all*** partnership obligations, whether contractual or tortious in nature. Choice **A** is incorrect because Cook is personally liable to the full extent of all partnership obligations. She would, however, have a right of contribution from the other partners to the extent that her total satisfaction of a partnership obligation exceeded her proportionate interest in that entity. Choice **B** is incorrect because Cook is liable to contractual creditors of the partnership. Finally, choice **C** is incorrect because Cook is personally liable to tort claimants of the partnership

113. **C** Unless there is an agreement to the contrary, every partner is owed the return of his or her capital; the partners are obliged to contribute in the same proportion that they share profits the amounts necessary to allow the partnership to satisfy this obligation. Moreover, a partner is not entitled to any salary unless it is agreed upon. Thus, choice **C** is correct. Choice **A** is incorrect because, even though Jack and Jill agreed to share profits equally, Jill is still owed the return of her capital. Choice **B** is incorrect because it says Jack is owed for his services, and there is no mention in the facts of an agreement to that effect. (A small and heavily criticized minority of courts have, however, implied from an agreement to share profits in a situation such as this one an agreement to value the services provided by one partner as equal to the capital provided by the other and to make distributions accordingly.) Choice **D** is incorrect because it still leaves a portion of Jill's capital contribution unrepaid.

114. **D** Within the scope of the partnership business, the partners have equal rights to manage unless there is an agreement to the contrary.

If there is a dispute, a majority of the partners can resolve it. However, in a two-person partnership, neither partner constitutes a majority. Thus, each partner is free to bind the partnership in such matters as buying supplies, ordering inventory, and the like. Choice **A** is incorrect because Begonia did successfully bind the partnership—and, thus, herself and Pansy—in the event the partnership is unable to pay. Choice **B** is incorrect because the partners in a general partnership are, in most jurisdictions, jointly and severally liable for all of the partnership's obligations. (In a few jurisdictions, they are jointly liable for the partnership's contracts and jointly and severally liable for its torts.) Choice **C** is incorrect because, although Begonia was the only one who placed the order, she succeeded in binding the partnership, and, thus, both partners.

115. **C** Under many limited partnership statutes, the fact that a limited partner's name is in the name of the limited partnership subjects that limited partner to the risk of liability to those entering into transactions with the limited partnership without notice of the limited partner's status; the fear is that third parties will be misled and act in the belief that the named limited partner is really a general partner whose credit stands behind that of the limited partnership. Choice **A** is incorrect because choice **C** is true. Choice **B** is incorrect because most tort obligations do not accrue in transactional settings in which misleading about the named limited partner's status is likely to occur. Choice **D** is incorrect for the same reason; liability to tort creditors is unlikely. It is important to note that, even though the liability of a general partner will, under many statutes, be imposed on a limited partner participating in control of the limited partnership, there usually is a safe harbor for the activities in which X is described as engaging: acting as a shareholder, officer, and director of the corporate general partner. (The most recent version of the Uniform Limited Partnership Act provides that not even general partners will have liability for the obligation of the limited partnership. This version was promulgated in 2001 but had, by 2011, been adopted by only fifteen states.)

116. **C** It is true that converting a general partnership into a limited liability partnership provides the partners with protection from the personal liability to partnership creditors that attaches to general partners. That protection will be meaningless, however, if the "veil" of the limited partnership is pierced. For decades, courts have

pierced corporate "veils" for factors most prominently featuring undercapitalization; there is no reason to think that the same principles will not apply when courts turn to deal with unincorporated entities affording limited liability. It, thus, will be important for Peter and Paul to make sure that Pastries is adequately capitalized. The question states that its assets have been kept low and that Peter and Paul foresee a liability greatly exceeding those assets. Courts do, however, typically take insurance into account in determining whether a limited liability entity is undercapitalized. Thus, choice **C** is correct, and Peter and Paul should be advised that failure to maintain insurance could lead to a piercing of the veil of limited liability. Choice **A** is incorrect because (1) in light of the state of Pastries' capitalization, Peter and Paul may not get the result they are seeking, and (2) there is no necessary difference in management structure between a general partnership and a limited liability partnership (for all intents and purposes, they are identical in all respects other than the partners' liability). Choice **B** is incorrect for reason (1). Choice **D** is incorrect because, in many instances, exactly the same results can be achieved by either a limited liability partnership or a limited liability company. It is true, however, that the limited liability company form is available in all states, while the limited liability partnership form is not.

117. **D** The definition of a partnership is that it is an association of two or more persons to carry on as co-owners a business for profit. There is no requirement that those persons have the intention of forming a partnership; the name given by the parties to the relationship is not determinative. Thus, partnerships can be inadvertent. There are not enough facts available to know whether S will have sufficient power to be regarded as a co-owner. Although entitlement to a profit share is prima facie evidence that a partnership exists, this rule does not apply if the profits are received as interest on a loan. This does not mean, however, that no partnership exists—it simply becomes necessary to grapple with the issue of co-ownership. No facts are given about S's rights to advise, veto, make decisions, and the like. Thus, choice **D** is correct. Choice **A** is incorrect because A and B will not be sharing profits, only expenses. Choice **B** is incorrect because not enough is known about the rights of S to engage in activities indicative of co-ownership. Choice **C** is not correct because if two people are not sharing profits, they cannot satisfy the definition of partnership.

118. A At common law, partners owe one another "the duty of finest loyalty." This clearly extends to avoiding the unfair usurpation of partnership opportunities. Because Oscar approached Angus to offer an opportunity to Ogee, Angus almost certainly would have been required—at a minimum—to advise Babs of Oscar's offer and to give her an opportunity to compete for it. This does not mean, however, that Angus's act in accepting the offer binds Babs, because conducting an oil and gas business in State Z appears to be outside the scope of Ogee's business (conducting an oil and gas business in State Y). Thus, it is likely that a constructive trust would be imposed on 50 percent of Angus's profits from Geo, but Babs will have no liability for its obligations. Thus, choice **A** is correct. Choice **B** is incorrect; if the money contributed by Angus to Geo came from Ogee's coffers, it may strengthen the claim that a partnership opportunity was usurped and certainly imposes an obligation on Angus to account for the use of the money, but does nothing to change the scope of Ogee's business. Choices **C** and **D** are incorrect because choice **A** is correct. (It should be noted that, even if a statute purports to define a partner's duty of loyalty, it would be unlikely to change the analysis in this question.)

119. D Assuming there is no reason to pierce the veil of limited liability, formation of an LLC provides its members with protection against personal liability for the tort, contract, and other obligations the LLC incurs (although it cannot prevent imposition of liability for a member's own wrongful acts). In addition, LLC statutes generally provide that the members may agree to such control arrangements as they see fit. Thus, a provision limiting H's ability to enter into contracts should be permissible. This does not establish, however, that a third party learning that H is a member of an LLC would not be reasonable in thinking that H has the ability to act on the LLC's behalf in the making of contracts in the ordinary course of business. Choice **D** is, therefore, the correct answer, because H might enter into a contract with a third party lacking knowledge of H's limited authority. Choice **A** is incorrect because, within the scope of the partnership business, the partners have equal rights to manage—and, thus, to bind the partnership—unless there is an agreement to the contrary. If there is a dispute, a majority of the partners can resolve it. However, in a two-person partnership, neither partner constitutes a majority. Thus, each partner is free to bind the partnership in such matters as accepting orders, buying supplies, and the like. Choice **B** is incorrect because an employee may have the apparent authority to contractually bind the employer to a third party if the third party reasonably believes, based on the employer's manifestations, that authority exists. Those manifestations can include failure to correct a misapprehension that reasonably arises. If H enters into contracts approved by G, but without notice that G's approval was necessary, H may succeed in binding G to subsequent, unapproved contracts. Choice **C** is incorrect because choice **D** is correct.

120. C There are many state statutes and constitutional provisions specifically mentioning partnerships and corporations, but, because they predated the recognition of limited liability companies (LLCs) and limited liability partnerships (LLPs), failing to mention those more recent business forms. Courts must, in these situations, attempt to determine the purpose of the legislative or constitutional drafters and then invoke that purpose in deciding how to treat LLCs and LLPs. It appears that the drafters of the State Q constitution were concerned that liquor distributorships be licensed only if individuals were to be liable for the consequences of their operation. Because both LLCs and LLPs, like corporations, confer limited liability on the owners of the business, a court almost certainly would hold that they could not hold licenses to distribute liquor. Thus, choice **C** is correct. Choice **A** is incorrect because an LLP would cut off the liability of its partners, evidently in conflict with the intent of the constitutional drafters. Choice **B** is incorrect because an LLC would cut off the liability of its partners. Choice **D**, which combines choices **A** and **B**, also is incorrect.

Index

References are to the number of the question raising the issue. "E" indicates an Essay Question; "M" indicates a Multiple-Choice Question.

Agency, E17, M37, M38, M94

Agreements

See Contracts

Appraisal rights, M74, M75, M76, M77, M78, M79, M84, M86

Articles of incorporation

Amendment of, E5, E25, M35, M80, M100, M101

Board of directors, size and election of, E4

Debts, E5

Filing of, E16

Meetings, notice of, M42

Preemptive rights, E15

Removal of directors, E19, M46

Authority

Actual, E24, M119

Apparent, E24, M119

Inherent, E24, M118

Misrepresentation of, E24

Bankruptcy, *Deep Rock* **doctrine**, M33, M87

Board of directors

See also Directors and officers; Indemnification of directors and officers

Delegation of powers, M48

Election of, E4

Meetings, notice of, M42, M43

Powers of, E8, E22

Proxies for reelection of, M69

Quorum, M41

Ratification of actions by, E7, M7, M8, M39, M92

Sale of assets, approval of, M40

Setting aside of purchase, E9

Size of, E4, E5

Terms of, E4

Vacancies, E4, E18

Bond for costs in derivative actions, E3, M50, M53, M54

Books, inspection of, E3, E18, M71, M72

Book value, M25

Business judgment rule, E3, E10, E12, E13, E14, E15, E22, M44, M45

Bylaws

Board of directors, size of, E4

Inspection of books under, M71

Meetings, notice of, M42

Removal of directors, E19, M46

Transfer of sale of stock, M91

Voting, E4, E14

Capital, return of partners', M113

Cases

Diamond v. Oreamono, E9, E19, M14, M96

Perlman v. Feldman, M85

SEC v. Texas Gulf Sulphur Co., E19

Superintendent of Insurance v. Banker's Life & Casualty Co., E7

Taylor v. Standard Gas & Electric Company, M33

UTE Citizens of Utah v. United States, M20

Charitable giving, E27

Class voting, E25, M100

Committees, E22

Compensation of directors and officers, E13, M73

Contracts

See also Subscription agreements

Authority to enter into, E17

Inspection of, M71

Liability under, E17, E18

Preincorporation contracts, E16, E17, M6, M7, M8, M92

Promoter's liability for, E16, E17, M6, M8, M90

Rescission or repudiation of, E8, E17, M35, M36, M37, M38, M39, M43, M56, M94

Corporate opportunity doctrine, E10, E12, M56, M93

Corporation-by-estoppel doctrine, E10, E16, M9, M10, M11, M90

Costs, derivative actions, E3, M50, M53, M54

Creditors, liability of

See Piercing the corporate veil

Creditors, rights of, E3, E8, E17, M3, M76, M87

Cumulative voting, E5, E20, M26, M29, M46

Deadlock, E21

Debts of corporations, E5

Deep Rock **doctrine**, M33, M87

De facto corporation, existence of, E10, E16, M9, M10, M11, M90

Defective incorporation, E16, M9, M10, M11

De jure corporations, E16, M9, M10, M11, M90

Delegation by directors, E22, E27

Derivative actions

Generally, E3, E13, E14, M51, M55

Costs, E3, M50, M53, M54

Demand for redress, E8, E9, E13, E14, E17, M50

Directors, approval of, E4

Due care, duty of, E7

Indemnification of directors and officers, E13, M59

Independent litigation advice, M49

Loyalty, duty of, M23

Shareholders, approval of, M54

Standing, E9, E14, E27, M52, M53

Waste of corporate assets, M73

Diamond v. Oreamono, E9, E19, M14, M96

Directors and officers

See also Board of directors; Indemnification of directors and officers

Appointment of, M47, M48, M67, M70, M86

Authority of, E7

Business judgment rule, E3, E10, E12, E13, E14, E15, E22, M44, M45

Compensation of, E13, M73

Corporate opportunity doctrine, E10, E12, M56, M93

Delegation by, E22, E27

Due care, duty of, E1, E7, E8, E12, E13, E14, E17, E25, E27, M44, M45, M53, M99, M102, M104, M105

Duties to multiple clases, E25

Election of, M47

Loyalty, duty of, E1, E6, E8, E12, E13, E14, M23, M52, M56, M99, M103, M104, M105

Meetings of, E27

Merger, resignation on, M86

Mismanagement, E10

Powers of, E6, E17

Proxy to, E26, M88

Removal of, E3, E18, E19, M46

Special facts doctrine, E9, E12, E19, E23, M13, M14, M17, M18, M20, M21, M95, M96

Discount shares, E15, E22

Dissolution of corporation

Generally, E20, E21

Priority of claims, M34

Dividends

Common stock dividend, effect of, M29

Compelling payment of, E3, E20, E25

Cumulative, E25

Earned income, payment from, E14, E22, M27, M32, M81

Insurance, refusal to acquire to have funds for dividend, M44

Nimble dividends, E22, M30, M81

Preferred stock dividend, E25

Ratification of payment of, M54

Revaluation surplus, payment from, E15

Dodd-Frank Act, E6

Due care, duty of, E1, E6, E7, E8, E12, E13, E14, E17, E27, M44, M45, M52, M99, M102, M104, M105

Equitable subordination, M110

Executive committees, E22

Executive compensation, E6

Fair market value of stock, M28

Fiduciary duties and liabilities

Directors and officers, E1, E3, E4, E5, E6, E7, E8, E9, E10, E12, E13, E14, E17, M23, M99

Due care, duty of, E1, E6, E7, E8, E12, E13, E14, E17, M44, M45, M52, M99, M102, M104, M105

Loyalty, duty of, E1, E6, E8, E12, E13, E14, E25, M23, M52, M56, M99, M103, M104, M105

Promoters, M93

Shareholders, E3, E5, M110

Voting trusts, M82

General partnerships, E11, M108, M112

Hostile takeovers, E4

Inadvertent partnership, M117

Incorporation, defective, E16, M9, M10, M11

Indemnification of directors and officers

Generally, E13

Criminal conduct, M61

Derivative actions, E13, M59

Good faith, M58, M60, M61

Negligence, M59

Settlement of action, M58

Insider trading

Rule 10b5, E7, E9, E12, E19, E23, M12, M13, M14, M16, M17, M18, M19, M20, M21, M23, M57, M58, M95, M96

Rule 16(b), E9, E12, E19, M12, M13, M14, M15, M16, M18, M19, M20, M21, M22, M53, M57, M97

Special facts doctrine, E9, E12, E19, E23, M13, M14, M17, M18, M20, M21, M95, M96

Inspection of books and records, E3, E18, M71, M72

Limited liability, generally, E2, M106

Limited liability companies

Authority of members, E24, E26, M119

Compared to other entities, E2, M108, M109, M110

Dissolution, E21

Fiduciary duties of members, E26

Management rights of members, E2

Piercing the veil of, E24, M110, M116

Treatment as corporation for purposes of statute, E26, M120

Ultra vires doctrine, E26

Limited liability limited partnerships, E2, M107

Limited liability partnerships, E2, E11, E21, M107, M108, M109, M110, M116

Limited partnerships, M107, M115

Loyalty, duty of, E1, E6, E8, E12, E13, E14, E25, M23, M52, M56, M99, M103, M104, M105

Meetings, notice of, E27, M42, M43

Mergers

Generally, E5, M40

Appraisal rights, M74, M75, M76, M77, M78, M79, M84, M85

Creditors' rights following, M76, M77, M79

De facto merger doctrine, M74, M77, M84, M85

Short-form mergers, M79, M84

Misrepresentation theory, watered stock, E16, M3

Net worth, M13, M15, M19, M24, M31

Nimble dividends, E22, M30, M81

Officers

See Directors and officers

***Pari delicto* doctrine**, E18

Partnerships, E11, E16, E21, M11, M90, M107, M108, M109, M110, M112, M113, M114, M115, M116, M117, M118

Pearlman v. Feldman, M85

Piercing the corporate veil, E10, E16, M87

Piercing the veil of a limited liability company or partnership, E24, M110, M116

Pooling agreements, M83

Preemptive rights, E5, E9, E12, E15, M51, M62, M63, M64, M77, M110

Preincorporation contracts, E16, E17, M6, M7, M8, M92

Promoters

Fiduciary duty of, M93

Liability of, E16, E17, M6, M8, M90

Notification of revocation of subscription agreement by, M4

Ratification by corporation relieves promoter liability, M7, M92

Proxies

Directors, E26, M88

Mergers, M78

Misstatement or omission in solicitation for, M69

Revocation of, E15, M65, M66

Rule 14a-8, E6, E18, M67, M68

Purpose, E21

Quorum, E27

Records, inspection of, E3, E18, M71, M72

Registration of stock, E13

Removal of directors and officers, E3, E18, E19, M46

Retained earnings, dividends, M27

Retirement benefits, E13, E22

Rule 10b-5, E7, E9, E12, E19, E23, M12, M13, M14, M16, M17, M18, M19, M20, M21, M23, M57, M78, M95, M96

Rule 14a-8, proxy materials, E6, E18, M67, M68

Rule 16(b), E9, E12, E19, M12, M13, M14, M15, M16, M18, M19, M20, M21, M22, M53, M57, M97

Sale of assets

See Mergers

Sarbanes-Oxley Act, E6, M99

Securities Exchange Act of 1934, E6

Security for costs in derivative actions, E3, M50, M53, M54

SEC v. Texas Gulf Sulphur Co., E19

Shareholders

See also Derivative actions; Stock; Voting

Derivative actions, approval of, M54

Fiduciary duties and liabilities, E3

Ratification by, M35, M47, M55, M73

Sale of assets, approval of, M40

Shareholder agreements, E3, E20

Special meetings, E4

Sole proprietorships, M111

Special facts doctrine, E9, E12, E19, E23, M13, M14, M17, M18, M20, M21, M95, M96

Special meetings of shareholders, E4

Statutory obligation theory, watered stock, E16

Stock

See also Dividends; Insider trading; Shareholders; Subscription agreements; Voting

Fair market value, M28

Options, E13

Preemptive rights, E5, E9, E12, E15, M51, M62, M63, M64, M77

Preferred stock, creation of new class of, M80

Premium for sale of controlling interest, M85, M86

Redemption of, E8

Registration of, E13

Repurchase of, E13, E22, M31

Rescission of transfer, E7, E8, M1, M2

Restrictions on alienability, E20, M89, M91

Right of first refusal, M89, M91

Treasury stock, resale of, E12, M63

Watered stock, E10, E12, E15, E16, M2, M3

Straight voting, E20, M26, M29

Strike suits, E3

Subchapter S, E2, M110

Subscription agreements

Liability under, M5, M98

Repudiation of, M4, M98

Superintendent of Insurance v. Banker's Life & Casualty Co., E7

Taylor v. Standard Gas & Electric Company, M33

Tax considerations, E2, M110

Treasury stock, resale of, E12, M63

Trust fund theory, watered stock, E16, M3

Ultra vires doctrine, E5, E13, E18, E26, E27, M35, M36, M41, M94

Unanimous written consent, E25

Undercapitalization, E24

Unincorporated entities, E2, E11, E21, E24, E26, M106-120

UTE Citizens of Utah v. United States, M20

Voting

See also Proxies

Class voting, E25, M100

Cumulative voting, E5, E20, M26, M29, M46, M101

Majority, exercise of control by, E5

Notice to directors, E26

Pooling agreements, M83

Quorum, E27

Straight voting, E20, M26, M29

Voting trust, M82

Waste of corporate assets, E13, E17, E22, M54, M73

Watered stock, E10, E12, E15, E16, M2, M3